MEETING THE ENEMY

MEETING
THE ENEMY

The Human Face of the Great War

Richard van Emden

B L O O M S B U R Y
LONDON · NEW DELHI · NEW YORK · SYDNEY

First published in Great Britain 2013

Copyright © 2013 by Richard van Emden

The moral right of the author has been asserted

Bloomsbury Publishing Plc
50 Bedford Square
London
WC1B 3DP

www.bloomsbury.com

Bloomsbury Publishing, London, New Delhi, New York and Sydney
A CIP catalogue record for this book is available from the British Library

ISBN 978 1 4088 2164 0

10 9 8 7 6 5 4 3 2 1

Typeset by Hewer Text UK Ltd, Edinburgh
Printed and bound in Great Britain by CPI Group (UK) Ltd, Croydon CR0 4YY

MIX
Paper from
responsible sources
FSC
www.fsc.org   FSC® C020471

To Mum

Contents

Introduction

Captain Robert Campbell was at a low ebb. Badly wounded and captured during the fighting at Mons in August 1914, he had been incarcerated at Magdeburg prisoner-of-war camp for the best part of two years. During that time, he had undergone several very painful operations on his face and a shattered arm, and now, to cap it all, he had just received an upsetting letter from Gladys, his sister, at home in England: their mother, Louisa Campbell, was dying.

The commandant at Magdeburg was a genial man, as far as any camp commandant could be, and Campbell had got to know him as well as circumstances permitted. On hearing Campbell's bad news, the commandant's sympathy went beyond mere words of consolation. He suggested that Campbell write to the Kaiser to ask whether he might be given special dispensation to return home to see his mother; the commandant would propel the letter up the chain of command with a recommendation that the application be granted.

Against all rational expectations a reply did come, and from the highest authority, allowing Captain Campbell to leave the camp. He would travel through Germany to Holland and back to England for a fortnight's leave. This would be permitted as long as he promised, on his honour, to return.

Campbell travelled home from the continent, arriving at Gravesend on 7 December 1916. What Louisa made of her son's miraculous appearance is not hard to imagine. Sadly she died the following February.

While Robert was still at his mother's bedside, a letter was passed to the Imperial Foreign Office in Germany. It was written by Friedrich Gastreich, a father and husband from the town of Kirchhundem, east of Cologne. His wife, Anna, was bedridden, suffering from tuberculosis and pneumonia: she was fading fast and her son was, like Captain Campbell, locked up in enemy territory. Twenty-five-year-old Peter Gastreich was held in Knockaloe internment camp on the Isle of Man. Would it be possible, his father asked, for his son to be given special licence to leave England for Germany?

The Imperial Foreign Office asked Britain through American intermediaries. Referring to the parole being given to Campbell, the Germans tried to work on the British sense of fair play to parole Gastreich in turn. The British were not willing to comply. 'Unable to agree to release of P. Gastreich. Capt. Campbell's case cannot be quoted as a precedent,' the Foreign Office official replied in a memo. Gastreich would remain where he was: his mother died just a week after the initial request, although this news had not been communicated to the British government when it made its decision.

It can be safely assumed that this attempt at a 'temporary exchange' was unique, owing to the refusal of the British to reciprocate. In October 1917, when a similar situation arose, relatives of another captured officer, Captain Bushby Erskine, petitioned for a temporary parole for him. The government's reply to the Erskine family was polite but negative. 'In one case the Germans permitted a British officer to visit this country on parole, but without consulting us. This case has since been used to support applications for German officers to visit Germany, which could not possibly be entertained.' The letter was forwarded to Captain Erskine's father by his niece. She wrote to the Foreign Office: 'I fear the result of the shock, as he [Erskine's father] had been led to believe, by irresponsible people, that there was a good chance of his son being allowed to return "en parole".'

There is no doubt that Captain Campbell was extremely fortunate, although his extraordinary return home was not reported in the national press: the Kaiser's seemingly spontaneous act of kindness was hardly the right sort of war news in 1916, and so only private communication could have brought the Campbell case to the attention of the Erskines.

As for Captain Campbell, no one would have blamed him had he chosen to stay where he was, in England, and by his mother's bedside. True to his word, however, he returned to the camp on time, where, released from his bond of honour, he set about trying to escape. He broke out of camp the following year only to be recaptured on the Dutch border. Thereafter, he remained in Germany until the end of the war.

Social, cultural and military ties between Britain and Germany were particularly strong before the outbreak of war. Germans made up the third largest immigrant population in Britain prior to 1914 (behind Russian Jews and the Irish); they set up businesses, commercial and industrial; Germans constituted by far the largest group of foreign students: forty-three matriculated from Oxford University in 1912 as compared with just three students from France; in London's upmarket hotels and restaurants young Germans were conspicuous by their presence, working front of house (10 per cent of London's waiting staff were German). They intermarried, settled and had families. Elsewhere, German academics, musicians and writers featured large in pre-war musical and literary circles.

Within the armed forces, ties were particularly convivial. Kaiser Wilhelm was Colonel-in-Chief of a British regiment, the 1st (Royal) Dragoons, in whose dress uniform he was photographed while on a private visit to Aldershot in 1894. Through the German military attaché in London, he kept in touch with the regiment, while its Colonel, George Steele, regularly sent him greetings and regimental news. On 3 June 1914 the regiment took part in a garrison parade to celebrate the Kaiser's birthday and each year the Kaiser sent a laurel wreath to 'his' regiment in commemoration of the Battle of Waterloo. In thanking the Kaiser for his 'unfailing thoughtfulness', Colonel Steele wrote, 'I venture to express the hope of all ranks of the Regiment that next year [1915] being the centenary of the Battle, our Colonel in Chief would, on that occasion, still further extend his kindness to us and himself affix the wreath to our standard.'

The Kaiser was one of many German military personnel invited to visit British counterparts. A month before the outbreak of war, the same London military attaché was a weekend guest at the barracks of the 4th (Royal Irish) Dragoon Guards. At the Cowes Regatta on the Isle of Wight at the end of July, Prince Henry of Prussia, a career naval officer and younger brother of the Kaiser, was due to stay with Commodore James Butler, 3rd Marquess of Ormonde. Reluctantly, he wired cancelling the visit owing to the spiralling international crisis. 'Au revoir, I hope,' he wrote to his friend.

And just as Germans came to Britain, so Britons went to Germany. It was almost a prerequisite for would-be British businessmen to spend time in Germany, learning the language and the business ethos of such an important trading nation, while other young men spent time studying at respected German universities such as Göttingen and Münster. In 1911, Sir Ernest Cassel, a Cologne-born naturalised British businessman and close friend of the British monarch, founded the 'King Edward VII British-German Foundation' to help promote better understanding between the two nations through funding young British and German graduates to study for a year in each other's country.

At the highest echelons of society, there was much social interaction and intermarriage. The Emperor Kaiser Wilhelm II was the grandson of Queen Victoria, who was herself married to a German (Albert) and had a German mother (Victoria of

Saxe-Coburg-Saalfeld). Visits from various German princes and dukes to Britain, to London's theatres and to the opera, were regularly reported in the Court Circular column of *The Times*. The Kaiser visited Britain frequently between his accession to the throne in 1888 and the outbreak of war, and both King Edward VII and George V returned the courtesy, George V visiting Germany as late as May 1913.

Yet familiarity bred a level of contempt. Economically, Germany had expanded rapidly since the 1870s under the careful guidance of Bismarck, the founding father of a unified German state. However, the Kaiser was an entirely different man. On coming to power, he sidelined the ageing Chancellor, and started to exert increasing influence over Germany's civil powers, and most importantly over successive Chancellors, who, until the defeat of Germany in 1918, were ultimately responsible only to the Emperor.

Bombastic, jealous and emotionally fragile, the Kaiser had a love-hate relationship with the English, envious and admiring in almost equal measure. He was, after all, the son of an English mother (Victoria, the Princess Royal), yet his main influences in life came from his father's side and an overly disciplined upbringing among Prussian aristocracy that venerated the military. There were few English influences, and he blamed his mother (irrationally) for his physical disability, a withered left arm. To compensate for this, he developed an arrogance and an exaggerated self-confidence combined with an innate restlessness and desire to assert his will; these were not good character traits for a man bent, if not on outright war, then at least on confrontation. Always careful to hide his arm, he would appear in public with a pompous desire to swagger and show off, as Percy Johnson, a twelve-year-old boy, recalled of the German monarch's visit to Britain in 1911. King George was riding down London's Oxford Street but it was the man next to him who attracted Percy's attention: 'Who should be with King George but the Kaiser, stuck up there wearing a great big cape and a helmet and wonderful medals on his chest. Well, our own King George, he looked absolutely way out of his depth.'

The Kaiser never sought to endear himself to the British public, and the press gradually turned against him as he contributed to his own unpopularity by reported blunders of foreign policy and diplomatic gaffes. These included an interview he gave to the *Daily Telegraph* in 1908. He had intended to give his views on Anglo-German friendship but, in the end, was quoted as saying, 'You English are mad, mad, mad as March hares': he also managed to insult France, Russia and Japan in the same interview.

Yet it was the well-documented naval arms race in the fifteen years prior to the outbreak of war that underlined to the British people where the threat to peace in Europe lay. The British press was obsessed with international ship-building, especially German, with tables drawn up and published annually of newly built foreign vessels, with the name, type, displacement and shipyard all noted. By 1910, Germany was reckoned to be, after Britain, the second strongest sea power in the world: it posed a genuine threat to Britain's maritime supremacy and by definition her ability to protect colonial interests of which the Kaiser was supremely envious.

The naval arms race and the rising consternation this caused in Britain did not, however, fracture relations at the highest level of society, and civility was maintained. Ironically, Edward VII was an honorary admiral in the German navy and when, in June 1904, he visited Kiel, he was greeted not only with a display of German naval strength, and a twenty-one-gun salute, but by the Kaiser wearing his British naval uniform as an honorary Admiral of the Fleet, a status afforded him by Queen Victoria, along with his title of Colonel-in-Chief to the 1st (Royal) Dragoons. In welcoming his royal guest, the Kaiser made a speech in which he pointed out that the German fleet, while the 'youngest in point of creation' among the world's navies, was nevertheless 'an expression of the renewal in strength of the sea power of the German Empire . . .' The writing was on the wall. That year the British concluded the Entente Cordiale with France, an act that Germany took as a clear indication of where British loyalties would lie in the event of war.

There had been perennial tension between France and Germany since the war of 1870 and the ceding to Germany by treaty of the valuable French territories of Alsace (including the city of Strasbourg) and part of Lorraine. The loss of this territory was an open wound for the French, and renewed conflict between France and Germany was all but inevitable. Indeed, long before 1914, Britain's General Staff anticipated a German invasion of France through neutral Belgium.

Despite the day-to-day cordiality that existed between British and German military officers, there was a growing presumption among the General Staff that the Germans also wanted war with Britain and were only waiting for the right moment to usurp Britain's position as the dominant world power.

The General Staff in London predicted it would come in 1915 once the Germans had widened the Kiel Canal to take modern battleships. Even so, there were German-induced war scares in 1911 and 1913 and *Der Tag* – the day – when Germany would attack was on the lips of many, years before August 1914. When young Percy Johnson returned home from watching the parade on Oxford Street that summer morning in 1911, he told his father that he had seen the Kaiser in all his grandeur. 'Oh,' said his father, 'there's going to be a war, and not very long either. That bloke's not here for nothing.'

Meeting the Enemy tells the story of what happened when these two great economically and socially intertwined nations were sucked into war. Few foresaw, or cared to envisage, the consequences of embarking on a truly international war, from the inevitability of prodigious loss of life to the terrible long-term dislocation of civil society that would result. It is, in part, the social cost of war that this book will examine, on the Western and Home Fronts but always within the context of Anglo-German relations.

My previous book, *The Quick and the Dead*, explored the circumstances surrounding the death of soldiers in the Great War and the families who were left behind to mourn; *Meeting the Enemy* will look at what happened to those who, in the main, survived: survivors who were both the instigators and perpetrators of conflict as well as those who were required to bear the brunt of war's vagaries and its vicious unfairness.

It would be easy to infer from the title alone that this book is about *direct* contact with the foe, that it begins at the point of the bayonet and ends, in the normal state of affairs, in a soldier being killed, wounded or taken prisoner. Likewise, as friends to whom I have mentioned this book have suggested, it must include, surely, the famous Christmas Truce – it does, but not just that of 1914, but, rather, the lesser known Christmas Truce of 1915. Then throw in a few spies, the odd temporary battlefield armistice to collect the dead and deserters who chanced crossing no-man's-land, and that would appear at first glance to cover the obvious eventualities.

In fact, indirect contact was as important as direct contact. Letters written by soldiers to the families of the enemy, fallen or wounded, were more common than might be expected; exchanging effects of the dead required no meeting either. At a governmental level, communication between Britain and Germany, while necessarily formal and businesslike, continued throughout the war, using Dutch, Swiss and American intermediaries: enquiries or protests were made, replies sent, agreements brokered and concessions granted. Surviving correspondence makes for fascinating reading, for much of the official communication is about the minutiae of daily life. This includes anything from the requested return of a Heidelberg professor's books, abandoned in Britain, to the proposed reciprocal supply of spectacles and trusses to prisoners of war.

War is nothing if not contradictory, abnormal and downright chaotic. It throws up the peculiar and the unusual as a matter of course, and provides a platform for highly improbable scenarios. Captain Campbell's parole to England from a German POW camp to visit his ailing mother is just such an example. Similarly, why, did a patriotic British professor, of British birth and descent, honorably enlist in the German army in 1915? The answer is strange and yet ridiculously plausible.

And, just as war is extraordinary, so it is often banal and trite. What happened to the many thousands of British women married to Germans living in Britain or abroad? What happened to those naturalised British subjects of German origin who lived in Britain, many for decades, in peaceful, lawful harmony with their neighbours? What was the position of their British-born children? With whom would their allegiance lie? The answers are as surprising as they are often mundane or simply sad.

As with the majority of my books, I have, wherever possible, used a chronological approach rather than a thematic one, as I believe this to be of considerable advantage in showing the development of key characters and their context as the war progressed.

This book includes many unpublished letters and diaries. It draws upon official government documents, largely untouched until now, to tell a new story of the Great War. The story slips back and forth from the Western Front to the Home Front; from prisoner-of-war camps to internment camps; from trench dugouts to terraced houses; from shell holes in no-man's-land to the drawing rooms of middle-class Britain. I examine fraternisation with the enemy and temporary armistices, reprisals and murder. And, as in all wars, the story will feature the nadir of human behaviour counterbalanced by the zenith of human endeavour and compassion. I am less interested in tactics or generals, weapons or strategy, than I am in human beings, and, when it comes to humans in war, one thing has become abundantly clear to me: you simply couldn't make it up.

I

The Age of Unreason

The dry summer heat had given way to a cool, pleasing breeze as the Reverend Henry Williams strolled to his flat in a side street off Berlin's famous Kurfürstendamm. It was Sunday evening, 26 July 1914, and the thirty-seven-year-old priest was on his way home from St George's Church where he served as chaplain. Built in the royal gardens in 1885, this very English church was physical proof of the close ties between Britain and Germany. It had been given as a silver wedding present by the then Prince and Princess of Wales, later King Edward VII and his wife, Queen Alexandra, to Edward's eldest sister, the Crown Princess of Germany and later Empress.

The church register revealed an impressive list of high-status guests: Queen Victoria had visited in 1888, as had her eldest child, also named Victoria, the German Crown Princess; their signatures so similar, Williams reflected, that they might have been written by the same hand. Edward and Alexandra had signed the book, as had their son, Albert, and in 1913, during the last royal visit to Germany, King George and Queen Mary had stopped by. But perhaps most interesting of all was the name of the Kaiser himself, signed not as 'Wilhelm' but 'William' in recognition of his maternal heritage. The Kaiser had visited St George's in 1904 as an honoured guest at the wedding of the British ambassador's daughter. Yet, while the Kaiser's English spelling was diplomatic, thoughtful even, to have assumed that his action was modest would have been wide of the mark, for his signature was made with a truly magnificent flourish, filling the entire page.

Ten years later, Anglo-German fraternity was about to be torn apart. The political skies over Europe had darkened rapidly after the assassination of the heir to the Austro-Hungarian throne. During a visit by the Archduke Franz Ferdinand and his wife, Sophia, to the Serbian capital Sarajevo in June 1914, a young Serbian nationalist had shot them both dead. One diplomatic crisis followed another as what at first seemed to be a local crisis in the ever-turbulent Balkans had instead spread the contagion of war across a continent. The European system of political alliances and military guarantees was awoken. In the event of war, Berlin would back Vienna in its dispute with Serbia. In response, Serbia would look to Moscow for support, and Moscow, in turn, would look to Paris; Paris looked towards London. On the afternoon of 23 July, the Austro-Hungarian Empire handed a ten-point ultimatum to Serbia. In effect, the Serbs were being ordered to cede sovereignty. They had forty-eight hours to reply or there would be war, with the implicit threat of invasion.

The Reverend Williams read the newspapers and fretted over the prospect of conflict. 'From week to week I had watched the threatening storm approaching without believing that it could ever burst.' The Kaiser had left for his summer cruise in Norwegian waters and, while he was there, thought Williams, 'What need to worry?' But the Kaiser was breaking off his cruise and returning to Berlin. That Sunday, as Williams made his way home, he could literally hear the drums of war.

> I had reached the Palace-bridge [when] I heard the distant sound of a band approaching, and stopped to see it pass. Borne aloft at its head was the eagle surmounted with its waving plumes and tinkling bells that always preceded the goose-stepping guards as they marched down the Unter den Linden on their way to the Palace, according to custom. But on this particular Sunday it was not the usual jaunty regimental march that was being played but

the Deutschland Deutschland über Alles, and that could have only one meaning, things were getting definitely serious – War, of which we had so often heard rumours, but which had always seemed so utterly incredible, might be really coming at last!

It was coming, and it was coming fast. Two days later, the Austro-Hungarians declared war on Serbia, and their forces immediately invaded the country. It was only a matter of time before Russia would enter on the side of its old ally.

The Kaiser arrived back in Berlin via Kiel and Potsdam and went straight to the palace. At the same time, the Reverend Williams walked once more to the city centre to see what was happening. The public excitement was extraordinary, and then he saw the Kaiser.

As his car drove up the Unter den Linden towards the palace, the crowd was so dense that it was forced to go slowly, and I found myself pushed so close to it as it passed that I could have touched its royal occupant. I noticed that he was wearing a brass curassier's helmet that covered the back of his neck as well as his forehead. His face looked bloodless and yellow, while his eyes stared fixedly ahead with a hard, almost fierce expression . . .

That evening, Williams returned yet again; the public clamour for war was almost tangible. 'I found Berlin gone mad,' he wrote.

Inside the Brandenburger Tor I got caught in a dense, shouting mob that was pressing forward. Groups of young men arm-in-arm yelling 'Deutschland, Deutschland über Alles', were eddying in the current of the tide of surging humanity that swept slowly forward carrying me with it. Somewhere near the corner of the Friedrichstrasse I saw a large printed placard bearing the fateful words 'ultimatum an Russland – Frage an Frankreich'. Now I knew what was urging the crowd to frenzy. The Day had come at last! When eventually I reached the Palace-bridge at the end of the Linden, the crowd was so solidly packed as to make any further progress impossible – it was about ten o'clock that a sudden roar of voices away ahead told me what I could scarcely see, that the Kaiser had appeared on the palace balcony. Though his words can scarcely have been audible in the prevailing din, he was believed to have said, 'Tonight our beloved Fatherland stands on the verge of war. I bid you all go home and say your prayers. God with us!' . . . 'Deutschland!' yelled the young men again and again, 'Deutschland über Alles!' screamed the crowd.

It was then that there came to me one of the strangest sensations of a lifetime – I seemed to be aware of a dark winged form hovering over that vast, frenzied crowd that filled the broad thoroughfare of the Unter den Linden from end to end and the thought came to me, 'How many of them will death not have claimed before this war that they are now hailing so jubilantly, and vociferously, is over?' And as I walked my two-mile way home, past open-doored restaurants and beer-houses filled to capacity, where everyone was frantically applauding the gesticulating speaker of the moment, I felt strangely depressed and lonely. For had not I alone, as it seemed, perceived the ghostly presence of the Angel of Death, watching and waiting as he brooded that night over a bawling multitude of the doomed and blinded in Germany's capital, and heard the rustle of his wings.

Two hundred and sixty miles away, in the city of Cologne, Harry Miles was staying as a guest of the Hahn family. This city, renowned in Germany for its liberalism and friendliness, was in just as much of a frenzy as the capital. On 29 July, Harry wrote to his father in England describing the developing crisis, how a continent teetered on the edge of a war the like of which had 'never been known and the result of which is too dreadful to contemplate'.

Those people here who want war are trusting that England will remain 'neutral' and leave Germany to wreak havoc as she surely will do if Russia intervenes . . . and those who are for peace are hoping that England will with that characteristic calmness yet iron firmness, demand the peace of Europe . . .

The last few evenings have been very exciting in the town. Crowds gathered round the newspaper offices eagerly awaiting telegrams from Sir Edward Grey and others – processions form with flags and parade the streets singing patriotic songs – the orchestras in the cafés strike up the Fatherland's anthem and the usual pandemonium follows. I'm sorry if I have bored you only you see all this has been intensely interesting to me here, on the spot, as it were.

Today Karl [Hahn], the son who has been doing soldier's training, has returned – though we didn't expect they'd let him owing to the 'trouble'. He says there were great scenes in the Barracks when the news came through. He is rather wondering how long he will remain at home!!

Three days later, on Saturday 1 August, Harry Miles quickly scribbled a card to his father.

Dear dad
    . . . am writing in the most extraordinary of all circumstances – such scenes as are passing are indescribable. Germany has mobilized. The official statements having arrived this evening! This has of course snapped the tendon which has held all Germany for the past few days. It is a sad thing this war declaration – every family here is affected and everything is very sad . . . but!

Most Germans welcomed war, according to British observers, but then those in favour were naturally more likely to fill the streets than the depressed and saddened. It was no different in Britain. *The Times* reported that holidaymakers had been attracted to London by the overwhelming 'desire to be present in the capital in this moment of grave crisis. They were eager for news and impatient to learn what part England was to play. Miniature Union Jacks and Tricolors were sold in the streets, and quickly bought . . . The demonstration of patriotism and loyalty became almost ecstatic . . .'

All along Pall Mall and in front of Buckingham Palace, surging crowds awaited the appearance of the monarchy. It was Tuesday 4 August, the day Britain declared war on Germany. 'Rule, Britannia!' was sung and 'God Save the King' and even 'the Marseillaise', and that was before Britain had even shown her hand.

'One hears on every side "We must stand by France" [in the event of war]. There seems little doubt that we shall go to war and no doubt that if we do we shall win,' reported the social observer and author Dorothy Peel. 'But still we hope that peace may be preserved. The statement "It will all be over in three months" seizes upon the imagination of the people, but no one appears to know why three months is the exact time which it will take to vanquish Germany.'

This war, long expected, had arrived and it was as if an emotional dam had burst across Europe. 'One could not stay in the house . . . there was a feeling as of an inner smouldering which at moments bursts out into intense excitement,' wrote a woman in London. In Münster, another English woman, known only as Miss Waring, recalled the astonishing emotion there, too. The town was 'packed full of soldiers and soldiers' families for the Mass of farewell', she wrote. 'At the end they sang the German Te Deum, "Grosser Gott, wir loben Dich!" It was thrilling at any time, but under the circumstances it bowled me over completely.'

Displays of intense national unity made foreigners feel isolated and vulnerable. Miss Waring returned to her home in Freiburg where at 5 p.m. a notice was pinned up: 'All English subjects must leave Freiburg at once'. Being British would, it might be assumed, be reason enough for the Germans to reach for lock and key, especially if the individual were young and male. As a priest, the Reverend Henry Williams would not have feared internment, as others did, but he was less certain about what might happen to his beloved English church.

I had given notice that a special service of intercession would be held the following morning and went to the church, which was 2½ miles from my flat in Charlottenburg, prepared for the worst. What, then, was my surprise when the verger told me that less than half-an-hour before my arrival an officer had come from the Palace with a personal message from the Emperor. It was that the church was to remain open and its services to be continued as usual, and that if any help were required it would be forthcoming. This good news was as unexpected as it was encouraging, and was in striking contrast to another action which, I was told, His Imperial Majesty took at about the same time, and not improbably by the same intermediary. It was to deliver at the British Embassy a badly packed brown paper parcel containing all his British decorations and insignia, with a message that while he had hitherto felt honoured to possess them he had now no further use for them.

Why did the Emperor show such extraordinary solicitude on behalf of the English church, of which he was never at any time a member? I can only credit one reason which I believe to be true, namely, that his mother on her death-bed extracted from him the promise that he would always protect her beloved church, and he kept his word.

Williams remained at liberty. The relative freedom afforded to a priest allowed him to use his influence to help British people stranded in Germany in the days and weeks ahead, as well as visiting the burgeoning community of British prisoners of war held in camps across Germany.

One Englishman looking to leave Berlin as quickly as possible was a fifty-one-year-old language teacher from Cheltenham, Henry Hadley. A former army officer in the West India Regiment, he took his cue to go on the outbreak of hostilities between Russia and Germany. Deciding to catch a train to Paris, he quickly sorted out his affairs in the German capital and then, the next day, returned to his rented apartment and packed his bags, leaving early the following morning.

Even in the febrile atmosphere of the time, a middle-aged English gentleman travelling through Germany should have been safe. Accompanied by his housekeeper, Mrs Elizabeth Pratley, he took a train from Friedrichstrasse station at 11 a.m. A German declaration of war on France was expected imminently and great crowds of German mobilised soldiers were being waved off by their families. Henry Hadley and his housekeeper were no doubt fortunate to find seats among such a throng of infantrymen.

The train left Berlin for Cologne. Here, Henry would pick up a connection for the French capital. The journey had been so far uneventful when, as the train neared Gelsenkirchen, Henry and Elizabeth went to the restaurant car. The service was slow. Henry became agitated, then angry with a waiter and a heated exchange took place in front of some dining German officers. Henry and his housekeeper abandoned lunch and the restaurant car to return to their seats. Then, shortly afterwards, he left the carriage once more, telling Mrs Pratley to look after the luggage; he would not be long.

In Schwalbach, Hilda Pickard-Cambridge was also trying to get home but her travel arrangements were complicated. She had arrived in Germany with her husband in early July and was enjoying some rest at the spa town while he dealt with business elsewhere. Hilda had noted the feeling of unrest at the end of July; there were rumours that ammunition was arriving at the railway station, and posters appeared on the trees alerting locals to the grave state of affairs between Austria and Serbia. 'During Saturday, 1st August, I saw consternation on every face, and in the evening after dinner, I saw a large red placard being posted up outside the Landrat's office. I ran towards it, and read that Russia had declared war on Germany, and that mobilisation was to begin in the morning.' Hilda was in a quandary. Within hours she received an urgent telegram from her husband. Rather than attempt to leave, she was to stay put and he would come for her.

> It was very difficult to know what it was best to do. I packed everything that morning, and was ready to start at a moment's notice . . . There was confusion everywhere. From every hotel the visitors were rushing to the station. All the cabs in Schwalbach were tearing backwards and forwards, to and from the railway. Groups of people were standing in the street, with their hand luggage, shouting to the carriages to come back.

Hilda's instinct was to leave but she had been told to remain where she was. The hotel, which had that morning entertained French, Americans, Dutch and Russians, was all but deserted by lunchtime; only two small parties were left. One was an American family 'half beside themselves, because they could not get petrol for their motor-car'. They were gone the moment they heard petrol was available in Wiesbaden. The other party consisted of an 'utterly wretched and frightened' French family which left on finding they could get a train that evening to Basle. Hilda Pickard-Cambridge was now on her own. That evening she stood outside her hotel hoping her husband might arrive. He never did. The journey had proved impossible.

Next morning Hilda was woken early by the noise of horses' hooves, passing incessantly. Lines of horses were being brought along each road into town to be sold to the army. Once purchased, they were harnessed in threes and led away for war service. 'It was extraordinary to see every avenue and open space entirely full of horses, instead of visitors sipping waters,' she wrote.

As Hilda waited in Schwalbach, Henry Hadley and his house-keeper were well on their way home and not far from either the Dutch or Belgian border. Their train, though, had stopped at Gelsenkirchen. After the altercation in the dining car, they had returned to their carriage but Henry had ventured into the corri-dor while the train was stationary. After about a minute, Elizabeth heard loud noises followed by sounds of a scuffle. She rushed outside to find Henry lying on the floor. 'They have shot me, Mrs Pratley, I am a done man,' he gasped. A German officer, later iden-tified as Lieutenant Nicolay, had fired his revolver at point-blank range, hitting Henry in the stomach. The Germans then turned on Mrs Pratley.

> Several men took hold of me and shouted, 'This your man, this your man?' I screamed with fright. Two policemen rushed in and took me out of the train into some room close by. A military officer came behind. They went back and fetched Mr Hadley into the same room and laid him on a stretcher. They telephoned for a doctor. After they had looked at some papers Mr Hadley had in his pockets, they took him to the [Gelsenkirchen] hospi-tal in an ambulance. I also accompanied him there. Mr Hadley was very anxious for me to stay with him there but they would not let me.

Elizabeth Pratley would not see her employer again. She was taken away for questioning while he clung on to life for another twenty-four hours. At 3.15 a.m. German time, on 5 August 1914, just hours after Britain's entry into the Great War, Henry Hadley died. He was the first British casualty of the Great War and the first person killed as a direct result of enemy action.

In London, the government heard of Hadley's death and an

explanation was demanded. Through intermediaries, the Germans rebutted all claims of foul play: the assailant, Lieutenant Nicolay, maintained that Hadley had been acting suspiciously. When asked, Hadley had been vague about his travel arrangements, he had been insulting to German officers on the train, and, when confronted, he was aggressive, raising a stick to Lieutenant Nicolay. Finally, although repeatedly told to raise his hands in surrender, Hadley refused to do so and reacted as if he was about to pull out a weapon. Even as Hadley was being removed from the train, he had 'resisted with all his might'. Lieutenant Nicolay was exonerated of all blame by the Germans and was subsequently promoted to captain. The British government considered the shooting nothing less than murder.

As the days passed that August, panic and fear gripped the small British community in Germany as soldiers were deployed along roads and railway lines. Hilda Pickard-Cambridge watched from her window as four sentries were posted near her hotel, all armed, stopping and levelling their rifles at any car that appeared. She heard that innocent people had been shot by overzealous officials and rumours proliferated of spies being caught and even executed.

I could see four men kneeling in the street, pointing their rifles at a motor-car which was coming down the hill. An officer gave two sharp orders, and I waited breathlessly for the signal to fire, when there were cries of 'Halt Halt!' The car came to a standstill at the very point of the guns, and the soldiers pulled one of their own officers out of the car! Then there were more shrieks, and the sentries turned sharply round, and pointed their rifles down the road in the opposite direction. Another car was stopped, and this time a party of French people, two ladies and two little boys were dragged out, and taken to one of the other hotels. I watched their car being carefully searched and taken away.

There was fury in Germany at Britain's declaration of war: fury but also a profound and widespread sense of betrayal. Before the war, wrote the Reverend Williams, Britain had 'continually bombarded Germany with assurances of good intentions and appeals for the improvement of friendly relations between the two countries'. This tended to create a strained and artificial atmosphere. 'In Berlin we had visits from Lord Haldane and various delegates of societies for international peace and understanding . . .' The attempt at understanding might have been misinterpreted by the Germans, 'as implying friendship under all circumstances and peace at any cost'. Williams was not surprised when, as war broke out, Britain was accused of deliberately betraying Germany's trust in her friendship, 'and King George the Fifth was portrayed on a particularly scurrilous picture-postcard, on sale, as "Der Judas von England"'.

War between France and Germany was long expected and much anticipated. Both countries had worked out detailed plans for the mobilisation and deployment of millions of men in the event of conflict. The French had their plan XVII, which envisaged an immediate attack on, and the recovery for France of, the disputed lands of Alsace and Lorraine. The Germans had their Schlieffen Plan, which anticipated the French strike. In response to this, a relatively small German force would be sent to engage and draw on the French forces, while a much larger force would be sent north through neutral Belgium in order to sweep south on Paris, simultaneously trapping French forces between German armies marching south-east and those already in action in Alsace and Lorraine. Given such a scenario, the French army would be quickly annihilated.

The Schlieffen Plan did not take into account the rapid deployment of a British force on the left flank of the French Fifth Army, an army that was urgently transferred from the eastern frontier to hold back the Germans sweeping through Belgium. In the event, the British Army sent just four divisions of infantry and one division of cavalry to the continent, a paltry number in comparison with the huge conscript armies of France and Germany; two further British divisions would arrive within days. Nevertheless, the embarkation of 70,000 men, with all the required artillery and transport, was a triumph of planning and logistics and, although small in number, the professional soldiers of the BEF (British Expeditionary Force) were a far more forbidding force than their token numbers suggested.

Although Germany had attacked France through neutral Belgium, most Germans believed that Britain, with problems of her own in Ireland, would stand aside. With Germany already at war with Russia and France, it appeared to Berlin that Britain had fallen on her 'friend' merely because it deemed the time propitious. It would not take much, or long, for this view to be transformed into a conviction that Britain had instigated the war all along. The Reverend Williams learnt on 'unimpeachable authority' that, so staggered was the Kaiser at the news of Britain's declaration of war, he was kept from fainting by the quick appearance of a glass of champagne. Whatever the truth, the American ambassador in Berlin, James Gerard, witnessed the public reaction and it was of almost uncontained 'rage'. A crowd attacked the British Embassy and almost every window was broken, with mounted police making scant effort to protect the legal sanctity of the building and grounds. Shouts of 'May God punish England' rang out.

The German press gave vent to the public fury. Lady Harriet Jephson was trying to leave Altheim but, without money or a return ticket home, she was stuck. In her daily diary she recorded the war from the moment that a young clerk had 'literally hissed' at her that England had declared war and shop window signs declaring 'English spoken here' were removed.

Next came the Press announcements, 'England who poses as the guardian of morality and all the virtues, sides with Russia and assassins!' Abuse of Sir Edward Grey, of our Government, and all things English, follows . . . The German press is full of the most virulent abuse of England, 'treacherous,' 'Hypocritical,' 'lying,' 'cowardly,' 'boastful,' there is no bad name they don't call her! Russia and France and Belgium get no lashings of scorn and fury and hatred such as England does!

Twenty-three-year-old Edward Sibbe was working in the manufacturing town of Chemnitz, when an elderly businessman, who had previously been friendly, stopped him in the street.

He enquired whether the English had gone mad, and I told him that I had not observed any traces of insanity when I left home. He then asked me why we had declared war on Germany, and I explained to him that I personally had had very little to do with it. He then got excited, and informed me, that if he ever saw me walking down the street with Sir Edward Grey, he would hang the latter on the nearest lamp post. He then expressed a desire to hang various British statesmen, but as I did not express any fear for the safety of the British Cabinet Ministers, he gradually cooled down, and expressed the hope that whatever happened we might always be friends, which, as I observed, was the only sensible remark he made.

On 5 August, Reverend Williams entered the embassy to find a large hall filled with unshaven British journalists and correspondents who had been ordered by the German police to remain there overnight, 'a strange sight', Williams recalled. He quickly became aware of the prevailing atmosphere of fear and excitement. 'I'm sure they mean to shoot us,' one individual said. Williams watched as one of the embassy secretaries 'who was afflicted with a stammer was doing his utmost to say something urgent on the telephone, but could only produce unintelligible sounds'.

Their fears were unfounded. The embassy staff, along with the journalists and correspondents, departed by train very early on 6 August, leaving the American Embassy under Gerard to handle British interests. This included looking after scores of distressed British citizens who had become stranded in the capital, living with the threat of arrest and internment. British subjects had already been picked up on their way to the British Embassy and now they would be stopped as they went to the American Embassy. Gerard remonstrated with the Germans when he discovered that British subjects 'without distinction as to age, or sex' were being removed to the fortress of Spandau for questioning.

After the death of Henry Hadley, Elizabeth Pratley had been whisked off for interrogation. Did Mr Hadley have picture post-cards or portraits with him of any kind? Had Mr Hadley been seeing other gentlemen while in Berlin? Her replies were deemed evasive or hesitant enough for her to be taken to Münster and a 'military prison' for further questioning by an officer. 'He hoped Mr Hadley had not been espionageing [sic] their ships. I said I was sure Mr Hadley had not. There was an interpreter there [and] he read a paper to me and said I was arrested as a spy.'

Elizabeth protested her innocence. After extensive searches of her luggage, she was finally released: they had all the information they required, she was informed. Elizabeth was by now in such a weakened and nervous state that she was taken to a Roman Catholic hospital to recover.

Not every Briton leaving Germany told stories of threat and harassment, of an enemy swelling with bellicose pride. Perhaps surprisingly *The Times* published readers' letters praising the kindness individuals had received in Germany. One lady, Florence Phillips, took the newspaper to task over a report by a correspondent who described 'ad nauseam' and 'in lurid terms the sufferings experienced by travellers in Germany in the last few days'. Travelling with a friend from Baden-Baden to Berlin, she maintained that that was not her experience.

> We met with much more than the ordinary courtesy extended to women travelling. I was very much impressed by the real kindness and chivalry shown to us on three different occasions by German men, who voluntarily gave up their places to save us from sitting on our bags in a crowded corridor, and who put themselves to much trouble to obtain food for us at the stations . . . I should like to put on record that during all those hours of intense excitement, with a nation newly called to arms, we did not meet with a single instance of rudeness in Germany.

In another letter dated 8 August under the headline 'German Kindness', the exotically named Bampfylde Fuller contended that, throughout a motor tour of Germany in early August, 'Our experiences have been wholly of kindness and helpfulness. We were stopped every few miles by armed patrols, our papers examined, our boxes sometimes opened, but on no occasion were we offered the least incivility.' As interesting as these counterpoints are, they are less interesting historically than *The Times*'s decision to publish them. Britain had yet to become as incensed with Germany as Germany evidently was with Britain. That time would soon come.

At her hotel in Schwalbach, Hilda Pickard-Cambridge was gradually feeling bolder. After a week she began to venture outside and was reassured by a somewhat perverse notice that English people should not be molested, just in case they turned out to be Americans. Hers was a strange existence. There were no guests at the hotel and so the maids were released and, with the exception of the proprietors, the building was deserted. Hilda waited, not knowing if she might be picked up by either her husband or the Germans. She looked out for war news but this was tainted by aggressive propaganda: it was said that Britain had declared war *before* Germany had invaded Belgium, that the British instigated the murder of the Austrian Archduke to pre-empt a war that would crush Germany. And then came the news from the front. The Germans were winning hands down, Paris would fall very soon and London shortly afterwards. It all made for dismal reading.

As Britain went to war, MPs voted to pass the Defence of the Realm Act (DORA) to secure the safety of the nation. It was a broad-sweeping Act, frequently modified, giving the government wide-ranging powers over public and press, with rights to requisition property and land and to control the transport network, including railways, docks and harbours. Individuals contravening the Act were liable to court martial with fines, imprisonment and even death as options.

Notably, DORA forbade communication that would endanger in any way 'the success of the operations of His Majesty's forces'. With Germans constituting the third highest immigrant population, it was self-evident that specific legislation was needed to control the movement and activities of foreign nationals and enemy aliens in particular, the perceived threat from whom the press would quickly and vociferously highlight.

On 5 August, Reginald McKenna, the Liberal Home Secretary, presented legislation to the House of Commons restricting the movement of all foreigners (the Aliens Restriction Act), and was greeted with broad cross-bench support. Hansard recorders included in parentheses the cheers that met his speech. McKenna assured Members that arrangements had been made to cause as little disturbance to the daily lives of 'alien friends' as was possible under the circumstances (that is, the lives of foreigners who were not German, Austrian or Hungarian), while at the same time helping to root out dangerous spies (loud cheers and cries of 'shoot them'). In another example of early calm, McKenna pointed out that there was 'concern that Germans who were long resident in the country should be protected'. MPs responded with questions.

> Mr [Joseph] King (Somerset, North) – As one acquainted with many German subjects, some of whom have been resident in the country for many years and are much more British in sentiment than German (hear, hear), I should like some assuring words from the Home Secretary that some regard will be had for these persons. There is a very great deal of apprehension among such persons at the present time. (Cries of 'Agreed')
>
> Mr McKenna (Monmouth, North) – Alien enemies against whom there is no reason whatever to suppose that they are secretly engaged in operations against this country will be subjected to nothing further than registration and the provision that they may not live in the prohibited areas.

In those first days of war there was no uniform, headlong rush to condemn everything German or Austrian. Newspapers such as the influential *East London Observer* still took on the mantle of guiding as opposed to being buffeted or swayed by public sentiment. On 8 August, the same day that *The Times* had published letters from Florence Phillips and Bampfylde Fuller, the *East London Observer* spoke to its readers in a tone that was both considered and measured.

> The East London German Colony is one which is an advantage and credit to possess. Its members have formed in varying degrees life-long business and personal ties of mutual respect with the English natives, and we should regard it as more than deplorable if, by word, deed or implication any manifestation of personal sentiment against friends and neighbours, who hate and deplore the present war as much as anyone, should occur to wound their feelings . . . To the German Colony of East London we bear emphatic

testimony of their virtues of sobriety, industry and honesty; that we should find the two great nations at deadly war is a bitter grief, but in the indignation of the moment one must not forget to behave oneself justly, and like a gentleman and a friend.

The country's pre-war liberal tradition that might have opposed such measures as alien registration was conspicuous by its absence, with little or no protest from the left. Instead, it was the radical right that made the running, accusing the government through Fleet Street newspapers of not doing enough to minimise the threat from Britain's enemies. Public opinion, fearful of complacency, was won over by those championing tougher laws, and the relative tranquillity inside the House was to be disrupted by the irresistible force of popular will. McKenna's and King's calmer sentiments went the way of most things in war once the shooting started, and newspapers pressed for greater restrictions on enemy aliens.

McKenna's desire to 'root out dangerous spies' was hardly required. Before the war, the Germans had run an almost laughably ineffective espionage network through a British-born subject of German ancestry. His name was Karl Ernst and he owned a barber's shop in London's Caledonian Road through which all communication between Germany and its twenty-two spies was passed. Unfortunately for Ernst, he was known to the equally small number of officers who at that time formed Britain's pre-war intelligence and, according to a former officer named Dunlop, his activities were closely monitored.

His job was merely to drop all letters received into the nearest letterbox. His salary was quite small, about £12 a year. All letters were opened, read and forwarded on with as little delay as possible. In this way the names and addresses of all German spies were compiled and arrangements were so complete that on the day of the declaration of war only one of the German agents escaped.

Britain's counter-espionage services burgeoned during the war and, on the whole, maintained the initiative over the numerically small number of spies sent to Britain. The fact that not one proven act of foreign sabotage took place on British soil underlines the extent to which Britain's security had enemy espionage under restraint.

Quick and efficient arrests of Germany's pre-war spies contrasted with the charges of espionage levelled against others for whom the evidence was flimsy at best. On the first full day of war, the press reported charges against Germans or German sympathisers in coastal towns as far apart as Sheerness, Portsmouth, Falmouth, Penarth, Swansea and Barrow-in-Furness. Arrests were a precursor of what would develop into a frenzy of anti-German paranoia. Public fear of spies was inflamed by vocal backbench politicians and journalists working for daily newspapers and weekly journals. The power of the press to stoke 'spy-fever' pushed the government into introducing ever more stringent controls on enemy aliens, controls that seemed vastly disproportionate to the actual rather than the perceived threat. 'It is extraordinary how many people were infested with "spy-fever",' wrote Dunlop. 'Nobody who showed a naked light or used a typewriter which made a noise like a wireless transmitter was safe. None of these denunciations, no matter how foolish, could be disregarded as the nerves of the public were on edge . . .'.

All along the British coast, Boy Scouts and well-meaning if often overzealous members of the public acted as volunteer coast-guards, patrolling seaside paths and tracks on the lookout for the enemy at sea and spies on land.

Harry Siepmann, the son of Otto Siepmann and Grace Baker, was in Cornwall enjoying the August bank holiday weekend as a chance to have a break from his work in London. One evening, as he was about to make his way back to his cottage, a thick fog descended and he took a lantern to help light his way. It was only after he had gone some distance that a shadowy figure emerged from the gloom. Levelling a doubled-barrelled shotgun at Harry's chest, the figure asked him what he was doing.

> I swallowed my resentment and introduced myself.
>
> 'I see,' he said, apparently satisfied. 'I had better take your name and address to put in my report.'
>
> That was unfortunate. In 1914, names of Germanic origin did not inspire confidence. In the glow of the lantern I could see the man's expression change, and the gun was once more levelled in my direction.
>
> 'I think I had better take the lantern off you,' he said.
>
> I was so shocked that I just gawped. Incredulously I listened while it was explained to me that I was now suspected of being a spy who had gone out to the cliffs to signal with a lantern to a ship, or more probably a submarine. I was promptly arrested.

Harry Siepmann was taken to Falmouth Castle from where he was quickly released. No one bothered to ask why a man would attempt to signal to a submarine with a lantern in fog dense enough to reduce visibility to a few yards.

For the first time, Harry felt acutely conscious of his name and the national hostility to all things Germanic. In his own mind he was English: he had been educated at Rugby School and joined the Officer Training Corps (OTC) there before going up to New College, Oxford. He graduated and in 1912 he had become a civil servant employed at the Treasury. Suddenly, he was under suspicion. At his father's home in London, windows were broken and slogans daubed on walls even before the declaration of war, acts of stupidity that Harry assumed would abate. But family friends turned vindictive and spiteful and, after the incident in Cornwall, Harry realised that his optimism was misplaced. He determined to join the army. 'At least my father would be able to point to that mitigating fact the next time a brick landed on the sitting-room floor.'

No one could have predicted the rising public excitement when MPs passed the Aliens Restriction Act requiring foreigners to register themselves with the police. Nationwide announcements in the press circulated the information and by 10 August the *Manchester Guardian* reported a motley queue of people outside Tottenham Court Road police station including: 'many quiet looking old ladies, probably teachers, young German girl students, tourists caught without money, barbers, stockbrokers, shipping clerks, waiters, bankers and some of the much less reputable occupations.'

Their number included one London-based German, name unknown, who joined a queue, little realising the confusion that lay ahead:

> . . . Yesterday morning [8 August] I went straight to the police station to register myself which I thought would take me 1 to 2 hours at the outside. Well, I joined the queue outside the police station at 9.10 a.m. and I got inside at 20 minutes to 7 p.m.!!! It was a terrible experience to stand there for 10 hours in an awful crush whilst it was raining all the morning and with nothing to eat since breakfast.

The cause of the delay was not one of numbers but the intricacies of the government form, bamboozling police officers unused to such detailed questions. Blunders were made in understanding the full requirements of the law. The anonymous German continued:

> I just had to go through it and left the Police station at 8.45 p.m. more dead than alive . . . As you will be able to see from the papers my position as a German here in London is a most serious one: whilst I have not the slightest wish or desire to do anything against this country I must be prepared to be arrested on suspicion. Of this I hope you are all convinced . . . I am very much

troubled, not for my own safety or comfort, but for the sorrow and disaster that will follow out of this terrible war which is caused by the folly of my countrymen!

Those registering gave details as to nationality, occupation, appearance, residence and 'service of any foreign government'. Quite reasonably, enemy aliens were banned from owning fire-arms, signalling equipment, carrier or homing pigeons or the means of conducting secret correspondence. They were also banned from owning cameras and naval or military maps. Germans had until 17 August to register and Austrians a further week; those failing to do so could be subject to a £100 fine or six months in prison – a harsh punishment for those who, ignorant of the law and fearing their neighbours, went into hiding, although, in reality, most were allowed to register late on expla-nation of the facts.

Julia Jacobitz was one of the 'quiet looking old ladies' who registered at her nearest police station in Bournemouth. A retired school governess, she had lived in the popular seaside town for sixteen of her twenty-three years in Britain. She was scrupulously law-abiding and on cordial terms with the local police. Several years earlier, her home had been burgled and ransacked and she now made a point of letting the police know whenever she went away and leaving them a door key should it be needed.

On registration, all enemy aliens were given strict rules as to where they could live and where they could or, more to the point, could not go. One provision of the Aliens Restriction Act forbade Germans from living close to the sea. Julia Jacobitz's whole-hearted cooperation with the police was, as she later pointed out, 'hardly the manner dangerous persons would adopt who wished, or had, to hide their business'. She was concerned that she might be forcibly moved and so was grateful when Bournemouth police reassured her that that would not be the case for someone such as her, living by herself and in her mid-sixties. She was a German who desired to stay in England and wished only to be left alone.

Many Germans who had lived in Britain for a generation or more wanted to be left alone, too, and hoped that Reginald McKenna's parliamentary reassurances to respect law-abiding enemy aliens would be honoured. Meanwhile, others were packing up. Leaving from Parkstone Quay, Harwich, was the German ambassador. On 6 August he was escorted to the port by an armed guard from the Rifle Brigade along with scores of embassy staff, their families, assorted luggage and prams. There were no restrictions on who left, then or during the following days, for the Act gave Germans until midnight on 10 August to leave from any of thirteen designated ports.

Princess Evelyn Blücher, *née* Stapleton-Bretherton, the British-born wife of Prince Gebhard Blücher, travelled with the ambassador's party. The Princess and her husband had been staying at their London home where a steady stream of friends and relatives had come to help her pack and say goodbye, including her brother Vincent, one of her four siblings who were serving as officers in the British Army. The Princess was taken to Liverpool Street Station.

Even at that early hour, we saw placards and papers everywhere announcing German disasters and 3500 Germans killed. The scene at the station I shall never forget, with 250 Germans and their luggage congregated on the platform, and the special train in readiness.

The Ambassador and Ambassadress arrived at the last minute and got straight into the train, the Ambassadress quite heart-broken, and making no attempt to hide her grief. The train steamed out of the station amidst a hushed silence, people on the platform weeping, and the men with hats off standing solemnly silent. It was as if a dead monarch was being borne away . . . it was difficult to realize we were going out of this country to become its bitterest enemy.

I could not face the departure of the ship, and went down to hide myself in the cabin. I could not look upon the shores – of my beautiful England fading from sight.

The ship reached open sea where it ran across a flotilla of British torpedo boats, one of which opened warning fire, a shell landing thirty yards away. The ship was meant to carry a German flag on the mainmast and a Union Jack at the stern, but the Union Jack had proved too small to be seen. The English captain of the ship hauled down the German flag to avoid any further repetition and the flotilla moved away.

'We made great friends with the Captain,' wrote Princess Blücher in her private journal,

and when he found out that I was English, and a sister-in-law to one of the Admirals whom he knew well, he became most friendly and sat in our cabin for a long time, giving us his views on the war, etc. He also promised to take some letters back to England for me, and to send a wireless message to my family to say we had arrived safely as far as the Hook.

We had many interesting conversations during the journey. The sadness and bitterness of all these Germans leaving England struck me intensely. Here we are, they say, being dragged away from the country that has been our home for years, to fight against our best friends. They all blamed the officials in Berlin, who had, they said, grossly mismanaged the negotiations.

By today's standards of migration, the exodus appears inconsequentially small, in thousands not tens of thousands during six days of 'grace'. The largest number left immediately on declaration of war between Germany and Russia, and then France. After Britain's entry, there had been no directive to stop Germans of military age returning home, although two hundred young men were halted at Folkestone on the morning of 11 August and later interned. However, as a government report concluded, Germans of military age 'had ample opportunity, to go home, if they so desired'. After 10 August only male Germans aged over fifty-five, along with women, and children under the age of seventeen, were given permission to leave.

The requirement for travel permits in Great Britain and Germany slowed repatriation traffic to a trickle. Germany forbade civilians of enemy nations to travel other than through Berlin and many foreign nationals feared going to the capital. Hilda Pickard-Cambridge eventually 'escaped' at the end of August with a family of Americans on whose permit she contrived to travel to Rotterdam. Elizabeth Pratley remained in hospital in Germany until, with the aid of a Friendly Society, she was given a permit to leave in November and would go on to tell her story about the murder of Henry Hadley to the British government.

After being stuck for several weeks, Miss Waring was finally authorised to travel to Switzerland at the end of September 1914. Beginning the war in Münster, she had eventually ended up in the famous spa town of Baden-Baden, in the foothills of the Black Forest. This town, she wrote, 'is surely one of loveliest places in the world, we could not have wished for a more beautiful "prison", but the lack of liberty spoils everything'. Then the German press began reporting their army's victories. Church bells were rung, flags came out and bands played in the street. 'Germans are bad victors, it makes them bullies,' Miss Waring opined, and, of course, the news was always reliable: 'One German lady told me their press could say nothing but the truth, because the censorship was so strict!'

'Bad victors' was an expression likely to have been on the lips of an English girl named Dorothy. Born in a country where the art of understatement had been honed to perfection – 'false modesty', other people might call it – Dorothy was surprised to receive a letter from her German friend Lotte in Görlitz. It was dated 14

September, and the first serious check to the Germans' offensive in France had yet to reach the press in Saxony. Lotte could not control her pride at news of German victories or her conviction that Britain's declaration of war had been anything other than cynical opportunism. It is worth quoting at length.

My dear Dorothy . . .

I write you now to tell you something about our victories, for we did not sustain only one defeat as you are thinking. Dorothy, I do not want all this to hurt you, but we know that you do not know the truth about the war, the battles and our people, you only hear cruel things of our soldiers and much of our defeats but all this is not true, I hope you will believe me. Your Government is only too cowardly to speak the truth, it hopes to make us more enemies by all these lies, but till now <u>we</u> are the conquerors and we shall slay them . . . I can tell you so many and so cruel things about our enemies, it is really terrible. The French and Belgian people had cut off the tongues of our <u>wounded</u> soldiers, their arms, their hands, they have struck them blind!

But you wish to annihilate our dear Germany, oh, you shall not succeed. We are so strong, much stronger than you can imagine. We must win, we want to win and so we shall win. If you could see the enthusiasm of our people that is resolved to give all for this country, or the soldiers how gayful they are going into the war, you would be astonished . . .

Oh, Dorothy you are all so very afraid of our dear Germany. In fourteen days we got seven declarations of war, but we laughed about them! And the eighth was that one of Japan – and this was your work! Dorothy, once I told you that I hated France and liked England. Today I shrug the shoulders about France but I despise England! Why did your Government declare us the war? Because we have broken the neutrality of Belgium. Now you may hear that France broke it much earlier, our soldiers found French officers at Liege, and your Government knew it surely but did not say one word, so that it was only a pretext for the war. You wanted the war with us because you are enemies of our navy and our power. Now you felt not strong enough to fight alone against us on the sea . . . You have betrayed us.

And not only that, you did not fight with us with honourable arms, our soldiers found at the French army and yours anti-social shots that make the terriblest wounds you can imagine. Sir Edward Grey disputes it, but he is a liar. I send you a picture of those shots. I hope you will be honourable enough to dispute the doing of your Government after knowing all this. All the English living in Germany now disputes his politics. Now when you can write me soon what are you thinking. Though your navy destroyed some of our ships we are not a bit afraid of it, we shall see which will be the stronger one, you have lost several ships too, perhaps you do not know it. But do you know that you destroyed one of our ships when it was lying in a neutral port? That was anti-social too, you may be ashamed of it . . .

I must go to dinner now so I must end the letter. Please tell your friends all I wrote you. Many greetings for you, your father and sister, Lotte

Lotte's letter lacks all subtlety but it does capture the prevailing Zeitgeist in Germany: the public impression of British betrayal and the sense of national euphoria at imminent victory.

It was three weeks since German and British forces had clashed just outside the Belgian town of Mons on 22 August, as forward units of the British Expeditionary Force met with advancing German forces of General Alexander von Kluck's First Army.

The first 'shot', a cavalry-on-cavalry engagement, saw British Dragoons overwhelm German Curassiers, ending with a number of enemy dead and prisoners taken. These men, their horses and a wagon full of lances were paraded past excited onlookers including troopers serving with the Queen's Bays, another cavalry regiment. Private Alfred Tilney, of the 4th (Royal Irish) Dragoon Guards who had taken part in the scrap, recognised a friend:

> He asked me where we had been. I pulled his leg, said we had been out to fetch a sample, and if they saw any chaps like these they were to shoot them, as they were Germans. When we reached the Regimental Headquarters, Colonel Mullens [the Dragoons' Commanding Officer] asked, 'Who caught this one?' I stuck out my chest and said, 'I did, sir'. He told me I was a damned fool.

The men should not have been taken prisoner. Mullens's order was that anyone surrendering was to be searched, stripped and turned away. Prisoners would hamper the work of cavalry on the move, especially when involved in such an important role as advance guard to the BEF. As it was, these Germans had to be passed back and up the chain of command. Before leaving, they had their wounds dressed by Captain Arthur Osborn, medical officer attached to the Dragoon Guards.

> Ploughboys in German uniforms – that was all they really were . . . I was not surprised, when I saw them, that several of these young Bavarians had turned tail. I could speak a few words of German and I asked them what they thought of the War. They said they did not know what to make of it, nor what it was all about. They had, they said, been called up for military training only a few weeks before War broke out . . . I asked one of the prisoners for a button, which he cut off – my first souvenir! Rather tearfully, he insisted that his brother had been shot in Munich for refusing to join up, and that he himself was very pleased he had been taken prisoner and would not have to take any further part in the war.

An Operational Order issued by Brigadier General de Lisle, commanding the 2nd Cavalry Brigade, congratulated those who had taken part in the 'spirited action' that resulted in 'establishing the moral superiority of our cavalry, from the first, over the German cavalry', which in this particularly brief and frenzied encounter was undoubtedly the case.

The next day the war began in earnest with British infantry battalions taking position on or close to the Mons-Condé Canal, a more than useful barrier on which to base a defence of Mons. Lance Corporal Alfred Vivian was there, serving with the 4th Middlesex Regiment. He had been sent with several others to a cottage on lookout. After finishing a morning wash, Vivian and his mates sat sunning themselves behind a wall when a sentry bounded in.

> 'Blimey! Corporal, grab your bloomin' pop-gun and have a dekko at the Kaiser's bodyguard prancing down the road, but be bleedin' careful' . . .
>
> Coming carelessly along the road towards us was a Uhlan patrol consisting of seven or eight men, then a scanty eighty yards away. The surprising nature of the sight robbed us of our breath and wits, and left us standing in a row gasping and looking like a lot of cod-fish.

In their astonishment, Vivian and his friends gazed on, and it was the enemy's officer who fired first. Brought to their senses by this brazen act, the Middlesex men returned the devastatingly accurate fire of professional soldiers, wiping out the German party 'with an ease that was staggering'.

> We stood aghast, overcome with horror by the enormity of the thing we had done. We had despatched fine, big, healthy men, full of the joy and the vigour of the prime of life, into the great unknown with scarcely a warning. We were all, I believe, absolutely stunned by the shock of this revelation. I felt, unaccountably, physically sick [and] I had a distinct fear of the consequences of breaking one of the most solemn laws of civilisation . . .

Accompanied by a volunteer, we approached the frightful scene slowly, and with great circumspection. On arrival, we found that, without any doubt, they had all been killed, the majority of them bearing at least two marks as evidence of the terrible accuracy of our fire. Neglecting precaution, we stood looking down at the sad fruits of our first clash with the enemy, the sight of these dead men exercising a dreadful fascination for me which I found very difficult to dispel. Thrusting aside its baneful influence, I pulled myself together with an effort, and we collected the peculiar headdress of these unlucky men.

The fighting at Mons that day was intense but brief. The men of the 4th Middlesex Regiment and neighbouring battalions defending the canal inflicted heinous casualties on the enemy. 'My sensations during this baptism were too numerous and confused to analyse,' wrote Vivian. 'I clearly remember being reduced to a profuse state of perspiration, the sweat pouring down my face and into my eyes in such volume as to render me temporarily blind. Gradually I became cooler, and the only sensation then noticeable was one of grim and increasing interest in the business of slaughter.'

The horror at such butchery was suspended if not dispelled. 'We had, in fact, become transformed into killers,' Vivian grimly accepted; the fields in front became littered with enemy dead. Only when the fighting died down and the audible cries and groans of the wounded reached the men of the Middlesex Regiment did humanity return. Yet just as the men were about to venture forward to offer help, the Germans attacked again. Once more they were cut down.

Parties of enemy stretcher-bearers made their appearance, greatly to our relief, and entirely without interference, and were permitted to carry out their errands of mercy . . . It was necessary for some of these to come within thirty yards of the hedge behind which we were entrenched and they interested us tremendously, especially when one or two of them hailed us in our own language. This resulted in a great deal of chaffing, which was given and received by all with great good humour.

One of our wags, very unfeelingly, with an immense lack of tact, implored them to inform him 'how they liked their eggs fried', which drew the extremely rueful reply that we were inclined to season them with a little too much pepper. As they were retiring on the completion of their job, one German, with a great grin, shouted 'Next time you will make the visits to us!'

The weight of attacks at Mons, and the risk of being outflanked by the numerically superior Germans, made the British positions increasingly untenable. To the astonishment of those who could see no more than the results of their marksmanship, a retirement was ordered, and the men fell back through Mons and on to the hot and dusty roads leading south.

Captain William Morritt was serving with his battalion, 1st East Surrey Regiment, on the German side of the Mons-Condé Canal, around three miles west of Mons. His battalion was deployed on the forward side of the canal, defending a railway bridge. During the engagement, he went to see some men on his right flank, returning to discover that those he had just left were falling back from their positions towards the canal. Morritt shouted to them to stop but was told that Germans were behind them and that they were in danger of being cut off. The enemy had managed to reach a rising embankment that led up to the bridge. If there had been an order to his company to retire, Morritt had not received it and he took the only course of action that seemed open: he ordered those men still under his command to fix bayonets and charge the Germans between him and the canal.

I got my revolver out to load. I had just done this when I was hit in the right wrist which knocked it out of my hand. I could not then draw my sword as I had no strength in my right hand, when I rushed forward I got a bullet in my calf and another just above the right knee which brought me down. I then had the satisfaction of seeing a German 20 yards off aiming carefully at me. I was saved by a miracle; the shot hit the solid hilt of my sword, square in the middle, bent it and broke it in halves, the bullet which otherwise would have gone through me was turned off. The shock of the bullet shook my body, and the German seeing that he had hit me, left me for dead.

Morritt remained where he lay for the rest of the day and night. 'Luckily I had fallen on my wounded arm and the arm being slightly twisted, I think the weight of my body stopped the flow of blood and saved me.' Morritt, and seven of those who survived, were picked up not by the Germans but by civilians who took them to a Franciscan convent for treatment.

A retirement became a retreat. Two days after the Dragoons demonstrated their 'superiority' over enemy cavalry, the same men, along with Lancers and Hussars, took part in a wild charge against German machine guns and artillery. It was a frantic attempt to stop enemy infantry from enveloping the left flank of the BEF. Success this time was measured in hours bought for hard-pressed British infantry but at the cost of De Lisle's 2nd Cavalry Brigade, which was temporarily scattered to the winds. On this occasion, they had been no match for such a blizzard of shells and bullets.

Lieutenant Alexander Gallaher of the 4th (Royal Irish) Dragoon Guards was brought down in this charge. His horse fell, pinning him to the ground until, in pain, he struggled free and crawled into a cowshed where three men were already sheltering. In no position to escape, they waited for the enemy to arrive.

A German officer and two German soldiers with bayonet on rifles, came through the doorway. In the officer's hand was a tiny pop-gun of a pistol, which he pointed at each of the four of us as he went from one to the other. Reaching my corner he stooped and relieved me of my revolver and my map-case, the later containing a notebook in which were an entry or two that I knew would hold his big, round blue eyes.

Running through my pockets he came to a purse with seven sovereigns in it. This he tucked back in the pocket of my tunic, then stepped out of the door to examine my notebook in the fading light. Other wounded men were brought in with those slightly injured taken away to help collect the dead and injured, both friend and foe, who still lay on the battlefield.

The more serious cases were taken to a convent in the village. A sergeant and myself were the last two to be moved. I was carried on the shed door. Before I was taken away the German officer, who spoke no English, came over to where I lay and gave me first a drink of water, then a drink of milk. Stiffly and awkwardly, he reached down and shook me by the hand as he departed. I never saw him again. Not a bad sort, I suppose. Meant well, probably.

A few hundred yards from where Gallaher was captured, a burial party was being assembled. Two men were being interred: one was Captain Ernest Jones, the other a drummer, Edward Hogan. The pair belonged to the 1st Cheshire Regiment, one of the battalions directly aided by the cavalry charge. Some of the infantry had got away; many had not, including a young private named Corporal Walter Crookes and his sergeant, Arthur Raynor. They had been caught in the same burst of fire that killed their two comrades, Jones and Hogan. Crookes, lightly wounded, had passed out, waking to find someone pouring wine down his throat. He looked around to find German soldiers everywhere, noting in a dazed way the numerals on their uniforms. Then he saw Sergeant Raynor talking calmly with the enemy.

The German Commander was interested in the Sergeant's ribbons. 'What ribbons are they?' he enquired. 'South Africa,' replied the Sergeant.

He became a person of great interest and respect to all the Germans. They had seen him make his bold dash for freedom from under their rifles; had seen him turn back under their fire to help a comrade, and had accepted his grudging surrender, when without ammunition he had been obliged to capitulate to their tremendous superiority in numbers. Now they recognised him as an old and seasoned soldier. He went round with a few Germans and collected his party, reporting all accounted for although the Platoon scout was lying behind a cornstook waiting for darkness and escape.

The Germans dug a shallow grave on the bank by the side of the road and prepared to bury the two men.

There was a sudden order and the Germans commenced to assemble the infantry in the road, the cavalry in the field behind them. The Sergeant saluted the German Commander and came over to me and a lance corporal. 'Fall in,' he ordered. I got up and fell in beside the Sergeant. In the trench lay the Captain and the Drummer. I watched the proceedings in a listless, apathetic manner. The German Commander took up his position on the other side of the grave, opposite the Platoon Sergeant. Behind him stood the Squadron Commander and another German officer. I stood next to the Platoon Sergeant, on his right the Lance Corporal. The Sergeant read some parts of the Service.

A command rang out in German. The Battalion and Squadron saluted, the German Commander and the two Officers behind him with drawn swords, at the Salute. Clear and decisive came the response from the British side of the grave, as if it were the changing of a guard. I admired the drill of the Germans, so smart. I looked at my Platoon Sergeant, straight and erect, smart, soldier-like, facing the Germans with all the pride and effrontery of an equal, not a prisoner. I straightened myself up and copied my Sergeant, facing the Germans squarely. 'Cheshires, Right Hand Salute!'

On this side of the grave stood the representatives of The Regiment and The British Army. Another German word of command and three volleys crashed into the air. The day was over, our first and last action had been fought and finished. The grave was filled in and the Sergeant, myself, and the Lance Corporal were taken to join a few other prisoners who were held at the other side of the road.

A grave marker was fashioned with the men's names and the words 'Faithful unto death' painted at the bottom. Later, perhaps after the war, the two bodies were moved to Witheries Cemetery where Jones's wooden cross was replaced by a Commonwealth War Graves headstone and, carved at the base, his family's paid-for inscription, 'For his bravery he was given a military funeral by the Germans'.

During these days of mobile warfare, contact between opposing sides was constant but not prolonged. As the British retreated, so the Germans, exhausted but jubilant at their success, pushed on, mopping up British stragglers. The equally shattered British infantry fought when called upon and then withdrew to be protected by a fast-moving screen of cavalry that came into repeated action, normally at short notice.

In the confusion, men became separated from their units. Overtaken by advancing Germans, a small number of British troops chose to go into hiding rather than surrender, secreting themselves in woods and barns and in the homes of courageous civilians. They hid, hoping that the tide of the war would turn and release them.

Because of his wounds, the Germans temporarily ignored Captain William Morritt. Along with the seven men from his regiment, he was treated in the nearby Franciscan convent. Three weeks later all the men were still there. 'Unfortunately there are Germans all around here,' wrote Morritt in a letter he hoped would be smuggled to his mother, 'and they know we are here. I hope I shall be able to escape them in a week's time . . . I cannot wait until the Germans call for me.'

Three photographs of Morritt survive, taken at the convent. In one he holds the sword cut in two by an enemy bullet. He appears well and wears the uniform in which he was wounded although, according to Morritt, civilian clothes were being made available to him to aid an escape. Unfortunately for Morritt, the Germans came knocking before he had fully recovered and he was removed to Germany and a POW camp.

Badly wounded men had little chance of escape during the Retreat from Mons and were left in the hands of Royal Army Medical Corps personnel who tended them in certain knowledge that their own capture was unavoidable. During the Retreat, Corporal Samuel Fielding of the 8th Field Ambulance crawled along ditches and through hedges in order to get away before he was commanded to remain with wounded men near a church. Within an hour they were spotted by a German patrol, the Commanding Officer making a visual inspection of the group, before letting them carry on. Then, later that day, staff officers appeared and Fielding was beckoned to speak to a German officer.

I must say he seemed to be quite a decent chap, and spoke good English. He said he had spent some years in England, and what a terrible thing it was that England and Germany were at war when they should have been friends. I told him that the Germans always hated the English. He said the reason for that was we were a volunteer army and had volunteered to fight against Germany . . .

While we were talking I saw one of the German troops lift his rifle and take aim at me. I said, 'What does that chap reckon he is doing? Is he going to fire at me?' The officer turned round and saw him still taking aim. He shouted to him and told him to come over. He then seemed to give him a good lecture and then showed him the Red Cross on the church and on my arm. He then slashed him across his face and head with his whip. While he was hitting him he was shouting at him. Then the soldier turned to me and started talking in German. Of course I had no idea what he was saying. He had some nasty weals across his face and neck and tears were running down his cheeks. The officer said, 'I have made him apologise to you and say he was wrong'.

Fielding and his comrades were left to continue their work with the wounded, waiting for the enemy to return at their convenience; in Fielding's case two weeks passed before they came back.

Coming across stragglers was the first opportunity for most Germans to see their enemy alive and in the flesh. Walter Bloem, a German officer who wrote in detail about the fighting near Mons, recalled how the cavalry rounded up 'whole squads of them out of farm buildings and houses'. These British soldiers were 'fine, smart young fellows, excellently equipped, but almost inso-lent in their cool off-handedness'. Bloem was introduced to two 'dishevelled but most gallant-looking' officers, one a colonel, the other a major. 'Putting on my finest manners I greeted them in my best English and told them I had the honour to consider them as my prisoners – a turn in their career to which they appeared to resign themselves in a most cool and matter of fact manner.'

One of those captured was a Gordon Highlander whose uniform, and in particular his kilt, intrigued the German soldiers. They assumed that the trousers must have been stolen by this Scotsman's own men, a misconception that greatly amused Bloem. The Gordon Highlander was an elderly man who had suffered a bullet wound to his right shoulder and a ricochet knock to the knee that made him limp. As he stood there passively, Bloem offered him his arm and the two of them returned to the German company who stood and gazed in blank amazement. 'I requisitioned a horse and cart, and a farm-hand to drive it, from a farmhouse nearby, and asked the colonel to get up into it, and I placed my third horse at the disposal of the major; so kind and thoughtful we still were in those days to the English.'

2

Best of Bad Friends

After the Battle of Mons, the Germans established a cemetery near the village of St Symphorien as a joint resting place for their own dead and those of the British. In this cemetery, now under the care of the Commonwealth War Graves Commission, there are three memorials erected by the Germans: one dedicated to the dead of both armies, one to casualties of the Royal Fusiliers, and, lastly, one to the 'Royal' Middlesex Regiment, probably in the mistaken belief that all British regiments were given the same prefix.

Respect shown to fallen comrades in arms is demonstrated well in this shared cemetery. In his memoirs, Walter Bloem implies that in these early engagements fighting, while hard, was honourable and detached: Colonel Mullens's order to turn away prisoners, once searched, is illustrative of this apparent lack of rancour. It could not last, and rough treatment was meted out by both sides soon enough. Lieutenant Gallaher, captured after the cavalry charge at Elouges on 24 August, recalled that the arms of his sergeant were black and blue from being beaten with a rifle butt 'delivered by a Hun for no better reason than that Hynes was the only one of a handful of wounded who had sufficient strength to sit up'. Even so, ill treatment during or shortly after action, when stress of combat had yet to abate, was understood by fighting soldiers though not necessarily condoned.

It was the incidence of 'dirty tricks' that hardened battlefield attitudes. Lance Corporal Alfred Vivian's description of German stretcher-bearers at work, and the comradely banter between themselves and the enemy, preceded an episode in which British stretcher-bearers were fired upon while on an 'obvious errand of mercy'. A corporal was killed. 'Many were the curses and oaths to avenge the unfortunate corporal that filled the air,' he wrote, the chance for which came with the Germans' next attack. When enemy stretcher-bearers reappeared this time they were shot at, not 'actually at them, but close enough to induce them to hop back to cover'. Whether the Germans had deliberately opened fire on British stretcher-bearers is a moot point. Bitterness towards the enemy quickly inveigled itself into soldiers' hearts and minds if they chose to believe what they *thought* they saw or, more often, if they chose to believe rumours that quickly spread among them.

Given the vast stakes wagered by Britain and Germany in going to war, it was only a matter of time before accusations of foul play were levelled against troops of both sides. One of the first and the most persistent was the allegation that dum-dum bullets were being used, Lotte's 'anti-social shots', which she had mentioned in her letter. The dum-dum bullet, so called after its invention by the British at the Dum Dum arsenal near Calcutta, was a soft-pointed bullet that expanded on hitting the target, causing fearsome internal injuries. The Germans first protested against its use during the Hague Conventions of 1899 and 1901. These Conventions hosted the first international attempt to formalise laws of war and of war crimes, during which use of the dum-dum in warfare was banned.

In 1914, not everyone was clear as to what exactly constituted a dum-dum bullet. Lieutenant Aubrey Herbert of the 1st Irish Guards, surrounded by Germans in woods during the Retreat from Mons, was in possession of flat-nosed rounds he believed were not dum-dums, but appreciated that they would 'naturally not make as pleasant a wound as the sharp-nosed ones'. Moments before capture he flung them away, as did others; he understood the wisdom of this when he heard 'Germans speaking angrily about flat-nosed bullets picked up in the woods, and how they would deal with anyone in whose possession they were found'.

British soldiers were not slow to make counter-charges. The Germans, for their part, reversed their bullets in the cartridge case, exposing the flat lead base. Too many were found for them to have been made ad hoc, and it was assumed 'reversed' bullets were manufactured in Germany and shipped to the front for use as dum-dums. Whatever their purpose – and there is evidence that they could be effective against snipers' shields at very close range – simple aerodynamics ensured that they could not have been fired in the normal course of trench warfare. As one RAMC (Royal Army Medical Corps) doctor, Henry Kaye, wrote, 'I should like to have a rifle expert's view of reversing a solid bullet in the case, for one would imagine it would then fly anywhere between third man and square leg.' Nevertheless, the grave suspicion that they might be used in close-quarter fighting darkened the general mood.

Abuse or misuse of the white flag of surrender was another mushrooming accusation, and once more it was difficult to separate fact from fiction, allegation from actuality, as John Harrison, a private serving with the 1st Cheshire Regiment, discovered. He was wounded and captured on 24 August 1914 shortly after the estaminet from which he was shooting was surrounded. He was accused of firing from beneath a white flag and was physically abused and fortunate not to be shot out of hand. Questioned by a German officer, he claimed 'there was no white flag over my house, but there was one over the house next door'. Similarly, Private George Allen of the Rifle Brigade, captured around the same time, recalled a German general driving up in his car hurling abuse in German and English 'accusing us of firing on the white flag', something denied by the Tommies.

In early September, both sides continued to accuse each other of misconduct, when surrendering German infantry resumed an attack on discovering the enemy's numerical weakness. At least that was the British version of events as witnessed by men of the

2nd Royal Sussex Regiment. The Germans claimed their men had in fact been fired upon without provocation. These accusations and counter-accusations preceded a series of alleged assaults upon British troops captured the following day. One of those assaulted was Private John Cooper of the 1st Coldstream Guards.

> We were taken to an officer who was, I think, a general. He was very angry about some incident having to do with the use of a white flag. He spoke very good English. We knew nothing about the incident, but apparently it had something to do with the Sussex Regiment. This general talked about shooting the men and hanging the officers. Finally he gave an order, and two or three battalions of Germans, armed, lined both sides of the road, and we were made to run between them for a distance of about 400 yards, and they set about us with their rifles and big sticks.

Stories of foul play were meat and drink to the press. British newspapers not only reported abuses of the white flag, they accused the Germans of driving prisoners in front of their own advancing troops and, furthermore, that their infantrymen had been wearing Red Cross brassards on their arms. Such accusations would inevitably make life in Britain much more difficult for enemy aliens and in particular German civilians. Similarly, the German press reported outrages by British and French troops that stirred up civilian resentment, which manifested itself in a spate of attacks on prisoners of war. As the propaganda war became ever more heated, each government condensed newspaper 'lies' of the other side and circulated them at home and on the Western Front. One German booklet entitled 'The Lying News of Our Enemies' was printed on lavatory paper for emphasis.

Germans believed that Britain's opportunistic union with France and Russia made her guilty of dirty tricks before a shot was even fired. Add to this the popularly held view that Britain's professional soldiers were little different from mercenaries beholden to a politician's will, and a toxic anti-British mix was distilled. One British soldier listened intently as Germans shouted across, 'You fight for money, but we fight for the Fatherland'; another that British soldiers were 'paid murderers'. In fact, Germans were ignorant of the reason many British soldiers joined up. Had they known, 'you fight for food and shelter' might have been more accurate.

It was all right, in German eyes, for a man to be called upon to defend his country. In this regard, French soldiers were deemed relatively blameless; Germany had, after all, declared war on France, and France, since the days of Napoleon, had also relied on conscription. RAMC Corporal Samuel Fielding and his comrades were to suffer the impact of this considerable difference when they were transported to Germany.

> As soon as they knew we were English they tried to slash us with their whips. They ignored the French ... At one station a hefty big German Unter Officer got into our truck, he appeared to be half drunk. He brushed by the French troops shouting 'Englander'. We were all at one end of the truck. He came up to a chap next to me, shook him and banged his head against the side of the truck and flung him to the floor. He then came up to me, looked me up and down, got hold of my arm and saw the Red Cross which I was still wearing. He then passed on to some more of our fellows, hitting them left and right with his fists.

Time and again during interviews given by exchanged British prisoners of war, officers and men gave a similar story, that prisoners had faced verbal or physical abuse at railway stations between the German frontier and prisoner-of-war camps. Captain Thomas Sotheron-Estcourt of the 2nd Dragoons (Royal Scots Greys), captured on 12 September 1914, contended that 'the whole way along, until we reached Magdeburg, there seemed to be an organised demonstration against us. People stood on the footboard and shook their fists at me, cries of dum-dum etc almost at every station.' Another officer, Captain Peskett, captured on 2 September, recorded that 'Someone had thoughtfully written in German on our cattle truck "English Prisoners", this at once brought the mob up who cursed us, our King and Country and our parents and consigned us to the nethermost regions in German and English.'

Public indignation was further stoked by the deliberate misinterpretation of enemy weapons. The German *bête noire*, as reported widely in their press, was the pointed marlinspike (used for splicing rope) which formed part of the clasp-knife carried by all British soldiers and marines. Despite its innocuous role, it looked sinister. Rifleman George Winkworth, captured just after the Battle of Mons, recalled how a German sentry had got hold of one of the knives 'and at every station exhibited it, saying that we used it to cut out the eyes of the wounded. At all the stations the civilians came to the doors [of the train] and spat at us and howled.'

The British press was not beyond such tactics either. The British were 'horrified' at the German saw-bayonet, a pioneer's bayonet with a vicious but practical serrated edge. Journalists did not know or deigned to forget that it was the British who had invented the saw-bayonet during the Crimean War. The enemy were endlessly castigated for its use until, in 1917, the Germans acceded to international pressure and ground down the teeth. The British also made a fuss over what appeared to be a cat-o'-nine-tails carried by German officers. This, it was claimed, was used to whip their own (German) men but was in fact used by officers to flick mud off their own uniforms. On both sides there was nothing to be gained by letting the truth get in the way of a good story.

All prisoners felt relieved to escape the battlefield in one piece but, being unarmed, they also felt vulnerable, being at the behest and mercy of the enemy. In years to come, lurid stories were told by returning British POWs, tales of threats and maltreatment, too many for there not to have been considerable truth in the accusations.

As Fielding finally reached the German city of Münster, he and the other prisoners were ordered to leave the train. 'Here were two women dressed in deep mourning. One of them, as soon as she saw the wounded, burst into tears. The other who was more hard-hearted called us Englander Swinehunds. When I got near them, still carrying a wounded fellow on my back, she spat a mouthful of phlegm in his face.' It was hardly edifying but at least prisoners believed that they had certain rights guaranteed under international law. Whether these rights would be respected was another story altogether.

That autumn the Reverend Williams had watched with interest as captured British artillery was paraded through the Brandenburg Gate and down the Unter den Linden: bands were playing, drums were beating to the accompaniment of stamping horses' hooves and the clatter of wagon wheels. An excited civilian throng lined the entire route. Russian and French guns had arrived a week earlier to far less pomp; 'special honour, it seemed, was to be paid to the trophies representing the British army', which were given centre stage in front of the Royal Palace. Chalked along one gun barrel was the inscription, 'This Gun belonged to the Regiment of the English Crown Prince – Hurrah!'

British guns were singled out for special attention, in much the same way as captured British troops, although, on this occasion, German press reports that British prisoners would be made to walk alongside the guns had not materialised.

The object of German propaganda, according to the Reverend Williams, was to vilify England in the eyes of the people.

In the window of practically every bookshop I saw in every town, I saw the same sort of books displayed. Most conspicuous among them was one bearing on its cover a lurid picture of Kitchener in a Scotch kilt grasping a bag of gold in his hands and wading through a sea of blood in which floated the corpses of women and children. Wherever I went, I found myself confronted by a huge poster showing a leering, drunken-looking British soldier, also in a kilt, with a pipe between his protruding teeth and a bull-dog between his bandy-legs. Above him were the words 'Who is guilty?' And beneath 'He is guilty'.

It had not taken long for the British press to influence government policy towards enemy aliens. Within weeks, headlines appeared reporting that stronger action [25 August] was to be taken against German and Austrian civilians. Fleet Street set the agenda, with news reporting and editorial opinion worryingly uniform. 'The public even now seem scarcely to realise the great gravity of this matter,' wrote one *Times* journalist of the perceived menace from espionage. The journalist quoted official figures of 50,000 enemies at liberty in the United Kingdom, 34,000 within the Metropolitan Police District, including 7,000 German and Austrian men of military age. He continued:

Thousands of resident Germans – waiters, barbers, and the like – have lost their employment since the outbreak of war; the adage concerning work for idle hands naturally occurs to the mind. Many of the East-end Germans are known to the authorities as ex-criminals; some of them are regarded as dangerous men . . . It has been remarked by the observant that German tradesmen's shops are frequently to be found in close proximity to vulnerable points in the chain of London's communications, such as railway bridges. Some such alien tradesmen have already been moved on. The German barber seems to have little time for sabotage. He is chiefly engaged in removing the 'Kaiser' moustaches of his compatriots. They cannot, however, part with the evidences of their nationality altogether, for the tell-tale hair of the Teuton will show the world that new Smith is but old Schmidt writ small.

Could this be the same East End German community described in such glowing terms by the *East London Observer* not three weeks before? The paper had commended that community as honest and productive.

The government believed German spies or sympathisers would attack key state infrastructure, with docks, power stations, waterworks, railway tracks and bridges principal targets. With this in mind, soldiers patrolled railway lines and station platforms while Special Constables, civilians appointed part-time to the force, guarded anywhere else deemed vulnerable. 'Probably, this ceaseless vigilance of the Specials, regular policemen, and soldier sentries frustrated the organised plans of the enemy's agents,' wrote a former Special in a history of the London Special Constabulary published in 1920. Or perhaps there were no plans for attack, certainly not organised ones. The Metropolitan Police received nearly 9,000 reports of suspected espionage in the first month of the war, but in fewer than a hundred cases was anyone detained let alone charged. Despite public fears, there was not a single substantiated case of enemy sabotage during the war.

In London, Dorothy Peel noted just how far spy mania gripped the public's imagination.

It was suggested that enamelled iron advertisements for 'Maggi soup,' which were attached to hoardings in Belgium, were unscrewed by German officers in order that they might read the information about local resources which was painted in German on the back by spies who had preceded them. True or not, this story was generally accepted, and screwdriver parties were formed in the London suburbs for the examination of the back of enamelled advertisements.

Inevitably, the finger of suspicion came to rest on those who did not appear to fit parochial standards of familiarity. The Reverend Andrew Clark, living near Braintree in Essex, recorded in his daily diary the anxious triviality that was part and parcel of local life. In September, an elderly woman with a German accent was arrested in Little Waltham as she was selling lace. She was jailed for a night while her claims to be a doctor's wife were investigated before being substantiated. Four weeks later, overzealous civilians detained an official working for the Ordnance Survey as he toured the countryside. When a Special Constable arrested this unfortunate man, he finally threw up his work, seeking out the protection of a local Justice of the Peace. Other outsiders, such as members of the Royal Commission on Ancient Sites and Monuments paying 'visits of enquiry' to outlying farms, were met with grave suspicion in Braintree, while a tramp was picked up during a 'spy hunt' as he rested by a haystack. Finally, in December, a 'foreign-looking' local was the target of an elderly lady's half-brick, thrown in the belief that he too was a spy. 'She missed him,' wrote Clark, 'but fetched the policeman a fair "crack" on the side of the head.'

Public anxieties were visited upon towns and villages up and down the country. It was at times almost funny – almost, but not really, for the repercussions were serious. Britain's German community was marginalised at almost every level. When representatives from London's golf clubs discussed what to do with German and Austrian members, it was hoped that such 'aliens' would take the hint that they were not wanted and withdraw without recourse to formal expulsions. In entertainment, a meeting was concluded of senior British musicians, including the musical adviser to the London County Council. While it was agreed that it might be difficult to ignore German music, German musicians were ripe for boycotting. 'For many years foreign musicians had usurped the positions which really belonged to Englishmen, and taken the bread out of the mouths of the rank and file of British musicians,' they agreed. And so it was thought only fair (expedient) that the war could be used (as an excuse) to restore an imagined status quo, with theatres and restaurants encouraged to employ only home-grown talent.

German music was removed from concert programmes, often from fear among the management of halls and churches that audiences would boycott an evening's musical entertainment if German composers were included. One who spoke out against the trend was Charles Eshborn, born in Urmston in Lancashire but the son of German parents living in Manchester. In late September he wrote in disgust to the editor of the *Manchester Guardian*.

What have these poor composers done? The family of Ludwig van Beethoven, as the name implies, is traceable to a village near Louvain in Belgium. He lived at a time when England and Germany were supporting each other, and his fame in England was often a source of great comfort to him, especially after his last illness, when the London Philharmonic Society assisted him when he was in very straitened circumstances and all help in Germany had been refused. Wagner was for a period an exile from Germany and in 1855 conducted concerts of the Philharmonic Society with great success. Handel left Germany at an early age, and, as everybody must know, became a naturalised Englishman. Bach, Gluck, Haydn, Mozart and Mendelssohn all lived in times when England was a most staunch supporter of Germany. Besides, what is to be gained by banning such great music as that of the above composers? Probably most of the people who are demanding the exclusion of these composers are perhaps under the impression that some of them are in command of some German Regiment destroying ancient churches and killing women and children.

The *Manchester Guardian* published the piece but exercised its editorial judgement and cut the last sentence. Given the excited times in which he was writing, Charles Eshborn also asked that they use his *nom de plume* 'Thomas Lorei'.

The excising of Germans from British life continued unabated. By October 1914 there were announcements analogous to advertising, confirming to customers that no Germans or Austrians were in the employment of the Savoy, Claridge's and Berkeley hotels, nor, indeed, at the Strand Palace Hotel, J. Lyons and Co. and the Palmerston Restaurant. Another press announcement made it clear that 'No Germans or Austrians, whether naturalised or not, remained in the employment of the Carlton and The Ritz Hotels, and the Princess Hotel and Restaurant.' Diners could rest assured that food was uncontaminated by enemy hands, diners' ears spared foreign musicians, conversations no longer eavesdropped by spies.

One who felt the icy winds of change was Richard Noschke, an East End German living in the borough of Newham. The capital had been his home for twenty-five years and he had married an English girl in the 1890s. Noschke was typical of those described by Joseph King MP in the Commons as being 'much more British in sentiment than German'; indeed, so good was Noschke's English that nobody except his works manager knew he was German. After the outbreak of war, Noschke dutifully registered himself with the police at Limehouse police station, being warned not to travel further than five miles from his home without a special permit and subjecting himself to a 9 p.m. curfew. Despite these restrictions he continued to work at the pharmaceutical company in which he had been employed for many years.

'The newspapers soon started their campaign of hatred against all Germans in England,' wrote Noschke. 'Everybody was termed a spy, and every employer was warned not to employ any German as they were all spies.' This agitation became so strong, according to Noschke, that eventually, out of fear, his boss discharged him. His next job lasted just four days before he was sacked once more.

I looked around for work, almost frightened by the attitude of the people, it was no easy matter, as most places had notices up that no German need apply, and most shops had notices in their windows, 'No Germans served here,' the feeling of the lower classes became so bitter by this time that they would almost throw a man from the top of an omnibus or out of a running train if they knew he was a German. At last one morning at Canning Town Labour Exchange I received a card to go to a place where a man was wanted [to make varnish], the official put my name on the card and said to me, 'your name sounds Russian,' I said, 'Yes, it is,' and he put right across the card Russian subject.

Thirty-seven-year-old Richard Druhm was in similar difficulties. A German by birth, he had lived in London for fifteen years, working long hours to establish his hairdressing salon, moving from Camden to Hampstead as his hard work paid dividends. He married a London girl, Ethel Norris, in April 1905 and they had a daughter, Elfreda, born in September 1910.

My father had arrived at the turn of the century and had done extremely well. He had never gone back to Germany, because he liked it here. Then he met my mother and they were married; both my parents worked in the ladies' hairdressing shop. I know that my grandmother, Elizabeth Norris, didn't approve of the match. She, as well as my aunts, strongly frowned upon the engagement, and in revenge they didn't go to the wedding. Well, there wasn't a wedding really, it all had to be hush-hush because nobody wanted her to marry a German.

Our shop was smashed within weeks of war breaking out and we had to leave because there was so much hostility. I was there but I can't say I remember it happening as a proper memory as I was in bed, but I do know that we cleared out of that house very suddenly. Father was taken away and interned, and Mother left at the same time. We had nowhere to go and we had to find furnished rooms quickly. Mother never said much about that night as it was a very painful part of her life. She had to leave everything behind. There was one relative who tried to help, a husband of my aunt, and he helped dispose of certain things, the furniture and the lease on the shop. He sold the furniture but got very little for that. My grandmother lived nearby as did one aunt, but they did little to help, which caused a lot of bad feeling for years.

My mother tried to find work telling the truth, saying who she was, why she was looking for a job and where her husband was. Nobody would help because she was married to a German, even though she was totally English and had only once stepped out of the country. So she changed her name to Miss Norris, her maiden name, and as soon as she went as Miss Norris she was employed at a salon in Oxford Street.

Newspaper stories of battlefield atrocities helped keep army recruitment high in September, October and November and continued to poison public opinion of Germans and Austrians living in Britain. One of the few who took a more objective view of the newspaper reports was a seventeen-year-old Kitchener volunteer, Charles Carrington. Like many boys of his age he could not wait to get into the army and had lied about his age to do so. He was also mature enough to have a healthy and sceptical view about some of the more lurid stories – Belgian babies bayoneted to church doors, for example – emanating from France and Belgium. 'German atrocities are being taken absurdly seriously and I get much abused if I remind people that our Allies include the slave drivers of the Congo [a reference to an influential report condemning Belgian atrocities in the African colony], the Cossacks and the Serbians.'

Carrington wrote to his mother that 'distraught refugees and drunken "Tommies" will tell all sorts of tales', and that he had never heard an authentic account of an atrocity at first hand. 'The papers are full of witnessed accounts,' he penned, 'but the papers have to get copy from somewhere.'

Enemy aliens were not completely cut adrift. In August 1914 the Society of Friends, the Quakers, set up the 'Emergency Committee for the Assistance of Germans, Austrians and Hungarians in Distress'. It launched a national appeal for funds and raised an initial but useful £5,500, including donations from the Archbishop of Canterbury, Randall Davidson, Sir Edward Goschen, the last pre-war ambassador to Berlin, and Viscount Richard Haldane, the Lord Chancellor and former Secretary of State for War; Haldane was later ousted from office in 1915 after being accused of pro-German sympathies.

The Friends' Emergency Committee (FEC) set up in offices lent to them in St Stephen's House, a building overlooking London's Embankment and so close to Parliament as to be in the shadow of Big Ben. Ironically, the FEC shared the building with the newly established Parliamentary Recruiting Committee but there was little friction despite a growing number of Germans, who, in pursuit of help and protection, spilt out of the FEC's offices into communal corridors and stairwells. In 1920 a record of the FEC's work at St Stephen's House was published. Written by a leading light of the organisation known only by the initials ABT, it gives a detailed and frank account of the charity's work.

Hundreds of discharged waiters flocked to us begging for work. Many of them had excellent references showing years of service in the best London hotels. Now in response to popular clamour they were destitute. Many had lost not only their jobs but their lodgings too, and were sleeping in the parks. Fortunately, August of 1914 was fine and warm, but soon the autumn rains of an exceptionally wet winter set in, and these poor people suffered. We arranged a soup kitchen for them and strove to help them in other ways.

Whole families came to us also, father, mother and little children. Sometimes they were faint for want of food, for many would not ask for help whilst they had a crust remaining. We saw people in the pangs of hunger – people who fainted whilst being interviewed – people who looked at us with sad despairing eyes and burst into tears at the first kindly word. Careful arrangements were made for investigating the truth of their stories and we required at least two reputable references before giving anything beyond an emergency grant.

To meet the first needs we were able to obtain a considerable number of offers of hospitality, and many Friends and others entertained these distressed people for days, weeks or even months at a time. Two furnished houses were used by the Committee as hostels, and a lady furnished a roomy garage as a temporary shelter for some of the cases when delayed in London waiting for their travelling permits.

Many of those the FEC helped were holidaymakers caught out by the declaration of war; others were attending summer schools as teachers or students. As German banks in London closed, many Germans were stranded without access to funds; they would have to be housed while travel permits were obtained. Like Britons trapped in Germany, these visitors were susceptible to irrational fears; they heard that railways in France and Belgium had been destroyed: they would be turned out into the fields to walk; there were agents of the white slave trade working on Dutch trains preying in particular on young girls. More credible were threats from fraudsters and opportunists, including one who came to the attention of the FEC. This man wrote to desperate aliens claiming to have been commissioned by their families in Germany to bring them home although an upfront fee of £10 would be required if he was to help them.

For every unfortunate visiting Britain, far more, like Richard Noschke and Richard Druhm, were permanently domiciled in London or the provinces. Of those helped by the FEC, eighteen years was the average length of residence in their adopted home.

The FEC was not the only charity helping enemy aliens; others included the Central Council of United Relief Societies, the International Women's Relief Committee and the Prisoners of War Relief Agency, all remarkable organisations swimming against the fast-flowing river of public resentment and animosity.

Their impact was generally to ameliorate the worst effects of government policy particularly in respect of internment and the effects that imprisoning the chief breadwinner had on family life.

Unfortunately, much of the government's policy of internment was fashioned without much thought as to the practicalities of imprisoning thousands of enemy aliens. After the period of grace granted to all Germans to leave Britain, the procedure that August was to intern all male enemy aliens of military age, seventeen to forty-two. The numbers interned rose gradually. From just 4,300 at the end of the month, the figure accelerated as news reached Britain of the BEF's military setbacks in Belgium and France, and the public grew correspondingly nervous. The numbers rose again to 6,600 by the second week of September and then almost doubled to 11,000 seven days later. The press reported the numerical rise just as the authorities ran out of available accommodation, the War Office suspending the arrests of civilians as figures, including prisoners of war, touched 14,000 by 23 September.

Ironically, it was because enemy aliens were hounded from their homes and jobs that internment became the best and most practicable option. It would be far easier to feed and clothe enemy aliens in one place and to grant allowances to their destitute families than to have them spread out in the wider community and at the mercy of the more troublesome elements of society.

Kitchener recruit Charles Carrington went to view one of the earliest camps at Deepcut in Surrey mistakenly assuming that it was for German spies only.

There were several hundred of them [Germans]. They live in tents in a huge square on the top of a moor with the finest air in England and one of the finest views. They are protected by two barbed wire entanglements. The whole space is I should think 300 yards square. The inner fence is 10 feet high of tight barbed wire guarded at the top by live electric wires. At each corner are platforms for sentries and at intervals inside the outer fence which is a barbed wire entanglement five feet high and thick, are arc lights on poles. Inside are tents and a few sheds and plenty of room where the men were playing football. Some of the better class Germans looked fed up already. We were allowed to walk round and stare.

Internment began again in early October when gruesome and largely unsubstantiated tales of enemy atrocities caused public outrage. Within days, perennial problems of accommodation caused authorities to backtrack and Chief Constables were once more instructed to halt arrests while accommodation was found. The War Office would notify Chief Constables as beds became available, allowing arrests to resume. In fact the government did not revisit the issue of internment until the next bout of anti-German paranoia hit Britain the following May by which time, conversely, 3,000 enemy aliens had been released back into the community to ease the pressure on space.

The government's logistical problems were mostly of its own making. In peacetime, Britain's regular army numbered 250,000 men, but of these well over half were stationed overseas on garrison duty in such places as India and South Africa. Britain relied on its navy for national security and the regular army was small in comparison to those of its European counterparts. On the outbreak of war the new Secretary of State for War, Lord Kitchener, set out his stall for a New Army made up of civilian volunteers. In five months nearly 1.2 million men responded to the call to enlist, swamping the army's ability to house, let alone train and equip them. Out of necessity, 800,000 soldiers were billeted in private dwellings by the autumn, while hundreds of thousands more were living in existing or hastily erected camps. Many men, rather than being billeted in huts, were still under canvas; all right in summer but with autumn rains and colder nights, these once happy-go-lucky civilians were becoming disgruntled soldiers slopping around ankle-deep in mud.

While poor living conditions bedevilled camps for Kitchener's volunteers, there was little chance that the authorities were going to expend energy on the comforts of enemy prisoners and internees. With suitable accommodation at a premium, civilians were packed into anything available and this varied greatly in quality. The War Office, for example, requisitioned nine transatlantic liners at a cost of around £75,000 a month. The ships retained their three classes of accommodation and fortunate was the German who could afford to pay for the privilege of a first-class suite and, if he was prepared to find six shillings and sixpence extra, even better food and waiter service. This was a far cry from the worst examples of accommodation such as that given over to 700 civilians sent to an old wagon factory in Lancaster. The floor, made of wooden blocks, was filthy; there was no heating or artificial light and scant bedding or furniture of any kind. Sanitary arrangements were inadequate and fresh water in short supply. At Newbury racecourse, internees slept in horse boxes, six or eight stretched out side by side. All were locked up from sunset until morning with no heating and the grounds a quagmire. Only when a large camp was constructed at Knockaloe on the Isle of Man were unsuitable camps closed.

Private Thomas Hughes, a recruit serving with the 1/28th London Regiment (Artist's Rifles), was sent with other men in the battalion to mount guard at the Olympia exhibition centre. Here, as on the transatlantic liners, position and relative wealth made a difference, however small, to a man's quality of life.

> The wretched Germans are herded together in pens in the annexe, with a large pen at the far end, called the House of Lords, where about 20 men were, owing to their blood and wealth. [These men are] kept apart and allowed chairs to sit on and to buy extra food beyond the half pint of tea and two slices of bread and butter allowed to the proletariat, who only get meat once a day. Five men had blood of such blueness or purses of such length that they were allowed to go out into the yard for an hour a day with a sentry. The

rest only walk round and round the main hall in fours for an hour every afternoon, a grim procession of lost souls.

At Olympia, as elsewhere, internees became the target for repeated degradation and even physical violence, much to the obvious disgust of Private Hughes:

> Only one man, an Irish Guard, was a sufficiently advanced cad actually to knock the prisoners about and he only just hit the very small ones who were unlikely to retaliate, but every humiliation was turned upon them. They have to give up their blankets and mattresses every morning and have them dealt out again at the point of the bayonet every evening. There are not enough of either to go around and they get different ones each night so that the talk of keeping free from vermin is well nigh impossible.

Britain's policy of internment brought retribution. After remonstrating with the British government, its German counterpart announced on 6 November that all unnaturalised British male civilians of military age would be held. But there were fewer than 3,900 Britons in Germany who were eligible. One huge camp on Ruhleben racecourse, near Berlin, was turned over for their confinement. Here, too, internees were forced to sleep in brick stable buildings and haylofts until a vast complex of huts was eventually built.

Finding suitable secure accommodation for prisoners of war was a greater struggle for the Germans than it was even for the British. With its requirement that all young men undertake at least two years' military service, and very commonly three, Germany had a large number of barracks that could be used to hold prisoners. The problem was that Germany was also calling up vast numbers of young men and they would also require accommodation. The Germans were also fighting a war on two fronts, and with substantial and easy victories against the French in the west and the Russians in the east, 815,000 prisoners only exacerbated the difficulty. These men arrived in Germany at an average rate of over 100,000 per month, vastly more than the 7,000 German soldiers removed to Britain over the same period. Indeed, prior to the Battle of the Somme in July 1916, the British held fewer than 14,000 German prisoners of war.

Private Charles Duder, serving with the 4th Royal Fusiliers, described his POW camp at Sennelager. It was September 1914 and the men lay in the open, with no tents or mattresses.

> This lasted some two or three weeks, during which time we got two dirty old blankets. The food was bad and insufficient . . . Afterwards we got into tents, accommodation very bad, very wet, lying on straw, which got like floating mud. We soon got covered with vermin. After being in the tents some time we went to Senne II. First of all we were in stables and then as soon as the huts were built, we were moved into them; this would be some time in December.

The living conditions for British POWs were shaped in part by the German belief that their own prisoners were being ill-treated. The American ambassador in Berlin, James Gerard, went to Britain to see conditions for himself, reporting back that prisoners were being reasonably treated, thereby improving conditions in Germany. Soon afterwards an agreement was reached that, on giving reasonable notice, the American ambassadors in London and Berlin or their representatives would have the right to visit POW camps in either country and converse with prisoners out of the earshot of camp guards. This sounded good in theory. However, owing to the federal nature of the German state the quality of POW camps varied immensely. Germany had been divided into Army Corps districts, each district presided over by a corps commander who had virtual autonomy, to the effective exclusion of outside civilian officials. It was *his* attitude to prisoners that dictated how good or how bad a camp became for its inmates.

By the beginning of September 1914, nearly 10,000 British officers and men were missing or captured. Their number included Major Charles Yate of the 2nd King's Own Yorkshire Light Infantry, taken prisoner at the Battle of Le Cateau on 26 August. This officer's story was remarkably similar to that of Captain Morritt's last-ditch bayonet charge. Cut off, his ammunition exhausted and with all other company officers killed or wounded, Major Yate led twenty survivors in a bayonet charge against overwhelming odds. He was captured when a German officer kicked his revolver from his hand.

It was believed that Major Yate had been wounded, although a photograph taken shortly after his capture shows the forty-two-year-old surrounded by German infantrymen. He looks exhausted, but if he was wounded his injuries were slight. There was even an unsubstantiated report that Yate had tried to shoot himself rather than be taken prisoner and that the German officer's action in knocking the revolver from his hand forestalled a suicide attempt.

Major Yate was sent to Germany with a number of officers, including Captain Walter Roche and Lieutenant Jocelyn Hardy, both of the Connaught Rangers, and Captain Arthur Hargreaves of the Somerset Light Infantry. All these officers testified that they received very rough treatment on their journey through Germany, as well as being jostled and heckled by civilians in the streets of Torgau, as Hargreaves reported.

On our arrival there, a vast crowd was assembled at the station. From the station to the Brückenkopf barracks (where we were to be imprisoned) was a seething mass of screaming men, women and children. The anger on their faces was terrible to see. They shook their fists, spat at us, and yelled themselves hoarse. I heard a woman (of the upper classes) shout out 'Recht fur die Schweine!'

Unlike his travelling companions, Major Yate faced an uncomfortable and serious allegation of spying, serious enough, it seems, for two German officers to be sent from Berlin to interrogate him. There was some substance to the Germans' suspicions of the major. Before the war, Yate had served at the War Office and the Germans were aware that not only was he fluent in German but that he had made numerous visits to their country. Taken to the camp commandant's office, Yate rebuffed searching questions, according to Lieutenant Breen, a prisoner with whom he shared a hut.

> Yate came to me to say that he was not quite clear as to what the German Military Authorities were aiming at, but that the German officers had tried by cross-examination to obtain an admission on his part that he had been engaged on Intelligence work in Germany before the War. He did not know what the next step would be. He was very reticent on this subject, and he did not say definitely to me whether he had been engaged on work of this kind or not. I remember that I reminded him that the usage of war and, I thought, even a definite clause in the Hague Convention, precluded the prosecution of a prisoner of war for espionage committed before the outbreak of hostilities. We agreed however that the matter was serious and that the German Military Authorities were not likely to recognize any usage or written convention when they had decided on a course of action.

The son of a German mother and English father, Charles Yate was born in Mecklenburg in 1872. His parents had moved back to England by the time he was two, but he spoke German with his mother and considered himself fluent in the language. In 1892 he enlisted in the British Army, serving on the North-West Frontier and during the campaign in South Africa. In 1904 he was attached to the Japanese army in Manchuria during the Russo-Japanese War and was awarded the Japanese War Medal. Significantly, it was while he was in Japan that he became influenced by the Japanese military tradition eschewing surrender. 'It worried him considerably that he had been captured unwounded,' wrote Breen, 'in his opinion no officer should surrender while conscious.'

The camp commandant at Torgau was a reserve officer by the name of Brandes. He was also Professor of Entomology and Director of the Zoological Gardens in Dresden. As camp commandant he was out of his depth and ineffectual, and camp security was, temporarily at least, lax, as Breen well knew. 'The German Authorities,' he wrote, 'showed little discrimination then, in their choice of Camp Commanders and Officers.'

Yate set his mind on escaping to Switzerland, believing that security would tighten as the war intensified. He would walk to Dresden, procure a bicycle and ride over the border. His determination to leave as soon as possible was reinforced by news that he was about to be interrogated again. As if to underline the porous security, workman's trousers, a loose cloak, soft hat and black boots were procured for Yate who swapped his safety razor for a cut-throat razor so that it could double as a blade.

The dangers of escape were very real. Even if he got away from the camp he might well be stopped and asked for identification papers, which he did not possess. The mood of the local population had been established by the treatment received on arrival in Torgau: 'Yate was convinced,' wrote Breen, 'that an Englishman, speaking fluent German, would be inevitably murdered by ignorant peasantry as a spy.'

On the night of 19 September, Major Yate was helped over the high compound wall by Captain Roche and Lieutenant Breen and lowered into a moat. In the dark, a sentry passed within two paces of their concealed position but saw nothing. Both Roche and Breen waited, listening intently for any disturbance that would indicate that the game was up. Nothing was heard.

Twelve hours later, Major Yate's bloodstained clothes were returned to the camp for identification. It was reported that he

had committed suicide, camp authorities refusing all requests for
an RAMC officer or British chaplain to examine the body. The
funeral took place four days later and, although the Germans laid
a wreath on behalf of Yate's comrades, not one British officer
attended the interment. The camp commandant cited the volatile
attitude of civilians as reason enough for his refusal to permit prisoners outside the camp. The burial took place at dawn (5 a.m.) so
as to avoid any possible friction with local people.

The secrecy surrounding Yate's death sparked rumours that he
had been murdered. On hearing the news, the British government
protested, demanding more information. The Germans held firm
that Major Yate had been responsible for his own demise, as
described by eyewitness testimony. Major Yate had been spotted
crossing an estate by the manager of a sugar factory, Herr Brottwitz,
who became suspicious. 'I was cycling towards Cosdorf, between
10 and 11 a.m., when I met a strange looking man walking on a
path under some trees. The man wore a shabby cloak much too
short for him, workman's trousers and was hatless. I hailed him
but got no answer.' Brottwitz called to a group of men who were
walking to work, giving one of them his bicycle so that he could
overtake and stop the suspect. The others hurried in pursuit. It
seemed to them that the suspect's features were 'those of a gentleman' and did not correspond with the shabbiness of his clothing.

> The workmen pointed to his hands which were small and obvi-
> ously unused to hard work. I asked the man whence he came and
> got the answer 'Schleswig Holstein'. I asked for papers, he said he
> had none. 'You know you cannot travel without papers in wartime.'
> The workmen removed the man's cloak and were proceeding to
> unfasten rather roughly a haversack, which he had fastened to his
> back by cross straps, when he suddenly took a razor from the inner
> pocket of his vest and drew it several times across his throat. The
> action was utterly unexpected; we all drew back in dismay, and
> nobody interfered when, dropping the razor, the stranger

commenced to walk away. He walked on some forty yards when he suddenly collapsed and died at once.

Major Yate's body was removed but returned to the estate in which he had first been stopped, and buried; an oak cross was erected over his grave. His belongings were eventually returned to his wife. Two months later, in November, Major Yate was awarded the Victoria Cross for his outstanding bravery during the bayonet charge at Le Cateau.

In the febrile atmosphere of the times, Yate had been accused of being a spy, perhaps with some justification. More significantly, his case exposed what might happen to an escapee if caught by civilians. In a post-war investigation into his death, Herr Brottwitz was interviewed and asked specifically what he recalled about the incident.

> The peasantry were naturally excited and handled the man roughly, asking him questions, shouting 'You are a spy'. Asked if he thought Major Yate was liable to be ill-treated if he had not committed suicide, he replied, 'You know the feeling of the people at the time . . . I cannot say with certainty but I should think he would have been roughly handled and possibly severely beaten when the men discovered from the contents of his knapsack that he was not a German'.

Such threats did not put off officers from escaping, and many made the attempt. Captain William Morritt, who had been surrounded and shot during a bayonet charge against the Germans, was one who remained undeterred. He made several attempts to escape, on one occasion being recaptured on the Dutch frontier. The Germans placed him in solitary confinement, put him on short rations and sent him to increasingly secure camps but his urge to escape remained undiminished. On 27 June 1917, Morritt made yet another attempt but as he emerged from an escape tunnel he was spotted by a sentry and shot. He died of his injuries minutes later and was buried near Hanover. This time fellow officers were permitted to attend the funeral.

The Schlieffen Plan of invasion had envisaged German forces enveloping Paris in one great sweeping move. Diverging from this overall strategy, General von Kluck, in command of the First Army, altered his line of advance to the east of the French capital in order to pursue and destroy elements of the BEF. In bypassing Paris, von Kluck's right flank was exposed to counterattack. The Germans, exhausted by their 200-mile fighting march from Mons, were dangerously overstretched. When the French attacked with a new, hastily formed Sixth Army, the Germans had no option but to fall back to the first defensible position on high ground north of the River Aisne. Here the opposing armies rested briefly. In an attempt to outflank each other, the Germans and the Allies engaged in a 'race to the sea' that eventually brought them by leaps and bounds to Nieuwpoort on the Belgian coast. A thin and primitive line of trenches had been established by both sides, with a strip of no-man's-land between them. The British Army, in moving back towards the safety of the Channel ports, ended up at a small but pretty Belgian town called Ypres. The open and fluid nature of warfare, as conducted during August and September 1914, was about to change. Now men took to the ground as a matter of personal protection and of tactical defence.

In October and November, the regular soldiers of the BEF, increasingly reinforced by the Territorial Army, held the ground in a tightening salient in front of Ypres. The Germans once more strained every sinew to break the British that autumn. Mass, almost suicidal, shoulder-to-shoulder assaults by German infantry were broken up as the fast and accurate fire of professional soldiers took its toll. Charlie Parke, an NCO serving with the 2nd Gordon Highlanders, was astonished at the tactics.

The Germans wore grey uniforms which, when massed, gave a suggestion of a blue hue, with matching circular hats. Their packed formations were four rows deep, each row barely a foot behind the one in front; it was a stunning sight.

They started advancing at a fast march pace firing their rifles in the air whilst at the port position, an exercise that killed nobody but was just another of the Hun's frightening tactics. At 800 yards the British started intermittent firing, approximately six rounds per minute; it was like shelling peas from a pod, the Germans were so closely massed. At 400 yards the enemy increased the speed of charge to a slow double but at the same time we switched to rapid fire. It was bloody murder: the grey masses fell like nine-pins, the man behind climbing over his dead comrade and continuing the advance. It was as though those brave men had been told by their ruthless, ambitious Kaiser that they could walk through bullets.

Fighting raged for weeks around Ypres, the Germans breaking the weakest points in the Allied line and British troops trying to plug the gaps or retake lost ground before the Germans consolidated their gains. The fighting was often confused, as Lieutenant Colonel John Hawksley revealed in a letter home on 23 October. Hawksley commanded a battery of guns close to a convent where one of his subalterns, Lieutenant Macleod, was on observation. In the morning the men woke to heavy firing and shouting. The convent had been surrounded and Macleod, as Hawksley saw, was shot at. Macleod dodged behind a wall.

Presently he found a German officer coming towards him. The officer saluted; Macleod saluted. The officer bowed; Macleod bowed; and then they all bowed to each other. My subaltern then was searched, his military equipment taken from him, and his revolver bullets examined, presumably to see whether they were expanding bullets or not. His private property was given back to

him. Then he and other prisoners were marshalled in the courtyard and put under escort of about twelve men and given some of
the English rations which were captured in the convent. Someone
(either ourselves or the Germans) began shelling the convent, and
they were put in the cellars. After an hour or so of this, someone
shouted in English, 'Hands up'. A party of East Lancashires had
made a counter-attack, retaken the convent, and taken about 100
prisoners as well. So my subaltern was released. He had the satisfaction of taking his own glasses back from the neck of the N.C.O.
who was escorting him.

As battle raged, the Germans varied their battery fire, and fuses
in shrapnel shells were adjusted to explode twenty or thirty feet
from the ground. Shrapnel shells were intermixed with high
explosive, wrecking trenches and causing mayhem and fear among
defenders. All the while, Charlie Parke remembered, 'the enemy
never eased up on their fear tactics; they would make sure the
British knew when they were about to charge by sounding off
with bugles and whistles and the German officer's loud commands.
The Germans knew they had vast superiority in numbers and
demoralisation was a tool they never ceased to use.'

The fighting continued until late November when winter
weather caused operations to be suspended. Britain's regular and
territorial soldiers, bolstered by men of the Territorial Army, held
on, but only just. 'I believed then and I still believe,' wrote Parke,
'that the Germans lost the war at Ypres in 1914. If the Hun
couldn't pass a thin line of troops, then how were they going to
stop hundreds of thousands of British reinforcements later on?'

Both sides hunkered down for winter. In the front line, trench
walls crumbled and an oozing, cloying mud caked itself onto the
men's feet and legs. Wood stripped from the finest houses in Ypres
was used as makeshift flooring but in sub-zero temperatures there
was nothing to do but feel miserable as men clapped their hands
and stamped their feet. Charlie Parke was fortunate. He was sent

out of the line to train reinforcements in musketry, fine-tuning what these men had learnt. They were taught to fire, he recalled, in the prone, kneeling and standing positions, to simulate, as he assumed, 'the different stages [depths] of trench preparation'. No one foresaw just how long 'standing' remained the predominant posture of the war.

On Christmas Day 1914, the Dean of Durham Cathedral, Hensley Henson, addressed the congregation. The subject of his sermon was 'The Paradox of Christianity' and he spoke of how empty and pointless it felt to sing Christmas carols to the 'accompaniment of the cannon' and the 'clamours of battle'. Yet, rather than be depressed, his congregation should be impressed by the 'vigour and volume of protest' that Germany's crimes had aroused, for despite 'a fearful repudiation of the principles of Christendom in Germany' – the 'ruin of Belgium' and of towns 'shamefully attacked' – other countries had stood up against this naked aggression and that was a cause for celebration.

That morning at the Temple Church in London, the Master, the Reverend Henry Woods, spoke, too, of the unavoidably saddened Christmas festival and of the suffering of fighting men. 'Unfortunately,' he told his congregation, 'it had been found impracticable to arrange a Christmas Truce, but they [the soldiers] could at least hope that there was a lull in the trenches, so that the men might have an opportunity for a quiet moment with their God.'

In Rome, Pope Benedict XV sought to silence the cannon by proposing a Truce in the hope that politicians of warring nations might take the ceasefire as an opportunity to negotiate a fair and honourable peace. His influential words failed to yield results, at least not as he envisaged them, for that Christmas morning a truce of a very different kind was already under way on the Western Front, albeit informal, haphazard and completely unauthorised. The truce was a spontaneous decision taken by the soldiers in the

line to have a day off: an opportunity to celebrate a festival that
was important to both nations. Frank Sumpter, a young private
serving with the 1st Rifle Brigade, was there.

> We heard the Germans singing 'Silent Night, Holy Night', and
> then they put up a notice, 'Merry Christmas'. Then they started
> singing, and our boys said, 'We'll join in'. So we joined in with a
> song and when we started singing, they stopped. So we sang on
> and then we stopped and they sang. The Germans waved their
> hands, 'Happy Noel, Tommy'.
>
> One German took a chance and jumped up on top of the
> trench and shouted out 'Happy Christmas, Tommy!' No one
> fired a shot, which was marvellous, as before then you couldn't
> put your finger up without it being blown off. Of course our
> boys said, 'If he can do it, we can do it'. The sergeant major
> came along and said, 'Get down there, get down there.' We
> stuck our two fingers up at him. 'It's Christmas!' and with that
> we all jumped up and the Germans beckoned us forward to the
> barbed wire and we shook hands. I spoke to one German and he
> said, 'Do you know Islington?' He could speak very good
> English. 'Do you know the Jolly Farmer's pub in Southgate
> Road?' and I said, 'Yes, my uncle has a shoe repairing shop next
> door,' and he said, 'That's funny, there's a barber's shop on the
> other side where I used to work before the war.' He must have
> shaved my uncle at times and yet my bullet might have found
> him and his me.

Meeting the enemy in no-man's-land spread to other units and,
given it was Christmas, soldiers exchanged presents across a
hundred, perhaps two hundred yards of grubby, stubbly and
lightly shell-pocked fields: there were German cigars for British
tins of bully beef, buttons for newspapers, cigarettes for plum
pudding. It was extraordinary how many Germans spoke English
well but then many of the lads with whom the British Tommies

shook hands or with whom they posed for pictures were the London waiters, Manchester barbers and Hull pork butchers who had used the period of grace offered by the British government to go home and enlist. Captain Sir Edward Hulse of the Scots Guards met four Germans in no-man's-land who crossed over to the British front-line wire.

They were three private soldiers and a stretcher-bearer, and their spokesman started off by saying that he thought it only right to come over and wish us a happy Christmas, and trusted us implicitly to keep the truce. He came from Suffolk, where he had left his best girl and a 3½ h.p. motor-bike! He told me that he could not get a letter to the girl, and wanted to send one through me. I made him write out a postcard in front of me, in English, and I sent it off that night. I told him that she probably would not be a bit keen to see him again.

Rifleman Graham Williams was one of the few soldiers from among the British Army's rank and file who could speak German well. Williams began translating for those around him.

As I was talking, a chap came up to me, and he actually greeted me with the words 'Watcha cock, how's London?' I said, 'Good Lord, you speak like a Londoner', and he said, 'Well, I am a Londoner!' I said, 'Well, what on earth are you doing in the German army?' and he said, 'I'm a German, I'm a German Londoner'. Apparently he had been born in Germany, but had gone to England almost immediately afterwards with his parents, who had a small business in the East End of London somewhere, and he'd been brought up in England and gone to school in England. As by German law he was still a German national – he'd never been naturalised – he had been called up to go to Germany to do his national service: they did three years at that time. And afterwards he had come back to London, joined his parents and got a job as a porter at Victoria Station. He told me all this. He spoke absolute Cockney! It was most extraordinary.

The truce was an opportunity for both sides to compare notes. There had been so much propaganda that no one was entirely sure where the truth stood. It was a chance to set the record straight. Leslie Walkinton, aged just seventeen, was serving with the Queen's Westminster Rifles, a territorial battalion in the London Regiment.

I talked to a German-American who seemed a very pleasant sort of lad. He had never been to England actually, though his ship had anchored off Plymouth. We tried talking war, but I found he was full of newspaper propaganda, as I suppose I was, and we couldn't make any sense of it. He thought that the Germans had made a successful landing in England and were marching on London. I laughed. I told him that we expected to beat Germany by Easter and he roared.

'They firmly believe they are winning and that they will soon have the Russians beaten,' wrote Rifleman Ernest Blake of the 3rd Rifle Brigade to his mother.

We told them they were losing all round but they would not believe it. One fellow said to us 'Today peace, tomorrow you fight for your country and I fight for mine.' There was several of them that came from London, and one asked us to write to his wife, and gave her name and address.

Most men thought it prudent to keep off some of the war's thornier issues, preferring to talk about home and family. Captain Edward Hulse was one of the few who addressed the issue of dum-dum bullets, and the 'ghastly wounds' they made.

They think that our press is to blame in working up feeling against them by publishing false 'atrocity stories'. I told them of various sweet little cases which I had seen for myself, and they told me of English prisoners whom they have seen with soft-nosed bullets, and lead bullets with notches cut in the nose; we had a heated, and at the same time, good natured argument, and ended by hinting to each other that the other was lying!

There was a reluctance to begin shooting again and in some places the truce lasted several days. There were expressions of regret on both sides that the fighting would recommence; some claimed to be fed up with the war, but the view expressed to Ernest Blake, 'Today peace, tomorrow you fight for your country and I fight for mine', was not peculiar or unusual. Those British soldiers rewarded with a tour of the German trenches took mental note of salient features useful when war began again. One man shared a cigar with a German who was regarded by comrades as the best shot in the German army. As he smoked he noted the position of the German's loophole through which, he had no doubt, the German had picked off many a British Tommy. He vowed he would get the German the following day.

One of the longest truces was upheld by the 1/6th Gordon Highlanders, a Territorial battalion. The Scotsmen had got on very well with the enemy since Christmas Day, discovering, as had so many others, that the German ranks contained men who had lived in Britain, including a waiter from London's Hotel Cecil. There were barbers, too, among the German ranks and the Scotsmen willingly succumbed to a free shave in no-man's-land.

The truce lasted until the afternoon of 3 January when a German officer, with an interpreter, approached the British line to be met by a captain of the Gordon Highlanders. The two saluted gravely, the German officer informing the captain that instructions had been received to the effect that the war must be resumed. Watches were compared and it was agreed the truce would end in one hour, after which a fusillade opened up all along the line. A message passed down the Scots' trenches confirmed renewed hostilities. It read: 'The Kaiser's dead'. Wishful thinking indeed.

3

The End of the Affair

Any Edwardian woman engaged to a foreign national ought to have thought carefully about her future legal status before committing to marriage. With such a huge empire to police, the British were rather prone to fighting wars, and no one could be sure when an ally might become a dangerous adversary; for a woman, therefore, marrying a 'home boy' was a much more prudent course of action. This naturally required some prescience; and love is, after all, blind. In particular, those engaged to marry Germans were, from any objective standpoint, dabbling with danger when the likelihood of war between Britain and Germany steadily increased in the years prior to 1914. Then again, the royal family had not baulked at marrying Germans and surely what was good enough for them . . .

The British legal system's treatment of women who went ahead and married a foreign national was paternalistic and inflexible and, in 1914, demonstrated that everything was far from fair in love and war. The law as it affected women was simple: anyone who married a male foreigner was deemed by Part Three of the Naturalisation Act of 1870 to have automatically adopted her husband's nationality. Any woman subsequently widowed or separated remained an alien subject. This new law was introduced to bring English common law, which had hitherto kept entirely out of such matters, into line with the legal practice on the continent, including both France and Germany. The Act of 1870 added one further legal contortion. Should a German man decide to take British citizenship then his British-born 'German' wife would be issued with a certificate of naturalisation to confirm her new legal status – as a Briton.

The Aliens Restriction Act, requiring enemy aliens to register with the police, resulted in a steady flow of Germans and Austrians brought before the courts for non-compliance owing, typically, to the defendant's ignorance of the law. With the expansion of internment in November 1914, British wives of enemy aliens were also required to register. Many women remained unaware of this fact or simply believed that the rules could not apply to them in the country of their birth, and so were shocked to be dragged through the courts to be imprisoned or fined.

That these women were no longer considered British was made explicit by the legal expectation that it was for the German government to provide welfare to British-born wives of German internees in Britain. Payment was made through the American Embassy and was a sum roughly similar to that paid by His Majesty's Government in separation allowances to the wives of soldiers serving at the front. This act of charity was reciprocated by the British government, providing welfare to German-born wives of British subjects in Germany.

This arrangement worked in Britain's favour owing to the fact that there were more 'Germans' to support in Britain than there were 'Britons' in Germany. Whether this dawned on the enemy is unclear; perhaps it was spite that caused them to terminate the agreement at the end of November 1914 when notice was given that funds would no longer be available to British-born wives of interned Germans. In response, the British no longer sent money to German-born wives of interned British men. Whatever the reasons for the change in policy, these decisions had serious ramifications. The law that imposed a husband's nationality on his wife stood, but suddenly, and through no fault of their own, these women were no longer entitled to the same support or protection given to all other wives.

In Britain, the Treasury channelled money through the Local Government Board to Boards of Guardians to support

British-born 'German' wives, although the amount paid was halved compared to separation allowances. In Germany the situation was more serious. Owing to the federal state, the German government told the British authorities that it had no mechanism to distribute monies to German-born wives of British internees and that they would have to throw themselves on the mercy of local charitable organisations for relief. As if British internees did not have enough to contend with, they were forced to write to their own government back home asking what they – the internees – were meant to do for their German-born 'British' wives and children cut off without a penny.

On 22 February 1915, Albert Cresswell sent an urgent letter from Ruhleben camp to the Home Office in London. His German-born wife had lost her British allowance and, on turning to the German authorities for relief, she was told that the only support she could expect would be inside an internment camp.

'The English Government are granting support to English born German women living in England, and leave it to the German government to likewise provide for the German born English women living in Germany,' he wrote, describing how the German government was abrogating its responsibility by leaving relief to local charities. 'I do not for a moment think that it is the wish of the British government that English women should be subjected to such treatment.' If his letter were made known in the right quarters, Cresswell believed, then surely financial assistance would be forthcoming. 'I am terribly worried on account of my wife as it is an awful feeling being penned up here and not knowing how things are at home [in Germany].'

There were two other signatories to Cresswell's letter: Arthur Harvey and Edgar Gillon. All three men were in similar circumstances although, if anything, Gillon's was the most pressing. His wife was due to give birth in five weeks. In a further letter, Gillon assured the authorities in London that his wife would travel to England as soon as possible but was in no position to do so while heavily pregnant. 'I have no means whatever, so trust in God for help from the Home Government without further delay. Remittances can be made to Mr Harris, American General Consul, Frankfort A/M to be forwarded to my wife.'

In an internal Home Office memo, a discouraging note was added to the file containing both letters. 'Unfortunately Mr Cresswell married a German girl', and so under the new arrangements there could be no help for her despite her legal status as 'British'. Meanwhile, the Home Office was still trying to establish the nationality of the wives of both Gillon and Harvey: both wives were German-born.

Paradoxically, while the British government would not countenance sending financial support to these wives in Germany, there was no restriction on their entry into Britain where presumably they would be entitled to some, albeit minimal, welfare. Cresswell's letter informed the British government that the wives of all three internees would 'leave for England as soon as weather and circumstances permit'. Undoubtedly the harsh reality of living in Germany, cut off from state support, must have been the primary reason for the decision to go. But just how bad were conditions that made women leave their homes, travel across Europe, presumably through neutral Holland, to land in a country that they might never have visited before and where they could probably not speak the language? For these three German-born 'British' wives, the fear of the unknown must have been excruciating and there were no guarantees as to their future health or security.

When David Russell, another Ruhleben internee, heard that his German-born wife and four children had been sent by order of the German authorities from Leipzig to England in January 1915, his concern turned to misery. Within a week of disembarkation his entire family had been forced to enter a workhouse in Hull. Mrs Russell did not speak a word of English and was destitute. Worse still, all four children, aged nine, six, two and one, were removed from their mother, as was workhouse policy at the time. David Russell wrote pleading that his family might at least stay together but received a perfunctory reply: 'It is not practicable to arrange that a mother and children shall live absolutely as a family in a poor law institution. Hull guardians have been instructed to allow Mrs Russell to see her children at reasonable intervals.'

The letter to David Russell was sent nine months and one week after Mrs Russell entered the workhouse. The only beacon of hope was a note that Mrs Russell's children had 'with other children chargeable to the Guardians, been at the seaside during the summer months', although sadly not, it appears, with their mother.

These four women – the wives of Cresswell, Harvey, Gillon and Russell – while legally British, were Germans moving to Britain in time of war. The indigenous population was hardly likely to be aware of, or be interested in, the subtleties of a law that altered without consultation a wife's nationality: the reception these women could expect would be, at best, cold and indifferent, and, at worst, aggressive and even violent. For all such wives, both in Britain and in Germany, the shock of being treated as pariahs and effective outcasts from the countries of their birth must have been deeply wounding and was tantamount to being stateless.

What is interesting about the Russell case is that the British authorities did not seem to have been aware of Mrs Russell's imminent arrival. She had met David Russell, a black Jamaican and British subject, in Leipzig and the pair had cohabited for eleven years, having two 'illegitimate' children before marrying and having two more. The Foreign Office paperwork states that Mrs Russell had been sent to Britain seemingly without discussion and not at the behest of the British. There was no policy in either country of enforced repatriation of women who purely through marriage had changed nationality. There was, perhaps, more than a whiff of racism attached to this particularly sad case.

In Britain, not every incident of family crisis was given equal attention by the Foreign Office or the Home Office. Yet to any family divided by war, their own plight was of the utmost concern and their insistence on official help just as ardent. Helen 'Nellie' Fuchs, *née* Jordan, had married Carl Fuchs, a cellist of world renown, in 1893. Her husband was born in Germany in 1865 but had moved to Britain in 1887, receiving British citizenship in 1899. In the intervening years he had become a well-known and respected member of the Manchester community. He was Professor of Music at the Manchester College of Music and was the principal cellist with the Hallé Orchestra and reports of his superb musicianship reached the national press. He knew Tchaikovsky and Richard Strauss, played under Brahms, and could count composers such as Sir Edward Elgar and the conductor Sir Henry Wood among his personal friends.

Days before the outbreak of war, Fuchs, accompanied by his family, travelled to Germany to visit his sick mother. So ill was she that Fuchs stayed by her bedside until she died in early September. By this time it had become almost impossible for a male enemy alien to leave, and Fuchs was duly arrested in November and interned in Ruhleben camp. In February 1915, Nellie and her two young sons were allowed to go home. Carl, although released from internment, was not allowed to return but was placed under effective house arrest at his sister's residence in Jugenheim.

As soon as Nellie arrived home, she began a dedicated campaign to persuade the government to exchange her husband for Otto Blix, an elderly German stranded in Wimbledon. To support her case, Nellie pointed out to the authorities the age of her husband, forty-nine, and the fact the family was entirely dependent on his earnings. To survive financially she made it known that she drew on the support of leading institutions, such as the Royal College of Music, as well as that of Sir Henry Wood and Sir Edward Elgar, both of whom forwarded letters in support of Fuchs's exchange.

March 1915
To the Under Secretary of State
Sir

Mr Carl Fuchs, now a civil prisoner of war in Germany, is well known to me and has been a personal friend for many years. I trust that everything possible may be done to effect an exchange for Mr Carl Fuchs who is a great artist.

I have the honour to be your obedient servant
Edward Elgar

The request was refused. In the first of a number of rebuttals, the Home Office replied on 26 March that it was 'not possible for His Majesty's Government to consider questions of individual exchange'. While strictly true, some flexibility was possible, as unrelated cases imply. Inflexibility was observed as and when it suited officials to stand firm. Besides, there was no reason why Fuchs could not have been added to a list of names for group exchange.

Nellie Fuchs would not be put off. She contacted the Home Office repeatedly, trying to find other avenues by which Carl could be brought home. Far from winning sympathy, she alienated the very officials she had hoped would work in her interests. The problem was that Fuchs was not interned. Being German-born and residing in the country of his birth was going to place him somewhere near the bottom of the Home Office's list of concerns.

'The more irons one has in the fire, the more likely is success I believe,' Nellie counselled a sympathetic supporter. 'And if Carl's name is mentioned again and again from different quarters, it should make more impression. Of course what makes me uneasy, and what Carl mentions too, is the fact that naturalized Germans are not particularly in favour with the Government here at present.'

Indeed they were not. No one was about to go out of their way to help Nellie Fuchs, as she gradually came to realise.

The stress placed upon married women in time of war was extraordinary, with husbands and sons away on active service, their men's lives in daily peril.

In 1913 Mary Newton married Arthur Harthaus, giving birth to a son the following year in Blackpool. At some point, probably around April 1915, Arthur was interned, forcing his wife to rely on eleven shillings a week in relief for herself and her child. Mary was forced to move from her home in Stockport to live with her mother near Durham. Serious domestic arguments ensued and, in October 1915, Mary took up a British government offer to 'repatriate' German women by birth or marriage. Mary travelled to Gotha in central Germany to live with her parents-in-law.

The move proved unsuccessful. Mary had no money of her own and her parents-in-law had little enough to provide for themselves. Within months she applied to return to England. 'I have decided to beg of you [the American Consulate] to communicate with England regarding my return as I am so very unhappy here.' The American vice-consul in Erfurt wrote to the American Embassy in Berlin: 'As Mrs Harthaus is a German citizen by marriage and evidently not entitled to a British passport, I have the honour to ask if I may advance her sufficient money to defray the expenses of her return to England if she is able to obtain permission to leave Germany.'

The British Foreign Office ordered a report from the Manchester City Police Force as to whether Mary's relatives would look after her and her son. Mary's brother-in-law, John Sutherst, claimed that he had no objections to her coming to stay, but she had to be in a position to keep herself and this was evidently impossible. He added that in his opinion Mary should remain in Germany. She had quarrelled with relatives and in all likelihood the same state of affairs would recur once she was back in England.

Two months after making her application, Mary Harthaus received the Foreign Office reply: 'Viscount Grey has the honour to state that His Majesty's Government regret that after due enquiry they do not feel able to grant permission for Mrs Harthaus' return.'

Why would the Foreign Office allow Mary Harthaus to return and become a financial burden to the state, especially when she was German and had opted to leave Britain at state expense? If this case appeared clear-cut, there were others in which absurdly punitive measures were adopted with no such rationale.

Annie Vinnicombe married an Anglophile German named Michael Reiser at a church in Marylebone, central London, in the summer of 1894. After four years of marriage the couple and their young family emigrated to Bordeaux where they set up a tailoring business called 'New England'.

Within weeks of war, Michael Reiser was interned and the business seized. Mrs Reiser was financially secure but by February 1915 the French government decided that as she was legally a German, she could no longer reside in France and would have to go either to Spain or Switzerland. Annie Reiser had contacts in neither country and feared that, instead, she would be sent to Germany where she was not aware of having any living family; she could not, in any case, speak the language.

Much distressed, she appealed for help to the British Consulate in Bordeaux. Arthur Rowley, a consular official, replied informing her that any British-born wife of an enemy alien interned in France would be given permission to return as long as they lived with relatives and were not a drain on state resources.

Annie had a brother and two sisters in England. Her brother, George Vinnicombe, a carman working for the London, Brighton and South Coast Railways, was contacted but he said that he was not in a position to support his sister and her children under his roof.

Annie might have moved in with her sisters but there was a further problem. Both lived within twenty-five miles of the coast, in areas prohibited to 'enemy aliens'. One sister lived near

Falmouth, the other near the village of Chailey in East Sussex. In a letter to Annie, the Home Office refused permission for her to live with either sister and consequently her return to Britain was effectively blocked.

The official rejection was sent at the end of February with a note suggesting the best solution would be if the French authorities allowed her to stay in Bordeaux. On 16 April 1915, the French government informed the British Embassy that they considered it impossible for her to remain as it would set an 'awkward precedent'. She would thus be removed to an internment camp. The British government then lost all interest in Annie Reiser. Their only concession was to allow her two oldest sons, as British-born subjects, to return home. Twenty-year-old Michael Reiser went to Paris and enlisted with the British artillery. Cecil, the second son, followed a year later and was posted to the 30th Middlesex Regiment, embarking for the Western Front in April 1918. Despite her sons' patriotism, Annie Reiser remained in France with her youngest son. She does not appear to have been sent to an internment camp.

In contrast to the British government's attitude towards Annie Reiser, the rights of German-born 'British' women to enter Britain were not restricted. David Russell's German-born wife might have had a miserable time in Britain but there was no question about her not being admitted. Elfride Robson, née Frick, was another arrival. Her position was much healthier than Mrs Russell's: Elfride had English relatives with whom she could stay in Birkenhead. Being on the coast, it was a restricted area for aliens but then, of course, Elfride was not considered an alien.

Elfride had met her English husband Alan in Hamburg where he was working as a company manager. They married and had a daughter, Muriel, born in 1915. Apart from a total of six weeks' holiday in England, Elfride had never been overseas and Muriel, owing to her father's internment, had had little or no contact with him. Mother and daughter spoke only German. In October 1918 as the tide of war flowed irrevocably against Germany, Alan applied for his wife and daughter to come to England. The government's reply arrived within a couple of weeks: 'His Majesty's Government have the honour to state that they have no objection to the issue of a passport to Mrs Robson to enable her to return to the United Kingdom with her daughter as soon as she has obtained permission from the German Government to leave Germany.'

Mother and daughter left Germany for Britain on 6 November.

By the start of 1915 the entire east coast and most of the south coast of Britain had been designated an area prohibited to enemy aliens. A surprise enemy naval raid on England in December 1914, and the bombardment of towns including Hartlepool and Whitby, fuelled suspicion that enemy agents were signalling to German ships in the North Sea, increasing pressure on the government to remove any Germans still near the coast. Around 2,500 enemy aliens were living in prohibited areas at the beginning of the New Year, with their continued occupation at the discretion of county Chief Constables. Permits were granted to those Germans considered unreservedly loyal or whose work was of such national importance that their presence inside the prohibited area was of more use than their expulsion. Permits were also given to enemy aliens who were elderly, blind or bedridden or who were confined to a hospital or asylum. In February, the Home Office explained these arrangements to MPs.

> On grounds of mere humanity, lone women with nowhere else to go . . . may be made exceptions . . . In rarer cases financial loss or ruin which might follow an expulsion may perhaps be accepted as a reason for indulgence, but in all cases the main factor is that the alien is an enemy, and, if any interest is to suffer it must be that of the individual and not of the country.

This statement should have reassured 'lone women' like Julia Jacobitz, the retired German school governess whose only wish was to be left in peace in her Bournemouth home. However, since registering with local police she had been systematically harassed. Within days of registration she received a letter requiring her to move, being given twenty-four hours to comply or face a fine she could not hope to pay. She remained where she was, only to be served with a further demand to go: this time she was threatened with up to six months in prison. Once again she ignored the order; she had no choice:

> Since my very existence as a decent human being was bound up with this little house of mine, to leave it would have amounted to being rendered homeless, destitute and ruined for life and I could therefore not comply with such an order any more than I could be expected to conform with one to commit suicide. I had therefore to prepare for imprisonment. For a whole day and night I sat up at the appointed time without food, or sleep, expecting every moment to be taken away.

Julia was given a reprieve but made subject to the five-mile travel restriction imposed on all enemy aliens. No sooner had she heard that she could remain in Bournemouth than she became the subject of a Deportation Order. Miss Jacobitz applied for an exemption, being obliged to reply to questions she felt 'far exceeded the requirements of the official application forms'. Only after she had endured five months of uncertainty was permission granted for her to remain, whereupon she was served with two further notices to move.

In exasperation, she wrote to the American Embassy's German Department asking for help.

> Having done no wrong whatsoever to justify proceedings against me, I beg to invoke [the] intervention of the Embassy on my behalf in their capacity as temporary protectors of Germans' interests, to prevent my being forcibly removed from my house. Ever

since the beginning of the war, I have been kept in a state of permanent anxiety and suspense: the present being the fourth official order to leave my house. For a woman of 65 years, like myself, weakened in health and placed in exceptionally difficult position by absolute loneliness, having to go through this nerve-racking experience all alone and unaided, passes torture in itself.

Julia Jacobitz had nowhere to go and no close friends with whom she could stay for any length of time. Her income was limited, an amount 'which any ordinary labourer would scarce accept as a living wage', and she lived within a carefully mapped-out plan of expenses. Normally she could manage but these were not normal times 'and I view with grave apprehension the possibility of the war outlasting the small saving which I am drawing upon now'.

She continued:

The Authorities have not stated what they are going to do with me, but recalling to my mind precedents and the manner in which they treated their own country's women, I do not entertain any illusions as to the treatment I shall receive at their hands . . . Broken in health and having grown old, I do not ask any more of life than to end my days in peace.

The American Embassy enquired into Julia Jacobitz's case but to no avail. The Chief Constable of Hampshire had ordered her removal and he proved impervious to all requests to reconsider. Julia was duly arrested for non-compliance with the order, as a letter written on behalf of the Under Secretary of State confirmed:

Miss Jacobitz received considerate treatment in being exempted from repatriation, but the grant of the further privilege of remaining at Bournemouth was within the discretion of the Chief Constable of Hampshire. The Secretary of State did not see his

way in this case to interfere with the Chief Constable's decision
which follows the general practice of requiring persons of enemy
nationality to remove to non-prohibited areas . . . Miss Jacobitz
has been ill-advised as to refuse to leave the prohibited area and
consequently was charged at the Bournemouth police court with
the offence of residing there without a permit when she elected to
be tried by jury and consequently she is now in the custody in
Winchester Gaol . . . She is said to have made no application for
bail.

The case came to court on 11 January 1916, with proceedings
being reported in the *Bournemouth Guardian*. While the Court
Recorder acknowledged that the defendant was no threat and that
he regarded the case as one of 'wrong-headedness' on her part,
nevertheless Julia Jacobitz 'seemed to think that her home was her
castle and that if that castle was in a prohibited area it made her
entitled to live in it. Of course that was not so.' Julia's defence
lawyer pleaded that his client subsisted on a government annuity
of under £60 a year, half of which went to rent her 'little cottage'.
Giving evidence for the police, a Superintendent Hack said that
Jacobitz was 'stubborn and obstinate' but conceded, too, that
there were no grounds whatsoever to suspect the defendant and
that the only reason she had been asked to move was because she
was an enemy alien.

The Recorder stated that the law had to be obeyed even if it
caused 'discomfort and hardship'. Julia Jacobitz was found guilty
and fined £75, which would be held over as long as she left the
prohibited area within a week. In the meantime, she would have
to report daily at Boscombe police station in Bournemouth.

The Foreign Office files do not contain any further material on
the case. Perhaps Julia Jacobitz moved; perhaps she ended up back
in Winchester gaol. On such a tight budget she could hardly have
afforded the fines. The only thing that is certain is that the retired
governess remained in Britain. She died of pneumonia in a

Southampton hotel on 14 December 1927, aged seventy-six. Her entire estate was worth £185.

Issues concerning nationality and statehood affected men as well, and not only vicariously through their wives. Men who took citizenship of another country automatically lost their former nationality and therefore citizenship, and the rights of protection under the law granted at birth. It meant, for example, that a German-born man, raised and working in Germany, who had, for whatever reason, accepted British citizenship, would be interned in Ruhleben camp as quickly as a British-born enemy alien. But irrespective of the perverse position in which many people found themselves, it is unlikely that there were many cases as odd as that concerning an uninterned British academic and Munich University lecturer, Wilford Wells.

His story came to light when the Secretary of State for Foreign Affairs received an urgent letter from a friend of Wilford Wells, Thomas Smith, a former lecturer at Erlangen University in Bavaria. In August 1914, Smith wisely chose to return to Britain but Wells, who was unmarried, remained overseas. Then, in late 1915, Smith's attention was drawn to a short newspaper article.

> I see by the *Fränkischer Kurier* [a Nuremberg newspaper] for October 29th 1915, that Mr Wells has been called up to serve in the German army. He is about 36 to 38 years of age and as he was a personal friend of mine, I am convinced that he has never taken this step of his own free will . . . [or] that he ever took out papers of naturalisation.

There was no longer an American consul in Munich, the last incumbent having been removed, Smith claimed, because of his pro-German sympathies. As a result, there was no one obvious to whom Wells could directly appeal. The Foreign Office, Smith suggested, should look into the case through the offices of the American Embassy in Berlin.

Born in September 1878, Wells left Britain for Germany in 1901, taking a position as an English lecturer at Munich University in 1906. Four years later Bavarian law changed: certain jobs, including teaching, were to be deemed government posts and attracted, for those foreigners who held them, Bavarian nationality. Both Smith and Wells knew that they were now considered Bavarian civil servants but, they believed, with only 'complimentary citizenship and pension rights.' 'At the time,' wrote Smith, 'I enquired from the British Consul in Nuremberg whether it made any difference to my [British] nationality and he replied in the negative.' Yet, according to Bavarian law these were not complimentary rights but full rights and, as a Bavarian subject, rights came with obligations.

Wells held a valid British passport obtained on the outbreak of war from the British vice-consul in Munich and assumed, logically, that he was ineligible for active service in the German army. In January 1915, to his surprise, he was called for a medical examination. Wells went to see the Secretary of Munich University and was informed of a two-year period of grace during which he should have given up Bavarian nationality in order to keep British citizenship. This he had failed to do. In a statement to the American vice-consul, Wells gave his side of the story:

> Subsequent enquiries at the University showed that I had in fact been for two years a subject of both states, but through my neglect to apply to the British Consulate for permission to retain my British nationality beyond this time, I had lost my British nationality. I was then asked unofficially whether I should object to serving against the Russians and was confidentially assured that I should not be employed in the West. I considered the matter and said I would serve. Since 1912 I evidently have not been a British subject.

Naively, Wells never checked as to whether or not the British considered him a subject, merely accepting that the British vice-consul had made an error in giving him a passport in August 1914.

Although it transpired Wells had British nationality, he decided to enlist rather than be seen by the Bavarians as avoiding his obligations. He did not 'wish to antagonise the German authorities'. Wilford Wells was conscripted on 2 September 1915 and took the oath of allegiance eleven days later. His army records show that he was considered 'fully fit for active service' and that his conduct was 'excellent'. It is interesting to note that on his records appear the words: 'May only be deployed on the Eastern Front', in line with his request. After training he was sent to join his unit, the 2. Bayerische Infanterie Regiment.

'So far as I could gather,' wrote the American vice-consul to the British Foreign Office, 'Mr Wells' own attitude is that he took the military oath of allegiance voluntarily, in the sincere belief that having lost his British nationality it was his duty to do so; that under these circumstances he does not wish to take any action, or to have any action taken on his behalf.'

The British government's response to Wells was characterised by mounting indifference. Officials concurred that it was probably useless making representations as the German army would be unlikely to let him 'out of their clutches' and that Wells should have acquainted himself with the laws of the country in which he resided. 'Besides,' wrote one official, 'he is a queer sort of an Englishman, if he is one at all, except in name and I don't think he is very deserving of assistance.' In the end the Foreign Office sent a letter to Thomas Smith: 'In the circumstances we do not propose to take any further steps in the matter.'

Wilford Wells was the youngest of four children born into a middle-class London family. He and his brother Norman attended Dulwich College in south-east London, but while Wilford sought a life in academia his elder brother followed the family tradition and set up a practice as a solicitor. It is not known how either his surviving mother or his siblings reacted to news of Wilford's actions but an indication of Norman's feelings may be inferred from his immediate decision to enlist.

Although just six months short of his fortieth birthday, and with three young sons of his own, in November 1915 Norman Wells applied for a commission entirely on the basis that his brother was serving in the German army. This was rejected and so he dissolved his practice and attested, being called up for service in January 1916 and posted to the 1/28th London Regiment (Artist's Rifles) to serve as a private. Within seven weeks he had been sent overseas, serving with C Company in France, having requested an immediate posting after basic training. In August he was awarded a commission, transferring to the Army Ordnance Corps, rising to the rank of temporary captain. He remained in France until May 1919.

Wilford Wells survived the war but his wish to serve only on the Eastern Front may not have been honoured. In May 1916 he was sent to join the 3rd Company, 1st Battalion Landsturm Infantry Regiment on the Eastern Front, serving during operations near Pinsk. He soon fell ill with pleurisy and was sent to a field hospital at Cobryn (in present-day Belarus) and after convalescence returned to Munich. Then, in December 1917, he joined the Bavarian Reserve Infantry Regiment, deployed that winter to fight in Flanders, where it remained for the rest of the war. It appears that Wells may have served in Flanders until February 1918, when he returned to Munich to see out the war. Whether he was aware that his brother was on the other side of the line is unknown, nor if he ever saw or spoke to his sibling again.

Of all the incidents that inflamed Anglo-German hostility, the torpedoing of the Cunard liner RMS *Lusitania* was the most serious and had profound repercussions for Germans living in Britain. On 8 May 1915, the liner, returning from the United States, was torpedoed eleven miles off the west coast of Ireland and sank in eighteen minutes. Of 1,959 passengers on board, 1,198 drowned, including almost a hundred children. The attack on this civilian liner was portrayed in the British press as unprecedented, unwarranted and without warning. There was a public outcry, prompting furious and sustained attacks on Germans and German property across Britain.

Nowhere was anger more heartfelt than in Liverpool, which considered the *Lusitania* one of its own. The 'Lusy', as she was affectionately known, moored at Liverpool's docks before each Atlantic crossing, guaranteeing that the crew, including the captain, were overwhelmingly Liverpool men. A journalist writing for *The Times* on 9 May reported the arrival of survivors at Liverpool's Lime Street Station, some two hundred in all: there was a handful of petty officers, some engineers, stewards, trimmers and firemen. 'Some had bandages round their heads, some were limping, and a few more seriously injured had to be carried away in motor-cabs. They all came in such clothes as they happened to have on when their ship was taken unawares . . .'

It was a pathetic scene. A noxious mix of fury and grief was inevitable. As the Union Jack was lowered to half-mast on Liverpool's City Hall, mobs attacked German shops, with police using batons to break up rioting crowds in Everton and Birkenhead. In places crowds swelled to two or three thousand with police powerless to halt wholesale looting and burning of German premises. Incidents were not confined to Liverpool but spread across the country. In Bradford, where Germans were still employed in mills, strikes were threatened unless all enemy aliens were dismissed – such demands were quickly acceded to.

In response, prominent German-born Britons felt compelled to demonstrate their loyalty. In Bradford a deputation of just such leading citizens handed to the mayor a signed statement that underlined their repugnance at the German navy's actions, and there were similar declarations made in Hull, Manchester and London. Others chose to write to the press. Sir Felix Semon, a naturalised British citizen of German extraction, and former physician to King Edward VII, wrote on 11 May that he had hoped that by doing his duty to his adopted country he would not need to make public an overt expression of loyalty. But, he continued, he was forced to act, hence his letter to *The Times* in which he wished it to be known that he 'emphatically abhor[red] the barbarous methods, one and all, employed by Germany'.

Sir Carl Meyer and Leopold Hirsch, leading London financiers, added their voices to the chorus of disapproval. Meyer wrote:

> I shall be very glad to join in a loyal address to the King to express on behalf of naturalised British subjects of German birth their feelings of detestation at the horrors committed by the German Army and Navy in the prosecution of the war, culminating in the cold-blooded murder of the innocent victims of the *Lusitania* . . . I take the earliest opportunity of declaring, in the most emphatic manner, that my feelings are no less strong and unequivocal than those of any British-born subject of his Majesty, and that I have lost all regard and affection for the country which is not ashamed of applauding such acts of infamy.

Leopold Hirsch made known his disgust and his wholehearted loyalty and devotion to King George V in whose country he had spent the previous thirty-six years. He pointed out that his son, John Hirsch, an officer serving in France with the 13th Hussars, was proof, if any were needed, of the patriotic feelings his family cherished.

Such feelings were justified. Sir Edgar Speyer, naturalised in 1892, headed the London bank Speyer Brothers. Highly respected, he had been part of London's economic and social life since the 1880s, being made a baronet in 1906 and a Member of the Privy Council in 1909. Speyer's brother, James, lived in New York, and was reported to have expressed pro-German and anti-British sentiments, but the odium that might have attached to James was, instead, visited on his brother.

Sir Edgar was attacked periodically in the press after August 1914 but the vitriol intensified after the *Lusitania*'s sinking. He was forced to resign from charitable boards, and from other business interests with which he was associated. Worse still, his house required police protection from crowds that harangued visitors. Speyer's children were forced from school because of a threat made by other parents to withdraw their children. When friends offered to take the children into safety, Sir Edgar had had enough. On 17 May he wrote to the Prime Minister requesting that his baronetcy be revoked and that he be allowed to resign from the Privy Council. Asquith rejected the proposals and wrote that he had full confidence in Speyer's loyalty, adding that he understood Speyer's 'sense of injustice and indignation'. The Prime Minister had known his friend 'long and well enough to estimate at their true value these baseless and malignant imputations'. Despite such support, Speyer packed up, and, judging German U-boats a lesser threat than the British public, left for New York.

For unnaturalised Germans and Austrians there was little likelihood of assuaging public anger. The sinking was just the latest in a catalogue of reported incidents, including the Germans' first use of asphyxiating gas on the Ypres battlefield, the alleged ill treatment of British prisoners and reports of escalating Zeppelin raids on Britain. On the same day as *The Times* carried letters from Semon, Meyer and Hirsch, all enemy subjects in Liverpool were told that they would be interned; even those who were naturalised were advised to leave the city and move 'inland'.

Great swathes of the national press, including the *Daily Sketch*, which ran a headline 'Lock Them All Up!', the *Globe* and the *Evening News* called for the internment of all unnaturalised Germans, as much for their own safety and for the preservation of public order as for their likelihood to cause mischief. The fear of social disorder frightened conservative newspapers. The public's antagonism towards enemy aliens should not be a reason for 'hooliganism', cautioned an editorial in *The Times*. 'If men are sufficiently able-bodied to attack Germans and to loot their shops, they should be in the trenches in Flanders with rifles in their hands.'

On 12 May 1915, a Conservative MP, William Joynson-Hicks, presented a petition to the Commons, signed, he claimed, by a quarter of a million women, demanding the internment of enemy aliens of military age and the withdrawal from coastal areas of all enemy aliens, male and female, to a distance exceeding thirty miles. Under mounting pressure, the Asquith government buckled. All unnaturalised male persons of hostile origin would be interned, the Prime Minister told MPs on 13 May. If over military age, they would be repatriated. Where suitable, women and children would also be sent home. Over the following six months, the number of internees grew rapidly once more, and included those men released the previous winter when accommodation was in short supply. Under reciprocal arrangements with Berlin, 9,300 Germans, women, children and the elderly, had left Britain since the start of hostilities: they would be followed by 10,000 more in the wake of the *Lusitania* disaster. Women of less than five years' British residency were automatically repatriated.

The pressure of living behind barbed wire grew ever more challenging for internees. To Doctor Adolf Vischer, a member of the Swiss Embassy and visitor to Britain's internment camps, it was becoming increasingly clear how endless confinement was already having serious ramifications for prisoners' mental health. His observations made for sober reading.

> Foremost is an increased irritability, so that the patients cannot stand the slightest opposition and readily fly into a passion . . . They find intense difficulty in concentrating on one particular object, their mode of life becomes unstable, and there is restlessness in all their actions.

Failure of memory is a general complaint, especially as regards names of people and of places with incidents occurring shortly before the outbreak of the war . . .

Very often people who are much affected brood for three or four days without uttering a single word. All in common have a dismal outlook and a pessimistic view of events around them . . . many are inordinately suspicious. I have met with complaints of sleeplessness in some camps in considerable number . . .

Prolonged confinement led to bizarre situations. Private Thomas Hughes, sent to guard prisoners held at Olympia in London, saw with detached amusement an internal court martial prosecuted by prisoners after one internee accused another of stealing a chocolate. Evidently no case was too small for men with time on their hands. Statements were taken, witnesses called and the prosecution and defence made their cases; even guards on duty at the time of the alleged offence were asked to give evidence. What the sanctions were Thomas never discovered as he was moved from Olympia before the verdict was in.

An internee's experience of captivity varied according to the prevailing ethos of the camp commandant. German-born Richard Noschke had avoided internment, working in a varnish factory. But then came the sinking of the *Lusitania* and on 23 July he was removed to an old jute factory in Stratford, a temporary holding camp, where, he claimed, conditions were poor and internees assaulted and harangued. The commandant, the Marquis de Burr, was, Noschke wrote, 'a very proud man, and a great German hater'. Burr was followed by a Colonel Lambert, who was 'even worse'. After three months, Lambert handed over to Colonel Haines, a 'perfect gentleman', Noschke acknowledged. 'A new life seemed to start in the camp, up until then everyone was depressed and downhearted.' Haines let the men build a skittle alley, allowed football matches and encouraged the formation of a choir and a band. He addressed the grievances of the internees and removed the rifles carried by the camp police. The improvement proved temporary, for Colonel Lushcombe, described by Noschke as being 'as bad as the first two', replaced Haines.

Anything that provided distraction or amusement for internees was welcomed but nothing compared to a visit from wives and children. Married men were normally transferred from camps like Stratford to more accessible places such as Alexandra Palace, north London, containing 3,000 internees. Richard Noschke was sent there, as was another internee, Pal Stoffa, who watched with melancholy and sadness the fortnightly family visits.

It was pathetic to watch the painful excitement of the men whose visitors were due in the afternoon: suddenly oblivious of the existence of their comrades, they were a prey to subdued suspense all the morning and as soon as the mid-day was over, they started their preparations, each man deliberately anxious to look his best. Long before 3 o'clock, which was the appointed hour for visitors, they assembled with their little bunches of flowers and toys for the children, and were then marched off to the visiting rooms.

I was once allowed to assist and shall never forget the scene: the men sitting at one side of a long table and the visitors filing in to sit down opposite; here a father with a child on his lap timidly peering into the face of the strange man, there an elderly couple hardly speaking, just looking and looking at one another with an intensity of longing that words cannot express. Elegant young women with a bevy of half-starved children, a grim looking solicitor with a pile of papers in front of him – visitors from another world bringing solace to some and tearing open the wound of others. It made me feel almost glad that I could have no visitors: it seemed cruel to allow the poor wretches to have their world so near to them only to be snatched away after a few minutes.

One child taken to see her father, Richard, was six-year-old Elfie Druhm. Her English-born mother, Ethel, was struggling to survive after their salon was wrecked in anti-German riots.

We used to visit him on Saturday afternoon for a few hours and I can still actually remember going through big gates with policemen on either side. In front of the building there was a flight of steps, at the top of which were long lines of German men, standing there looking out for their wives. We went in and sat down and talked for two hours. We weren't to take any foodstuffs with us, a policeman there was supposed to search us, but I don't think he ever did. My mother had a muff, in those days that was the fashion, and she could have hidden things in there but she thought that would be the first place they would look, so she stuffed food into the elastic of my bloomers, packets of chocolate, oranges even. All the men were receiving the same sort of smuggled food. We weren't being watched, or guarded. When we were in there, we were free to move around in what looked like a doctor's waiting room so it was quite easy to hand the food over.

In internment they were not badly treated. There was a little room where Father used to make little boxes, marquetry, decorated with tiny pieces of wood, to pass the time. The building was a grey, cold stone kind of place, it wasn't comfortable. The windows weren't barred as I recall, but the place was secure. I remember a big fence round the building and in the summer we used to sit outside in the garden along with the other men and their wives and I remember looking at that fence, but not really understanding what it meant.

As life experienced by an internee in Britain varied according to the commandant, so much the same applied to British prisoners of war in Germany. The genial commandant at Magdeburg POW camp, who helped parole Captain Robert Campbell to see his dying mother, presided over a camp that was in every way

different from that run by Karl Niemeyer, the vicious commandant of Holzminden camp. Both Karl and his equally unpleasant
brother Charles, also a camp commandant, were notorious enough
to be placed on a British prosecution blacklist for alleged mistreatment of British prisoners.

What provoked individuals to behave well or badly towards
British soldiers? The attitude of the District Commander was an
influencing factor, but faith in or distrust of war propaganda was
also key to their attitude and that of the men under their command.
The commandant's authority and his approach set the overall tone
of the camp and therefore of its guards. Nevertheless, as the war
progressed and casualties increased, so impressionable younger
guards were replaced by middle-aged men who were, in turn,
replaced by men who had been wounded in the trenches and were
no longer fit for active service. It was widely accepted by British
prisoners that former front-line soldiers were, on the whole, more
amenable and sympathetic to their charges than those who had
seen no action at all.

Circumstances at the front affected attitudes, too. The one-
time commandant at Wahn camp, General von Nestler, enhanced
conditions for prisoners after his son was captured by the British,
as did the commandant at Göttingen who, according to Private
James Harrold, made distinct improvements in the autumn of
1916 when he heard that his captive son was being well treated in
Britain. Likewise, General von Stienneich, who had fought in the
Franco-Prussian War of 1870, and whose two sons were prisoners
in England, 'tried to do his best for us', according to Lance
Corporal Herbert Lewin of the 1st Royal Berkshire Regiment.
'The General was very human, and was very satisfied with the way
they [his sons] were treated.'

And then there were those Germans picked out by prisoners
simply for exemplary behaviour. General Steinkie, in charge at
Münster III (Rennbahn camp), was excellent, according to Private
James McDaid, captured at Loos in September 1915. 'He was a

very good man and did all he could for the prisoners. He had a "kind of affection" for the English and used to point to us as an example of soldiers to other nationalities. Any complaint that went to him was reasonably dealt with.'

A number of Germany's camp commandants, doctors and guards had lived in Britain, and some returned to Germany as war broke out. Yet residency did not necessarily make Anglophiles of these men. Privates George Kitson of the Scots Guards and Patrick Leavy of the Highland Light Infantry gave interviews at the end of the war in which they spoke of an interpreter at Fort MacDonald, an infamous transit camp in Belgium. Here a German guard was recognised as being a former shipping manager from Scotland, a man described as being around thirty-five years old, slim, sallow, with rounded shoulders and 'vicious to our men'. His wife and children were in Britain and it was their likely predicament, and his family's enforced separation, that informed his attitude to British prisoners whom he regularly assaulted.

By contrast, others were humane. In Cassel, Doctor Noyes, one-time consultant at St Thomas' Hospital in London, looked after the sick and wounded as well as circumstances allowed. After Noyes left, Doctor Simon arrived, and was considered by prisoners to have been just as professional. Simon had friends in Manchester and was very keen that wounded men marked for exchange relayed to his friends that he was doing his best. In the same camp, a British sergeant major, a policeman in civilian life, recognised the camp's censor, a pleasant enough man, as an employee of the Deutsche Bank in London's Mincing Lane. The erstwhile constable had been sent to arrest this man but the German had given him the slip, leaving for home that morning.

Unsurprisingly a number of interpreters and censors were formerly resident in Britain. At Libau, the interpreter, Sadler, had owned a shop in London's Fleet Street. Leonard, the censor at Friedrichsfeld, had also been a shopkeeper, in Nottingham. In one

of the more curious episodes of Anglo-German relations, Leonard
cajoled prisoners into helping a visiting professor with his research
into dialects and phonetics. The professor, Wilhelm Doegan, a
graduate of Oxford University, asked men to speak or sing into a
gramophone; some refused but others did take part and their
efforts survive as an archive in both Berlin and the British Library.
Leonard had lived in Nottingham concurrently with the commandant of Langensalza camp, a former laceworks owner. It was said
that Hauptmann Alexander had been so happy in Nottingham
that he openly favoured men from the town, giving them the best
jobs on work kommandos.

Prisoners were not passive recipients of good or ill will. Those
who knuckled down, and did not kick against authority, had an
easier time than those who proved belligerent or resentful.
Commandants rarely tolerated impudence and, if ordered to transfer men to camps that used prisoners in coal and salt mines,
selected those they considered the obstinate and ill-mannered
first. Conditions in these mines were appalling and prisoners often
died of injuries and illness. By contrast, prisoners who showed
themselves not only amenable but cultured, too, could thrive in
POW camps and were permitted to construct theatres, form
bands and print newspapers.

Nonetheless, the claustrophobia of a POW camp and the
enforced communal life only helped to magnify resentments and
petty jealousies between fellow prisoners. Worst of all, not every
prisoner remained loyal to his comrades.

Only privates and lance corporals were expected to participate
on work kommandos. With this in mind, some prisoners added
two or more stripes on their arms to fool the Germans into thinking that they were senior NCOs and therefore not eligible for
outside work. This trickery threw the onus of extra work onto the
remaining men. Bona fide NCOs felt they could not expose the
fraud for fear that cheats would be sent to the salt mines. Equally,
they were angry that men who did not take the responsibility of

NCOs in the trenches were only too happy to take advantage in Germany.

Did all these NCOs really care about the plight of the men given extra chores owing to the selfishness of others? Or were they instead, as some privates and lance corporals believed, simply cherishing those privileges granted senior NCOs, and protecting their rights? At Senne, Sergeant Major Thomas of the Warwickshire Regiment was nicknamed 'von Thomas' because of his alleged enthusiastic co-operation with the enemy, to the detriment of comrades. It was easy for enmity against such men to fester. One old regular, Private Alfred Hoare, captured during the Retreat from Mons, let his bitterness slip during an interview he gave on returning home in 1918. Hoare had been held at Döberitz camp for most of the war.

> I was sent out on kommando when attending hospital. This was the fault of the English Sergeant Major who made it pretty hot for us. I could also tell tales of bad treatment by the NCOs and RAMC men but I prefer not to give any information as to this. The world is not very big and I might meet some of them after the war and if I do I will take the law into my own hands.

Those in camp who held privileged positions attracted dark suspicions from men who did not. Red Cross food parcels sent to Germany proved a lifeline for soldiers who could barely stomach the enemy's dire rations. These parcels were collected from nearby railway stations, stored, and then distributed by a parcel committee run by the prisoners themselves. At Cassel there were accusations that the prisoners who ran the committee were stealing from other prisoners' parcels, a view apparently confirmed when the hut and parcel records went up in smoke shortly after the Armistice.

With food in short supply, the smallest discrepancy in allocations drew vehement protest. At Ohrdruf Hospital, Private James

Harlock suspected Corporal Rowley of stealing from parcels. Rowley, as the principal member of the parcel committee, had the job of opening and overseeing the distribution of parcel contents. 'Frequently the tins were changed,' complained Harlock, 'in my case butter into margarine and meat pudding into jam . . . some [tins] were missing.' Harlock believed that Rowley sold tins to German guards who were, by 1917, very short of quality food-stuffs themselves. It was an accusation he repeated when inter-viewed at the end of the war.

> Sapper Milner told me that Corporal Rowley once showed him ten 20 mark German notes and was bragging about what he had got, and said he had got some cognac. He seemed to be in favour with the German Guards and to be able to go about and do as he liked. All of us in the barracks suspected him of making money out of the parcels, and he was still in charge of them when I left.

Hunger and mental fatigue undermined the morale and morals of weaker men. It would be no surprise that some prisoners availed themselves of the chance for an easier life at the behest of the enemy and at the expense of comrades.

The worst betrayal of all began when prisoners broke ranks entirely and aligned themselves with the enemy. In interviews with exchanged or returning prisoners of war, men picked out individuals who passed well beyond the boundaries of fraternisa-tion with the enemy, resorting instead to outright collaboration. 'Private Owen did not conduct himself as a comrade with the exception of a few of his own friends; he took the side of the German authorities and frequently declared men fit to work who were seriously ill,' claimed Private Ernest Barton, of the 2nd Manchester Regiment, insisting that the accused also assisted in the thrashing of two prisoners of war who had tried to escape. 'Owen's conduct cannot be too severely censured.'

Chalmers of the Gordon Highlanders was just as treacherous, claimed Alfred Amey, a crewman of HMS *Nomad* sunk at the Battle of Jutland in 1916. Amey assured his interviewer that Chalmers, who spoke fluent German, was given command of his hut and sorted out work shifts. In this capacity he was given an official title. 'The Germans issued a notice to say that he held the position of a German Unter-Officer and had an order put into the hut to that effect. Any man who struck him would be court-martialled and punished in the same way as for striking a German non-commissioned officer.'

Private Mark Nathan of the 2/7th Lancashire Fusiliers had no honorary rank bestowed upon him but he was 'very thick with the Germans in the Guardroom', according to Private Ernest Brown of the Machine Gun Corps. 'Nathan would not mix with us, drinking the Germans' beer and smoking with them.' It came as no surprise to Brown that Nathan was attacked by another prisoner, who was charged and given seven days' punishment. Like Chalmers, Nathan spoke fluent German and was used as an interpreter. He was seen, Brown said, as being very 'pro-German', getting rations reduced whenever a man went sick, or claiming that men were malingering.

Owen, Chalmers and Nathan might successfully have rebutted such accusations had they ever been asked to do so. Anyone acting as an intermediary with the enemy had to be shrewd and even-handed. It is possible that these men were attempting to ameliorate the more stringent German demands on British prisoners, but then failed to appreciate the negative image they portrayed to those around them. It is possible, but unlikely. Whether these men did collaborate with the enemy will never be known for sure. Their names and their deeds have passed into obscurity, unlike those of another man whose presence in several prisoner-of-war camps in 1914 and 1915 was to cause an international sensation.

*   *   *

Visitors offering help to British prisoners in Germany were likely to be warmly welcomed and remembered, especially if they were English-speaking. The American ambassador, or more likely his representative, John Jackson, was seen occasionally, busying himself with soldiers' welfare. Then there was the Reverend Henry Williams, the chaplain of St George's Church in Berlin, who used his special licence to move freely across Germany to pursue his ministry. And then came another English-speaking visitor who attracted attention for very different reasons. His name was Sir Roger Casement. With the active encouragement and material support of the Germans, this Knight of the Realm-turned-devout Irish Nationalist came not to offer help but to procure it from among Irish Catholic prisoners. The intention: to enlist a 'Brigade' of men to be used in a planned uprising in Ireland.

Although Dublin-born, Casement was raised by paternal relatives in Ulster. An Irish Nationalist in his youth, he nonetheless rose to become a British consul, employed in Africa. After the Boer War he became an anti-imperialist, yet continued working for the British government, compiling a report on human rights abuses in Belgian-controlled Congo, for which he was knighted in 1911. His findings helped recharge his own interest in the right to self-determination and Irish Nationalism. In 1913, after retiring from consular service, he helped form the Irish Volunteers, a group that would ultimately fight for Irish Independence in 1916. His decision to travel to Germany to raise a force to fight for Irish independence was a huge gamble and an act of high treason that ultimately cost him his life.

Casement arrived in Berlin on the last day of October 1914 and soon came to the somewhat startled attention of Princess Evelyn Blücher.

The wonder was how an Irishman, and an ex-consul of the English Government, could have found his way there. But we were more interested than most, as we knew him well. He had been in Africa with my husband, and we had also seen a good deal of him in London at various times. We knew his anti-English feelings well, and his rabid Home Rule mania, but we did not expect it to have taken this intense form of becoming pro-German . . .

My husband went to see him shortly after his arrival and tried to show him what a false position he had put himself in, and that he had better leave the country as quickly as possible, but it was no use . . . he was most enthusiastic and certain of success.

Casement received the cooperation of the German State Secretary for Foreign Affairs for his plans to form the Brigade. To begin with, Irish Catholics were separated from other British prisoners. In Sennelager, where 400 Irishmen languished, a German Feldwebel addressed the men, offering improved food, accommodation and clothing. The offer was resisted by senior Irish NCOs who did not want preferential treatment but, despite their protests, the men were moved into newly constructed huts.

If Casement was to make an appeal to 2,200 Irish Catholic prisoners then they would have to be brought under one roof. By mid-December all were concentrated at Limburg camp, thirty-five miles north-west of Frankfurt-am-Main and in a strongly Catholic region. The camp was one of the best in Germany with excellent sanitation, good quality wooden huts and plenty of blankets. Cigarettes were handed out freely and the men were addressed directly by Casement. Private Andrew Duffy was one of the men listening. 'He said, "I have come here to form an Irish Brigade, to strike a blow for Ireland". The men hissed and hooted at him. He saw it was no use and left, the men would have pulled him to pieces.' Private Tim Macarthy of the RAMC took note as Casement 'addressed us on how badly England had treated Ireland and why should the Irish fight for England'. The appeal fell flat. 'He told us we were no Irishmen. We booed him out of the place.' Only two men approached Casement to enlist.

The Germans made every effort to help procure the men needed. Those who agreed to join would be given all the comforts the Germans could muster, and absolved of all work. Posters were printed to convince Irish Catholics of their true allegiance, and it was not to the English. 'Remember Bachelors Walk' exhorted one poster, referring to an incident just days before the outbreak of war when British troops opened fire on Irish Nationalists, killing three and injuring thirty-two. A leaflet was handed out giving 'Reasons why you should fight for the Germans', followed by another: 'Reasons why you should not fight for the English'. Private Daniel Merry was given what he called an Irish 'manifesto'. This explained that fighting for England in Belgium meant no more to Irishmen than the Fiji islands. An Irish Brigade, it clarified, would be fully equipped and financed by Germany; in America 'brothers' were forming a league to help the Brigade and, after the war, anyone who wished to leave and settle in America would be given free passage and a grant. Finally, those who remained in Germany post-war would be welcomed on the streets of Berlin and treated as guests.

A recruiting office was opened at Limburg and twelve men at a time taken to see the sort of food they might eat, including roast beef and potatoes. In spite of all the incentives and arm-twisting, the men remained almost impervious to persuasion. This infuriated Casement. An Irish Brigade 'black book' was created and the names entered of those declining to help, so testified Private Cullen of the Royal Munster Fusiliers. 'Those men (of whom I was one) were given reduced rations and made to do all the "dirty work" in the camp.'

Those resistant to persuasion were sent away, as the Reverend Henry Williams discovered. Williams had made an application to visit Limburg but the camp commandant turned it down: 'My services were not required as all the prisoners were Roman Catholic.' Williams wrote in his diary that Casement had become convinced that a few loyalist ringleaders swayed potential volunteers and that if these loyalists could be identified, weeded out and removed, then the others would soon join the Brigade.

> The consequence was that week after week small parties of these supposed ring-leaders were singled out for punishment and sent to other camps containing several thousands of Russians but no British. It was in these camps that I met them and soon got to know their story. The presence of these small groups of Irishmen at Sagan, Spottau, Guben and other camps puzzled me at first.

Seventeen Irishmen were sent to Guben, where, on arrival, they were subjected to four days without food, mattresses or blankets. At Neuhammer camp, fifteen 'ring-leaders' were sent to live among some 20,000 Russian and Polish prisoners.

The testimony given by witnesses to Casement's campaign varied in peripheral details but not in key facts. Casement returned to Limburg and with the additional help of an Irish-American priest, Father Nicholson, sought more recruits but without success, and only a handful of men enlisted. One recruit, Corporal Harry Quinlisk of the Royal Irish Regiment, would come to acknowledge ruefully the failure of the entire enterprise. 'The Munster Fusiliers were more loyal than the English soldiers. Several Englishmen volunteered for the Irish Brigade, but we could never enrol them. Most of the men we interviewed asked how much money they would get.' In all, just fifty-six NCOs and other ranks joined up and, although some effort was made by the Germans to enlist officers, none succumbed.

The few dozen prisoners who joined the Irish Brigade would live in a sort of limbo, their numbers too small to be of any material use in an Irish uprising. As a group, they would wear a distinctive Irish Brigade uniform described as green with red cuffs, with a shamrock on the collar, cap and cuffs. Being so conspicuous hardly mattered: all their names were known to their erstwhile comrades. Eventually, in July 1915, they were taken from Limburg to Zossen camp, south of Berlin, where they remained segregated from other prisoners. James Gerard, the American ambassador, came across them in 1916. 'The Irishmen did not bear confinement well, and at the time of my visit many of them were suffering from tuberculosis in the camp hospital. They seemed also peculiarly subject to mental breakdowns.'

Little wonder. No one, least of all the men themselves, knew what the future would hold for those who had thrown in their lot with the enemy.

The Kaiser (left) rides alongside his cousin, King George V, during a visit to Potsdam in 1913. Contact between the royal families prior to the war was close but could also be fraught as the race for naval supremacy mounted.

Vast crowds pour onto the Unter den Linden to greet news of the outbreak of war. The Kaiser was profoundly shocked by Britain's entry into the war on the side of France and Russia.

Henry Hadley, pictured at Cheltenham College circa 1880. In 1914 this 51-year-old English teacher, was leaving Germany by train when he was shot and mortally wounded by a German infantry officer. He died at 2.30 a.m., 5 August, acquiring the dubious distinction of becoming the first British citizen to die by enemy hands in the Great War.

Reverend Henry Williams, priest at St George's Church in Berlin, left a detailed eyewitness account of the outbreak of war in the capital. He remained in Germany throughout the War, looking after the spiritual needs of British POWs.

Captain William Morritt photographed at a Belgian convent, holding the sword shattered by a German bullet. Wounded at Mons, he was eventually captured, and was shot and killed during an escape attempt in 1917.

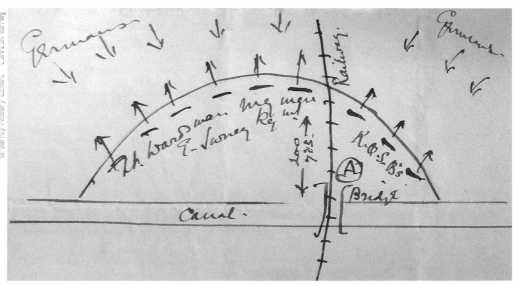

A map drawn by Captain Morritt while recovering at the convent. It shows the East Surreys' precarious positions during the fighting at Mons, as well as the ground over which he led a bayonet charge.

Major Charles Yate surrounded by Germans after he was captured during the fighting at Le Cateau. Weeks later, he committed suicide when a bid to escape from a German POW camp was foiled.

Exhausted British soldiers sleep in temporary billets during the retreat from Mons. In two weeks, they had walked and fought over 200 miles, halting the German advance on the River Marne in early September.

The harsh reality: the first news of enemy atrocities on the Western Front brought the 55,000 German civilians in Britain to public attention and unwarranted demonisation.

Businesses similar to the Druhms' hairdressing salon were wrecked in orgies of violence that spread across the country.

GERMAN PRISONERS IN A BARBED WIRE COMPOUND
WHERE MOST OF THE GERMANS IN THIS COUNTRY OUGHT TO BE. ::

Internment of enemy aliens helped allay widespread public fears of a dangerous 'unseen' enemy. However, the rounding up of thousands of German men led to an acute shortage of accommodation.

The sinking of RMS *Lusitania* with the death of 1,200 civilians caused outrage in Britain. Thousands of Germans were rounded up once again, many returning to captivity while their families chose to be repatriated.

A contemporary artist's impression of a meeting of internees and their families at an unspecified London camp. Fortnightly visits were hugely anticipated but caused immense heartache for the internees.

The Great Hall at Alexandra Palace. Several thousand Germans were held in cramped living conditions. Open-ended confinement caused serious mental health issues for men separated from their families.

In the better internment camps, men were given activities to keep them occupied. Marquetry was a favourite pursuit and exquisite gifts were made for visiting families.

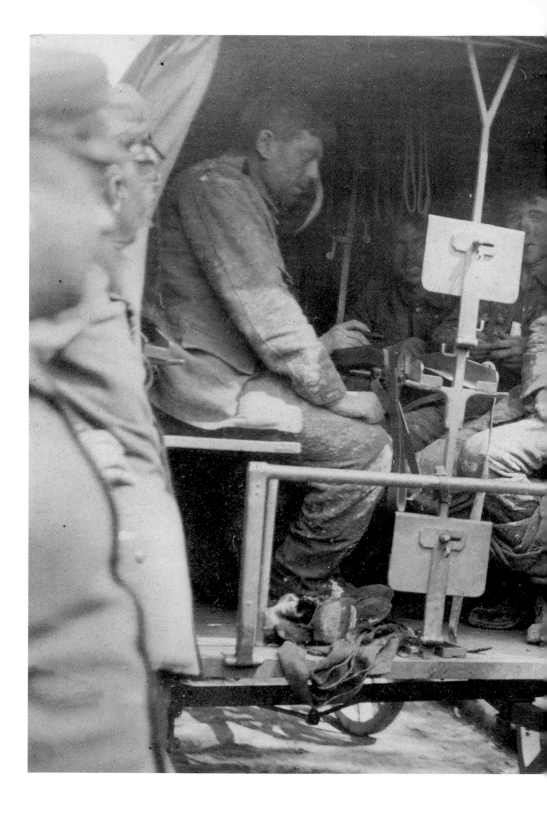

British prisoners pose for the camera before beginning their tortuous journey to Germany from the Western Front. In 1914 verbal and even physical attacks on British POWs were common, although as time passed, civilian attention shifted to the chronic shortages of food and fuel in Germany.

British internees at Ruhleben camp, near Berlin. Only one camp was used to house all 3,500 male British internees in Germany.

Living cheek by jowl: British internees had precious little privacy.

Queuing for food. Red Cross parcels were critical to the physical well-being of internees.

Under an agreement brokered with Germany and Britain, the US ambassador was permitted to visit POW camps. James Gerard, the US ambassador in Berlin, talks to British POWs, although the close proximity of German officers invariably stifled prisoners' free speech.

The ringleaders of the Irish Brigade pose for photographs in their new uniforms adapted with Irish insignia. Only around 50 men volunteered to join the Brigade.

DEAR TOMMY,

YOU ARE QUITE WELCOME TO WHAT
WE ARE LEAVING. WHEN WE STOP WE
SHALL STOP, AND STOP YOU IN A
MANNER YOU WONT APPRECIATE.

FRITZ

'Dear Tommy': a propaganda leaflet dropped over British lines during the Battle of Loos in October 1915. The bullish tone of the leaflet is in marked contrast to the conciliatory nature of the pamphlets the Germans dropped towards the end of the war.

Board put up by Germans to tell us of a big victory at Verdon against the French 4/3/16 Mount Sorrel

Copy of Printing on Board

"BIS GESTERN ABEND WAREN AN
UNWARENDEIN GEFANGENEN GEZAHLL
228 OFFIZIERE 17370 FERNER WARDEN
BESCHUTZE DARUNTER SCHWERX

A pencil drawing by Private Herbert Gibson of a German notice board placed in no-man's-land. The German wording on the board, probably inaccurately transcribed by the artist, boasts of German success at Verdun, including the capture of 228 British officers and 17,370 men.

A remarkable image taken looking out from the German trenches at Beaumont Hamel on the Somme, November 1915. In the distance, around 150 yards away, helmets of British soldiers can be seen looking over the top during a moment of informal fraternisation.

A day after the terrible British casualties suffered on the first day of the Somme Battle. An unarmed British soldier stands just in front of the German trenches at Beaumont Hamel. Permission to call a truce was forbidden by the Divisional Commander but went ahead regardless, as British soldiers crossed no-man's-land to collect the wounded.

In 1916 Captain Robert Campbell wrote to the Kaiser asking for permission to return home to see his dying mother. Permission was granted on condition that he returned to his POW camp in Germany within two weeks. Campbell kept his word.

April 1916: British and German officers attend the funeral of Captain Wilfred Birt, 9th East Surrey Regiment, at Cologne's Südfriedhof. Wounded at the Battle of Loos, Birt underwent numerous operations, winning the respect and affection of the German doctors and nurses.

After capture, a German soldier cooperates with British soldiers in an attempt to curry favour and lessen the chances of becoming a victim of summary retribution.

Souvenirs: two postcards taken from the body of a German soldier. The chilling note on the rear of the card explains the circumstances in which they were obtained.

A popular souvenir among British soldiers was the German pickelhaube (helmet). Richard Hawkins in the early 1920s, wearing a pickelhaube that he picked up on the first day of the Battle of the Somme. He is also holding a German Luger pistol.

4

The Lives of Others

Heavily laden soldiers funnelling through narrow, winding trenches understood that there was a claustrophobic side to front-line life. The twisting route up deepening communication trenches linking the reserve, support and front lines felt interminable to those who shuffled, puffed and grunted their way forward. Theirs would be a worm's eye perspective on the world, crumbly earthen walls, a parapet lined with sandbags, wooden duckboards on which to walk. Here, hemmed in by earth, they would feel relatively safe just as long as the trenches were sensibly located, properly constructed and deep. Men would stay here for three days or more, venturing out at night, using the protection of darkness to undertake trench repairs, strengthening barbed wire defences or patrolling no-man's-land. Only during the day was there time to rest, pen a letter home or chat to mates.

For those new to the line, the temptation to peer over the top was worryingly common: to take a quick look at no-man's-land and see the enemy's trenches. Some men were overeager to see for themselves where Fritz sat, maybe no more than a hundred yards away, perhaps less. Such curiosity was madness if the German trenches were near. To stick one's head up above the parapet for more than a second invited the attention of snipers, who were adept at taking advantage of such naivety. And what would a man expect to see? Hardly a German looking back at him. At best he might see a grubby, meandering line of enemy sandbags and straggling lines of barbed wire. In the early days, before the great battles of attrition destroyed the ground, uncut crops or long grass swayed in the breeze. Roofless houses stood with disintegrating walls, abandoned farm machinery lay idle, and soldiers' discarded tin cans and bottles littered the ground.

By late 1915 a complex, interlinking system of trenches, three lines deep, stretched over two hundred miles from the Swiss Alps to the Belgian coast. Long gone were the mere scoops in the ground dug by the men of 1914. Where the water table was low, trenches were dug eight feet into the earth, with 'dog-leg' turns every few yards. Sumps drained water away, and raised wooden duckboards kept the men's feet out of the worst of the mire. Where the water table was high, digging was restricted to a couple of feet and a trench wall constructed above ground with literally millions of sandbags.

Trench life was routine to experienced soldiers, but to the uninitiated stepping into the front line could be a thrill. Corporal George Foley of the 6th Somerset Light Infantry felt that frisson of excitement. 'There was no one between us and the enemy. It was a great moment for every one of us, and my diary announces with pride that on this night I "fired my first shot at them". It was merely a blind shot in the direction of the Hun trenches, some 300 yards away.'

Casualties put paid to such attitudes. Private Martyn Evans's first day in the trenches was marked by the unnecessary loss of good mates. 'Cook and Dyer were killed outright during the morning and several men were wounded because they would not stop from looking over the top,' he wrote. 'Strict orders were given that during the day, except in case of attack, no one was to use anything but the periscope for observing the enemy.'

Interest in the German trenches, and by extension the Germans themselves, remained pervasive, especially when sightings were infrequent and generally fleeting. On a quiet night the noise of German transport rumbling along the back roads might be audible, but the enemy himself remained hidden, tantalisingly so. 'It was queer seeing all those miles of trenches in front of us showing not a sign of life, and yet swarming with the enemy,' noted Evans, serving with the 1/6th Gloucestershire Regiment.

As a reminder to everyone that this was a deadly war, the artillery exchanged shells morning and evening to dissuade anyone from using the half-light to attack. Bouts of machine-gun and small-arms fire peppered the parapet or whined overhead, with the occasional crash of a trench mortar and crack of the sniper's bullet to ginger everyone up. At night, flares rose and fell for miles around, eerily lighting up no-man's-land, and distant, continuous gunfire rumbled; it was not hard for a man to appreciate that he was involved in a gargantuan struggle.

Of course it was possible, with the curvature of opposing trenches, and the ground's natural undulations, that a man might glimpse the enemy. Signaller Victor Cole, of the 7th Royal West Kent Regiment, was making his way along a battered, largely disused section of trench, looking for a break in a telephone wire, and as he went he took a quick look over the top. In two months on the Western Front he had yet to see the enemy. 'To my surprise I saw a German about three hundred yards away digging at the back of a trench. I watched him for a moment and thought, "Well, I'm entitled to have a shot at him." I aimed, pulled the trigger and saw a piece of cloth or leather fly off the side of his coat – he disappeared.'

In popular imagination, the Great War has come to symbolise a conflict in which suffering was unremitting, and conducted in a putrid landscape. Memoirs evoke scenes of carnage: the reek of cordite after a shell explosion and the shouts for stretcher-bearers. Diaries tell of the pitiless shooting of combatants in trench raids and fighting patrols and of men breaking down with shell-shock. These stories are just one side of a bigger, now forgotten picture. Eclipsed are the stories of humour, albeit much of it black, of passive, easy-going relations with the enemy and of the German-baiting fun that saved morale, particularly at critical moments. When the 1st Royal Scots were locked in desperate fighting at Ypres in April and May 1915, their response to ferocious German attacks was not to buckle but to raise a large piece of cardboard on which was the life-sized picture of a man's head in profile with an outlandishly large hand. The fingers were outstretched, the thumb placed on the tip of the nose: the meaning transparent enough. It lifted spirits in the British trenches and it was raised every time the Germans opened fire.

Trench life, in quieter and less contested parts of the front, was punctuated by only short periods of intense excitement and fear; otherwise it was dull. If one side looked for trouble, trouble was returned, and with interest, as Denis Barnett, a second lieutenant serving with the 2nd Leinster Regiment, was well aware. If German artillery opened up, British guns responded, but rather than searching out the enemy's batteries, the guns pummelled a village where it was known the enemy had billets. It was tit for tat but on an impressive scale.

> All these things work out on very human lines. If we turn a Maxim on to a German fatigue party, that night they'll keep firing to spoil our night's rest. If they try to pump water into our trenches, we fire rifle grenades where we see their smoke rising. It's all very amusing. If one side does not annoy the other, they live side by side in perfect concord without interfering with one another.

To break the daytime monotony, shouted conversations with the enemy were heard and might begin with a simple 'Morning, Fritz' and other pleasantries, or with bullish insults, depending on the mood.

'I had a conversation with a German the other morning,' wrote Barnett in a letter. 'It began just at dawn: "Guten Morgen, Allyman," and we soon got going. I told him about the Kaiser, and he said we were all sorts of things I didn't know the English for, and also one thing which is a favourite appel-lative among the lower orders of English society, which he was awfully pleased with.' Acknowledging that Germans had been the mainstay of London's pre-war restaurant and café staff, Barnett parted with a badinage with which he was particularly pleased. 'I shouted "Waiter!" and one sportsman said "Coming, sir, coming, sir!"'

It was usually boredom that made the fur fly, and not always between opposing trenches. When tedium got the better of two men in Barnett's platoon, the disagreement was settled on top of the parapet in full view of the enemy. The scrap was a welcome distraction for all, including the Germans who encouraged the two protagonists by cheering and firing their rifles in the air. There was no question of sniping at the men.

During daylight, both sides regularly inspected no-man's-land to see that there was nothing untoward. A visual inspection was undertaken with a variety of trench periscopes raised above the parapet or telescopes slid through a concealed hole in the sandbag defences, known as a loophole. Routine observation was that noth-ing had altered, although that did not prevent surprises. Brigadier Philip Mortimer, serving with the 3rd Meerut Divisional Train, borrowed a telescope belonging to a Machine Gun officer, and, as he peered at the German trenches:

> I actually saw as clear as daylight, the reflection in the top mirror
> of his periscope, a German officer's head as he searched our trenches
> through his periscope, a most uncanny sight – the grey peaked cap
> and face as he looked down into the bottom mirror could be clearly
> seen. It was decided to 'strafe' the periscope with a Maxim which
> after being trained on it carefully was let off to the tune of about
> 15 rounds. The periscope immediately disappeared.

Looking through binoculars, Private Percy Ogley, serving with the 1st York and Lancaster Regiment, was in a position to see beyond the enemy's trenches and was intrigued by a small cloud of rolling dust. It was a dispatch rider on a motorbike taking a message to the trenches and Ogley was able to observe the man dismount, run into a dugout then reappear a few minutes later when he was seen to strap a bag onto his back and ride off. On the Somme, in the summer of 1915, Lieutenant James Pennycuik, serving with the Royal Engineers, studied a German in the village of Curlu. Pennycuik was sitting in a French observation post and through a telescope watched with almost voyeuristic interest the sentry in front of a house. He recalled watching a 'rather sloppy individual' lounging about and talking to a lady. He also saw the Colonel's cook dressed in white overalls and an apron, as well as two other Germans, some children and a number of cows. It was, he claimed, an amusing half-hour.

Perversely, it was when the trenches were far apart that the enemy were more evident, lazily confident that distance made them safe even from excellent snipers. Private Sydney Fuller watched one German repairing a trench with sandbags. Judging the distance to be about 1,400 yards, he and another sniper set their sights. Their shots had no effect on the German other than to make him stop and glance up. Only later did machine-gunners use a range finder to accurately measure the distance; it turned out to be half Fuller's estimate. A Lewis gun was then brought to bear on the same spot where three Germans could now be seen; the first burst scattered all three.

Most marksmen considered any target over 400 yards as 'hard' and shooting over extreme distances was as much about having fun as anything else. Jack Rogers and Charlie Shaw, snipers serving with the 1/7th Sherwood Foresters, were sent to an observation post, Charlie looking through a telescope, Jack using binoculars. The two opposing lines were at least 1,500 yards apart, with the German trenches on a low crest.

'All of a sudden, Charlie said "Look!" and over the top, out over the German lines, two men appeared walking down the slope, both of them carrying shovels. They hadn't got down a long way before they started digging quite a large hole.'

It became apparent to Charlie that the men were digging a latrine, utterly unaware that they could be overlooked. 'They haven't got the cheek to build a toilet there, surely,' Charlie said. 'I mean nobody's going to use it, are they?'

'It wasn't very long before another soldier appeared,' recalled Jack. 'He came walking down to that toilet and began to pull his trousers down, sat on the toilet and had the nerve to pull out a newspaper.'

The German was the best part of a mile away and it was decided that Charlie would shoot and Jack would observe. 'Charlie loaded his rifle, got it poised. "Ready?" I said "Yes." "Right," said Charlie, "watch out", and he fired. I don't know how near he was to the German but that man never stopped to pull his trousers up. He just got up and tore away as best he could over the top of the hill out of sight.'

Private Tom Tolson, serving with the 8th Kings Own Yorkshire Light Infantry, had trained at the Second Army Sniping School. He was frequently sent to a hidden observation post (OP) keeping a log of what he saw, noting enemy machine-gun posts suspected, known and inactive. He also looked for enemy OPs, sniping posts, obstacles in no-man's-land, and the state of the enemy wire, its strength and depth. Finally, and as importantly, he watched the enemy, describing their activities and noting uniform insignia to aid identification of opposing units. Map references were written down with observations. 'Enemy seen bailing water out of trench at point F 19 C 05 50 . . . German showing head and shoulders, another handing sandbags up to him apparently strengthening the trench.' In noting what he saw, he also revealed the confidence with which the enemy openly carried on his activities:

1.05. Observed enemy looking over the trench for a few seconds and then disappeared wearing field grey uniform and round cap.

One man looked over this particular spot every fifteen minutes. F 19 C 1 1¼ 8¼.

2.10. Observed earth being thrown out of the enemy front line trench at different points.

2.45. Observed four Germans looking over the parapet. One of them wearing glasses and very stout. They were talking to our men and waving their hands. The conversation lasted five minutes. German got up and held a piece of white bread in his hand. Showed it to our men and then commenced to eat it with pocket knife in his hand.

9.30. Observed two German officers showing half figure wearing polished peak cap and grey uniform, smoking and laughing and waving their hands to someone in our trench. They drank something out of a bottle, remained in view for three minutes, then disappeared again. Could have shot them at F 19 c 1¼ 2¼.

Intelligence was keenly pursued and included night-time raids that would not only cause disruption and alarm in the enemy's lines but which offered an opportunity to seize a prisoner. Private Percy Ogley was involved in an attack on a German machine-gun post. The officer in charge led the men to within a few feet of the enemy, so close in fact that the Germans could be heard talking to one another while one man tapped the machine gun as if it were out of action. Then a German stepped forward, unfastening his trousers.

He saw us and stopped dead in his tracks. He was flummoxed. He didn't know whether to run, shout, or what to do. Our officer decided for him. Lifting his revolver, the officer took aim and fired at point-blank range.

Down fell the German. His pals in the outpost took to their heels, and legged it back to their trenches.

'Come on chaps,' said the officer. 'Quick as you can, lift him on your shoulders, come on, tout suite.'

Ogley was given the job of carrying the wounded German.

The officer and one man walked several paces in front and the other two followed behind. The poor Jerry was in some terrible pain, blood trickled down my back, and I felt ready to drop from exhaustion; all the time he groaned. The other chaps had their turns of carrying our prisoner, and finally we reached our lines, here we had a tot of rum, and examined the German's wound.

Raiding the enemy's positions was exceedingly risky, and could result in losses greater than those inflicted on the enemy. Private Ogley was involved in a further raid but the enemy's artillery was alerted and a hasty retreat made under fire. In taking cover in a shell hole, Ogley became aware of another man's presence; in the dark he took the man to be his officer, Lieutenant Thomas Bassett. As the gunfire died down, Ogley turned: '"Come along Sir," I said, "I think we can make it now." I had my face buried in my arms but when I looked at the chap next to me, I sent up a yell, jumped to my feet and off I went like hell.'

The man was a German in an advanced state of decomposition. The hideous sight galvanised Ogley into action but in his fright he ran the wrong way down a sunken lane where he was sent flying by a shell explosion. Shaken but relieved, he made the front-line trench where he was greeted with well-earned tea and a cigarette. Ogley reported what he had seen to Lieutenant Bassett who, to Ogley's dismay, asked to be taken to the shell hole to ascertain the dead man's regiment.

On our bellies we wiggled through the wet grass and up to the shell hole where I had seen the dead Jerry. By heck he was a tall chap. He must have been six feet eight inches. We two were like pygmies at the side of him. Our officer cut off the chap's epaulettes on which were stamped the chap's regiment, he also took a large canvas sheet from the chap's back, searched all his pockets and got all the information he wanted. He said the chap was a Bavarian.

Although the British Tommy broad-brushed the enemy as Fritz, Boche or Hun, he appreciated that there were significant regional differences among German troops. Prussian soldiers were noted for their aggression, and a feud was widely believed to exist between the Scottish regiment of the Black Watch and the Prussians over alleged battlefield atrocities. The Bavarians had a bad reputation although not as bad as the Prussians, while, conversely, the Saxons were broadly liked for their easy-going nature and quiet disposition in the line. Perceived fracture lines between regions could be exploited, especially with the more approachable Saxons, as Second Lieutenant Barnett recorded in a letter home dated May 1915.

> The other night a couple of men of the Rifle Brigade went up to the German wire with a newspaper account of how the Prussian gunners wiped out some Saxons who wanted to surrender. I hope our friends the 133rd [Saxon Regiment] will take it to heart, and do the dirty on their Prussian friends at the earliest opportunity.

As Anglo-Saxons, these men shared a common bond of sorts with German Saxons, and Saxons were not shy of reminding British troops of the link. It was the Saxons who initiated many of the festive truces the previous Christmas. And when large working parties were sent to work on the front line in January 1915, Lieutenant Graham Hutchinson, 2nd Argyll and Sutherland Highlanders, watched as Saxons shared a heavy iron-headed hammer with men of the East Kent Regiment, the tool being alternately thrown across the barbed wire.

Serving in the same battalion was Lieutenant Alexander Gillespie. He noticed how Saxons used the general surfeit of water to float friendly bottled messages downstream to British trenches.

And it was this placid nature that reasserted itself at the year's end when, in November, flooded trenches forced Saxons again to abandon their positions. This time they walked about quite openly, bailing and pumping water from their front line into a mine crater. The following morning the Saxons were in cheery mood as Lieutenant Frank Hitchcock, 2nd Leinster Regiment, observed.

> The enemy shouted out 'Good morning' to me . . . I watched six Germans coming up in the open, and getting into one of their advanced posts. Six more got out with their rifles slung, and with braziers in their hands, yelled 'Good-bye' to me and went back to their main trench. The relief started to try and fraternise with us immediately.

Second Lieutenant Barnett served in the same company as Hitchcock and had a soft spot for the Saxons, writing home about their cheerfulness and general bonhomie.

> Yesterday evening we brought up a new machine gun and opened fire with it just after dark. The Germans shouted 'try again', 'pretty good' and 'vot vos dat?'. It was quite amusing listening to them; they seem a very decent lot here (they're Saxons) . . . They are always singing and doing 'milk-o' calls, especially when we fire volleys in the night.

Beyond the Leinsters' trench stood a ruined farm that opposing sides visited in search of food. At night, when one of Barnett's men went without permission to take chickens, he did not bother to go armed. 'While so engaged he ran into a German [a Saxon] who was doing the same. As neither had a rifle, they nodded and passed on.'

Just as the British were keen to play on regional differences between the Germans, so were the Germans not averse to playing on fracture lines that might exist amongst the Allies. In the knowledge that the British were arriving on the Somme in the summer and autumn of 1915, the Germans were keen to sow discord, too. The only problem was that they were sometimes a little late: the French had gone, as Second Lieutenant Francis Smith discovered when his regiment, 1st Royal Scots, arrived in the line for the first time.

> Yesterday the Huns fired some very funny looking little shells across into A Coys trenches. They didn't explode but the nose cap of one came off and the cylinder was full of papers, giving the names of French prisoners taken, with the name and regiment of each man – page on page of names. There was also some printed matter, mostly stories and articles (all in French) showing Great Britain in a bad light. One was about Joan of Arc, telling how shockingly and treacherously and cruelly the English had behaved. Probably the Hun must have thought the French were occupying these trenches. The outside of the cylinder they fired them over in had 'gazettes' and also 'news' painted in white on the outside. We were very suspicious at first of some trick, and fired at the cylinders for some time (at a safe distance) to see if they would explode, but there was no explosive in them – just the papers.

When the British came to the Somme region, they found a front as quiet as any in which they had served. The Somme was a backwater; a place where the French and Germans indulged in short and sometimes intense spats, but nothing more. Private James Racine, 1/5th Seaforth Highlanders, arrived with his battalion in early September. At dawn on their first day in the line, the men discovered a welcome as cordial as any that could be imagined.

> We found on our barbed wire entanglements a piece of paper on which was a written request that two or three of our men would,

at a given time, proceed halfway across no-man's-land and meet a similar number of Germans in order to exchange periodicals and souvenirs, as the French had been accustomed to doing. After a consultation, our interpreter and two men agreed and, at noon, met the enemy halfway; the heads of the troops on each side were above the parapets and no firing took place. Later, when we left the trenches, we were paraded before the Commanding Officer and severely reprimanded. He stated that 'it was impossible to fight a man with one hand and give him chocolates with the other'. We were given to understand that any similar action in the future would be severely dealt with.

The level to which friendly relations developed could border on the preposterous, according to Captain John Laurie, 2nd Seaforth Highlanders, in a story that he heard and which he was inclined to believe. His battalion had come down from the Ypres Salient after suffering heavy casualties in the German offensive in April and May. The men had taken over the line east of Mailly-Maillet, a place where the former French occupants believed in neither raids nor shelling. Such was the rapport with the enemy that German officers came over nightly for a game of bridge, a game interrupted when, unaware of the relief, they arrived to find the British.

The British were there to stay. The real fun and games were about to begin.

There were men who wished for nothing better than to escape the war; men who looked forward to a wound serious enough to get them away from the fighting line, hopefully for good, but which did not mar their lives. One such man, a German, came to the attention of Private Frank Richards in March 1915. The German was using a trench mallet and, as he lifted the mallet, he deliberately left his hands and arms hanging in the air for a few seconds before bringing the mallet down. 'We saw what his game was,' wrote Richards. 'To oblige him we started to take potshots at his hands or arms.' Such a small target as an arm proved frustratingly easier to miss than to hit.

A small number of men not prepared to gamble on a light wound took their chances and deserted. They might be sick and tired of life in the line, their nerves frayed by continual danger, or they might be men whose allegiance to their country's cause was tenuous at best. Men from the formerly French-owned regions of Alsace and Lorraine were commonly ambivalent about fighting for the Kaiser against the French. And then there were those who cared nothing for international disputes, but who had nevertheless been dragooned into the forces. Whatever the reason, these men were hardly welded to the common endeavour and, given the opportunity, would be willing to give up without a fight. When Sergeant Dawson, serving with the 7th Somerset Light Infantry, became hopelessly bogged down in Somme mud, he little cared who came to find him. In his memoirs, Commanding Officer, Colonel Cecil Troyte-Bullock, recalled what happened next.

> He [Dawson] was found by a party of five Boches who proceeded to pull him out. He, of course, expected to be taken off to the Hun lines, but not a bit of it. They informed him that they were his prisoners and demanded to be taken across to our trenches. Sergeant Dawson had hopelessly lost his way and said so, but they said it was quite all right as they knew the way, and conducted him back to our advanced battalion headquarters. On the way back they picked up another of our men, also bogged, and took him along with them.

Deserters normally made their escape at night, slipping over the parapet to take their chances with a trigger-happy sentry on the other side. It was a risky policy. Lieutenant Andrew Buxton, 3rd Rifle Brigade, was present when one of his posts was

approached by a German at night, calling quietly 'Hi! Soldier!'
Buxton believed the man wished to surrender but equally it could
be a ruse to locate the post in order to bomb it; such tricks had
been used before, 'so the only answer was a bomb,' wrote Buxton,
'though no harm was done him, I think'.

Lieutenant Gillespie was reading by a dim light in his dugout,
when he heard a cheerful Scottish voice in the doorway announcing that he had a 'wee souvenir' for his officer.

> I looked up and there was a German standing in the doorway,
> in grey cap and tunic, with red piping. He was a deserter, a
> young Prussian who had crawled across in the dark into our
> wire, and when challenged put his hands up; then Fraser, our
> enormous subaltern, reached out a brawny arm, and swung him
> into the trench. He was not a bit frightened; he knocked some
> papers off a chair, sat down and asked for a cigarette. He was
> very anxious to talk, and I did wish my German had been
> better. He said he had come over because it was 'better over
> here' . . . He told me a good deal about the officers and sergeants
> and their strenuous life in billets, more in fact than I could
> understand, but we sent him in to headquarters and they would
> get all this information. He was a miserable creature – I do
> despise a deserter.

The confidence of this deserter contrasted with the one seen by
Captain T. I. Dunn, Adjutant of the 36th Field Ambulance, whose
contempt was no less marked than Gillespie's.

> A German deserter with eyes bound was led in followed by a
> crowd of interested Tommies. The guard with fixed bayonets took
> him into a large shed and we went and saw him . . . The deserter
> was still carrying in his hand a small stick and a large white pocket
> handkerchief which the guard told us he waved energetically,
> shouting 'no fire, no fire' as he approached . . . He was in a great

funk. On being searched he had some letters and postcards with his regiment written on them. He belonged to the Landsturm. He answered the questions smartly and willingly.

Asked why he deserted he replied that he could not get suffi- cient to eat as his Saxon comrades called him a Polish pig and gave him only the leavings of their rations. Many more of his compatri- ots would have deserted with him, he stated, only they thought that our trenches were manned by black troops who killed their prisoners and then ate them, so they weren't having that thank you. He stated that their troops had been officially told that peace would be declared on October 8th [1915] and on being asked the reason for this statement he said that they were reputedly informed that the Allies had no more men and were bankrupt. So you see peace is not far off!!

We left him talking with a sergeant and eating voraciously at smoked ham bread and butter that had been supplied to him while one of the officers gave him a cigar. It was amusing to see dozens of Tommies at the door looking in on the scene with the greatest curiosity and amusement muttering something about 'the ruddy Hun'. Then he gave away a lot of military information about their troops and lives.

There was another kind of German soldier who used the cover of darkness to slip across, a German whose motivation to serve his country was in direct and inverse proportion to a deserter's desire not to serve his. These men were spies, and in their chosen occupation they took an enormous risk of being shot on capture, for their capacity to cause mayhem in opposing trenches was very real.

Fear of spies percolating into British lines exercised the minds of senior officers to a disproportionate extent. In August 1914, Britain had given enemy aliens of military age a week-long open door to return home, and a number of Germans speaking perfect English had been met in no-man's-land that Christmas. Senior officers were certainly aware of the fact that many Germans spoke excellent English and that a number could pass themselves off as British officers.

Suspicion had circulated since the autumn of 1914 that verbal messages contradicting existing orders were sent by German spies intermingling with British soldiers. During the desperate fighting around Ypres in late October 1914, Captain Smyth-Osbourne of the Royal Welsh Fusiliers recalled that the whole morning 'messages in a perfectly correct form were passed along the line to me from the Officer Commanding A Company which was on my right; the order in every case was the same "You are to retire".' These messages continued to reach Smyth-Osbourne long after he discovered that the officer sending them was dead. Another officer captured around the same time claimed that he was even told by the enemy that greatcoats removed from his men after capture were being used for 'spy work'.

Spy fever caused excessive and bizarre incidents of suspicion. The 1st Royal Scots had a number of spy scares in mid-1915 culminating in the discovery of a 'wretched dog' in no-man's-land. 'The dog was brought in and thoroughly tested by the men who had heard of cunning dogs who carried information to the enemy under false skins! This animal was clutched by its skin by many horny hands and hauled over the place to its sorrow,' wrote an officer in the battalion. 'It was proved to be quite innocent, but deserted soon after.'

There were fears that German spies were living behind the lines, watching and reporting on the movement of Allied troops, or that there were French and Belgian collaborators signalling from their homes. Windmill sails or clock hands sent semaphore messages; lights were seen flickering from upstairs windows, washing was laid out to dry in such a way as to signal to enemy aircraft.

Details could be remarkably specific. Two weeks after landing at Boulogne, the 9th East Surrey Regiment was involved in a spy hunt at the French town of Humbert. The battalion's War Diary carries the following message:

> Instruction received of case occurring of two civilians driving around in car endeavouring to obtain information from troops:- car shabby and old. Roi de Belge open touring probably Darracq but with Darracq badge removed from radiator. Colour dark, radiator brass. Car noisy. Individual I Oldish going white scrubby beard, appearance French, speaks French; last seen brown cap, dark suit. Individual II well built 5ft 10" 40 years, pasty face, fairly heavy, black moustache. Both seen driving. Units warned to instruct guards on roads to stop and arrest individuals (whether they have passes or not). Separate them and send to Div HQ under officers' escort. If car seen and challenge disregarded, guards to fire at tyres. Duties detailed to Regimental Police, doubled at night. Police trap system. Guards Armed. Magazines charged. Guards warned that if these individuals are spies they will not hesitate to shoot.

In fact, far more British officers and men were summarily arrested than enemy spies, especially when rewards were offered for each captured spy.

'The 109th Brigade are all suspicious of everyone,' wrote Private Charles Heare of the 1/2nd Monmouthshire Regiment.

> They are told that if they catch a spy they will get ten pounds and a leave to Ireland. It is agony to go out at night. 'Halt, halt!' everywhere you go. Coming back from the trenches one night, a sentry stopped me and said, 'I'm off to Belfast.' 'What, sick?' I said. He says, 'No, I've got a spy a minute ago.' 'Let's have a look.' I did and nearly had a fit. It was our Colonel Bowen.

The presence of enemy spies was not entirely a figment of over-imaginative minds. Harry Siepmann, the artillery captain of

German descent, knew a little about spies, having almost been shot as one while walking on the Cornish cliffs in August 1914. Now in France and serving with a battery of guns, Siepmann found himself approached by two staff officers who were carrying out an inspection of battery positions. They asked to look around the guns, asking questions. When these were answered to their apparent satisfaction, they left, Siepmann, out of courtesy, walking them to the nearby road.

> For a moment or two I stood looking after them as they set off down the road, and suddenly it dawned on me . . . I had not the slightest doubt then that the two men in British staff officers' uniforms were German. A back view of the one who waddled might not have convinced me if I had not had in my mind a faint, indefinable uneasiness about the other one. He had asked, in fault-less English, too many questions; but in matters of pronunciation I had a trained ear, and in German idiosyncrasies I had some experience.

The two 'staff officers' disappeared from view. Perhaps it had taken a German, albeit a half-German, to know a German, but in the end Siepmann let the matter go. 'My reason for keeping my suspicions to myself were not so much a sneaking sympathy for the two masqueraders as the fear of being laughed at for causing a lot of fuss and bother about a cock-and-bull story.'

The military authorities were especially nervous about spies, for, on 25 September 1915, the British Army would engage in the first combined Allied offensive of the war, the British attacking the northern flank of German forces in France near the mining town of Loos, the French attacking the southern flank, in the region of the Artois. In that attack, the 9th East Surrey Regiment, part of the 24th Division, was to advance towards the German-held trenches near the village of Hulloch. In command of

A Company was a middle-aged officer, Captain Wilfred Birt, and in leading his troops he was shot and badly wounded in the left thigh.

Captain Birt enlisted in October 1914 at the age of thirty-four. A former pupil of Harrow School and a graduate of Oriel College, Oxford, he had risen, by the outbreak of war, to become the managing director of the Australian Mutual Shipping Company. On being commissioned, he embarked for France with the battalion on the last day of August 1915.

In the same battalion was Corporal Alfred Felton, a fifty-year-old building contractor from Battersea, south London. In 1906 he had married Jenny, twenty years his junior, and the couple had set up home in Brentford. By 1914 they had three children, Ethel, Winnefred and Alfred, the youngest being five years old by then. Quite why their father had felt the need to enlist in such circumstances, and presumably to lie about his age, is not known but in August 1915 Felton sailed on the same ship as Captain Birt for France and, weeks later, he was involved in the same attack.

Birt was reported wounded and missing; Corporal Alfred Felton was simply missing. The battalion had been cut to pieces and Birt and Felton were two of 452 casualties among the battalion's officers and other ranks, just short of 50 per cent of those who had sailed for France. Of Felton nothing further was heard, and six months later his death was presumed to have occurred on the day of the assault. After the war, however, some of his personal belongings were returned from Germany under unusual circumstances. Birt was more fortunate. Weeks after the destruction of his battalion, he turned up as a prisoner of war, his wife receiving a card from him in mid-November stating that he was being held in Wahn POW camp on the outskirts of Cologne.

A botched operation by a French doctor, presumably in a battlefield hospital, had left Birt with one leg an astonishing 11½ centimetres shorter than the other. Afterwards, he was taken to

Germany where he remained bedridden, in severe and continual pain, losing his appetite and smoking heavily. His weight dropped alarmingly.

Because of his condition, Birt was transferred to Cologne Fortress Hospital. The short night-time journey had been terrible, morphine injections failing to dull the pain. In hospital he underwent further surgery before being placed in a room with three other wounded British officers. The treatment he and the other men received was little short of exemplary, as Birt acknowledged. In return, the Germans admired Birt for his stoicism, and he quickly became a favourite among both fellow prisoners and German medical staff.

Slowly, Birt recovered his appetite and he began to put on weight, thanks in large part to the food parcels he started to receive from his family. His spirits rose, too, with the regular arrival of letters from home.

You can't think how, under these circumstances, one goes silly when a letter does come and I can tell you that I read the two I have received again and again until they're very dirty with my finger marks.

They're feeding me up here for a little operation which I'm going to have . . . Isn't it a nuisance about this leg? If it had been done properly at the start I should be walking about now. However as you know well, I've always been in some sort of similar trouble since I was a nipper – however it will all come right as it has before.

Two German specialists performed the complex operation to extend his shortened left leg. The surgery was carried out without anaesthetic but was highly successful and, according to the patient, only moderately painful. Birt was then encased in plaster of Paris from his left foot to his chest, although he still managed to pencil a letter to his wife the following day.

The doctor this morning lifted me off my bed and I stood up for the first time since the 26th Sept! Awfully dizzy business and I sat down after about 30 seconds. They've certainly done me most awfully well here and I look upon the doctors – especially my doctor Herr Maier – as awfully clever and painstaking. [This is a] proper first class German hospital with good doctors and careful attention.

Birt's eulogy to his surgeons could not have been more enthusiastic, and he looked forward, as he said in a letter, to one day coming home.

In the German city of Cologne a solemn cortège was wending its way through a large municipal cemetery, the Sudfriedhof, on the city's southern edge. The coffin was followed by a group of four prisoners of war, all officers. One of them, Lieutenant Charles Wilson MC, had served in France with the 10th Hussars in 1914 before joining the Royal Flying Corps, serving with 15 Squadron. Shot down over Ypres, he was a recent arrival in Cologne. Another, Mostyn Llewellin, a captain in the Monmouthshire Regiment, was a cousin by marriage of the man whose coffin they were following. As they walked along the pathway, the men passed by the graves of German soldiers who had died of wounds and who now lay at rest among the tall, dominating conifers. Then the cortège emerged into a clearing and a rapidly growing military cemetery containing the graves of British soldiers who had died in captivity.

That morning a new grave had been prepared, ready to receive the body of Captain Wilfred Birt. His death four days earlier was as sudden as it was unexpected, causing considerable sorrow among fellow prisoners and the German doctors and nurses who had treated him for months.

It was only a couple of weeks since Birt had sent a card to his sister thanking her for a parcel of food and asking for British bread. For reasons unexplained, he had written that he hoped their father was playing golf again. Birt's leg was painful and it was still being stretched after the operation but, all in all, it was getting better and he sent his love to everyone at home.

Wilfred Birt's leg was no longer the issue, however. Instead, doctors were now becoming gravely concerned about a serious intestinal problem. Two specialists were brought in and an emergency operation was performed, without success. Birt recovered consciousness but was now beyond help. Lieutenant Wilson, who shared a room with Birt and with whom he had become good friends, went to see the stricken officer. He noted that Birt stirred briefly but died that evening, peacefully and in no pain. The doctors maintained that the cumulative effects of his thigh wound had left him 'too weak to withstand the subsequent trouble'. His death certificate recorded death owing to 'cardiac weakness'.

The atmosphere at the burial service was in stark contrast to the hurried and covert committal of Major Charles Yate well over a year earlier. Then, no fellow officers were able to attend the funeral for fear their presence would stir up trouble among the civilian population. Public war fervour had calmed to such a degree that Captain Llewellin had been allowed to travel by public train from his camp in Crefeld to Cologne, a distance of forty miles. In a letter to Veronica, Birt's wife of six years, Llewellin described the funeral service.

The Commandant here received a letter from the Commandant of the hospital in Köln [Cologne] to say that Wilfred had died there, and out of respect for him he would like me to attend the funeral the following day . . . I gave my parole and went to Köln next morning arriving in time for the service in the hospital courtyard after which the coffin was borne by the English tommies (wounded) to the hearse. At the cemetery it was met by the General in Command at Köln and other military representatives. The funeral was very well done – nothing could have exceeded the attention and consideration bestowed by the Germans who were sincerely moved by his death – he had earned their deepest regard and admiration. The General for himself, and on behalf of the other officials, expressed his deep sympathy and condolence. There were nice wreaths including one from the Town of Köln. When the graveside service was concluded a Roman Catholic priest who had known him gave an address in English speaking of their high esteem for him – he told me he would see the grave was kept up . . . The doctors were very attached to him, and grieved at his death. It was most considerate my being sent to the funeral, and I was glad to be there.

Apart from Captain Llewellin, the three other officers are not identified in photographs taken at the time, yet one is clearly an officer of the Royal Flying Corps wearing the medal ribbon of the Military Cross. He is almost certainly Lieutenant Charles Wilson; the other two were probably officers with whom Birt had shared a room in hospital.

Birt's possessions were gathered up and forwarded to Veronica. As well as a letter detailing the precise cause of the captain's death and the general regret at his passing, a very personal eulogy was added by a German whose identity is unknown:

Captain WB Birt of the English Army was carried to his last rest at the South Cemetery having died of severe wounds. In the long list of military funerals which take place almost daily, this example would call for no particular notice if it did not deal with the case of one who through the uprightness of his character his truly chivalrous disposition and his unprejudiced understanding of German characteristics had won in the highest degree the respect of his adversaries . . . Grief for his death went deeply to the heart of friend and foe.

Among the many wreaths was one worthy of note: it bore a simple inscription by the doctor of the German garrison of the Fortress Hospital in Cologne in the name of the medical staff to the distinguished memory of one too early dead: 'Captain Birt's notes and explanations [as to the quality of his treatment] will be an efficacious means some day to help truth to prevail even in England and therefore his memory remains blessed by all who knew him.'

'Even in England'? What exactly was that truth? That the Germans were looking after all prisoners as well as they very evidently looked after Captain Wilfred Birt and his comrades? The picture on this point was decidedly mixed.

Despite the heinous casualties suffered by the East Surrey Regiment, the offensive at Loos did deliver some early success, with serious disorder in the German lines. However, the offensive ran into difficulties, with problems of supply and of battlefield control forcing the British on the defensive once the Germans recovered their poise and mounted strong counter-attacks. After heavy fighting, there was a pause before the British renewed the offensive in mid-October, but this was repulsed with heavy losses. With the onset of bad weather and the approach of winter, the battle was brought to a close. Once again, both sides faced one another as Christmas approached, and not a few must have wondered if there would still be enough seasonal bonhomie for another Christmas Truce.

Knowledge of the first Christmas Truce had spread quickly among the soldiers in France and Belgium. Within days the British public knew about it, too, for not only did sons and husbands write copiously about the extraordinary events, but their stories and personal photographs also reached the British press.

Newspapers ran images of smiling British and German soldiers at ease with one another, all wrapped up warm against the winter weather. The photographs appeared in newspapers such as the *Daily Mirror* and the *Daily Sketch*. And when photographs were not readily available, artists' impressions were drawn instead for the *Illustrated London News* and *The Sphere*.

British Army Headquarters were furious. Letters written by serving soldiers spoke of British and German soldiers 'arm-in-arm with exchanged caps and helmets', and having their photographs taken; '. . . they [the Germans] were jolly good sorts,' wrote one man of the London Rifle Brigade, his letter being published in *The Times*, and at length. 'I have now a very different opinion of the German . . .'

The images that hit the press went a long way to persuading the Commander in Chief to ban the use of private cameras on the Western Front and there would be stricter censorship of letters. The incident, they instructed, was never to be repeated and a year later firm orders were issued that no fraternisation with the enemy would be tolerated. The four battalions of 140th Infantry Brigade, 47th London Division, for example, were given the following warning: 'The Brigadier [General] wishes you to give the strictest orders to all ranks on the subject, and any man attempting to communicate either by signal or word or by any means is to be seriously punished. All snipers and machine-guns are to be in readiness to fire on any German above the parapet.'

The Germans were issued with much the same instructions so that no one was in any doubt as to the inadvisability of another truce.

Forty-one-year-old Captain Miles Barne had been made temporary Commanding Officer of the 1st Battalion Scots Guards three days before Christmas 1915. A week earlier the battalion's Commanding Officer, Lieutenant Colonel Lennox, had gone home sick and Captain John Thorpe who had taken over was now wounded, so it would be down to Barne to maintain discipline when the battalion was in the line near the village of Lavantie.

As Christmas approached, Barne was spoken to by the brigade major, 2nd Guards Brigade, Major Guy Rasch. He told Barne that orders issued by the Divisional Commander were that everything was to be the same on Christmas Day as on any other. With this information firmly fixed in his mind, Barne ordered two of his companies, B and C, to go up for a two-day spell in the trenches.

Private William Gordon had been in France twelve weeks, serving with B Company. As darkness fell, the men set off heavily laden with extra ammunition, extra water and sandbags full of charcoal for cooking. After the usual struggle along the communication trench, B Company reached two round-shaped forts, a hundred yards behind the front-line trenches being held by C Company.

It was a quiet night, dry and cold, with just the odd sniper's bullet to break the monotony. At about 9 p.m. the German artillery opened up with a short barrage of whizz-bangs, 14-pounder shells that caused considerable damage to communication trenches, but there were no casualties. Silence resumed, broken by the sound of Germans singing hymns and songs in their trenches. William Gordon listened intently.

Around daybreak the Germans began shouting 'Tommy Tommy Good Christmas'. The Scots returned the calls, followed by men of the 1st Battalion Coldstream Guards with 'Good old Fritz, Merry Christmas'.

As the darkness slowly disappeared, a Sergeant of the Coldstreams, away on our left, who possessed a most powerful voice, shouted out to the Germans and at the same time stood up on the fire-trench showing himself from the waist up and at the same time beckoning to the Germans in their trenches to do likewise.

C Company was commanded by a superb leader of men, Sir Iain Colquhoun. He was the British Army's lightweight boxing champion and he would go on to win the Distinguished Service Order twice. He was also well connected and in 1915 he married Geraldine Bryde, niece of the Prime Minister's wife. In his diary he records that the men were having breakfast at 9 a.m. when he was made aware that the Germans were actually walking towards the British parapet. Colquhoun immediately left to investigate.

> A German officer came forward and asked me for a truce for Christmas. I replied that this was impossible. He then asked for ¾ hour to bury his dead. I agreed. The Germans then started burying their dead and we did the same. This was finished in ½ hour time. Our men and the Germans then talked and exchanged cigars, cigarettes etc for ¼ of an hour.

Sir Iain's matter-of-fact record of the incident contrasts with the more excitable account of Private William Gordon who was enthralled by what he saw as both sides met in no-man's-land.

> I was observing all this from standing on top of the parapet of my trench. The Sergeant in charge of No 5 platoon was Sergeant [George] Moore, a fine type of pre-war soldier and a Boer War veteran who had been called up on the outbreak of the War. He had forbidden anyone to leave the fort but on my suggestion that I go forward to see what was happening, he let me go. Very promptly I shed my equipment and set off to the front line, wearing my leather jerkin on top of my ordinary khaki uniform.

Scots Guards officer Lieutenant Wilfrid Ewart was much closer. He had begun that day gazing over the parapet at a drab landscape, noting the rise and fall in the ground, the irregular line of trenches and the untidy sandbagged parapets. He could see a stream marked by 'a line of twisted brown willows bent to every conceivable shape'. The stream ran down the middle of no-man's-land, where the coarse grass hid 'little mouldering heaps of grey and khaki', like 'heaps of old clothes or fallen scarecrows'. These were the dead from the battles of Festubert, of Neuve Chapelle and Loos, and it was among the fallen that the Scots Guards and Germans met.

The men mingle together in a haphazard throng. They talk and gesticulate, and shake hands over and over again. They pat each other on the shoulder and laugh like schoolboys, and leap across the little stream for fun. And when an Englishman falls in and a Bosche helps him out there is a shout of laughter that echoes back to the trenches. The Germans exchange cigars and pieces of sausages, and sauerkraut and concentrated coffee for cigarettes, and bully-beef and ration-biscuits and tobacco.

They express mutual admiration by pointing and signs. It is our leather waistcoats and trench-coats that attract their attention; it is their trench-overalls, made of coarse canvas, that attract ours . . .

Confidences are exchanged in broken English.

'When's the war going to end?'

'After the Spring offensive.'

'Yes, after the Spring offensive.'

'What sort of trenches have you?'

'Rotten! Knee deep in mud and water. Not fit for pigs.'

'Aren't you sick of the war? We are!'

'Not a bit.'

And the information is even vouchsafed that our Christmas Eve bombardment had caused the Germans a lot of casualties.

Meanwhile, Private William Gordon was making his way to join the throng that he estimated to be around two hundred in number.

Within minutes I had reached the main crowd in No Man's Land, the Germans dancing to their harmonicas which they had brought with them . . . I got talking to a few Germans, some of whom could speak a little English. One especially, I liked, was a fairly tall young man who some years before the war had been a waiter in the Savoy Hotel, London . . . I suggested to him that we get busy and bury some of the dead that were lying around both German and British. These men were either killed during the May fighting or were killed whilst on night patrol, their bodies not being recovered. Anyway, the two of us got started, removing the identity discs from the British soldiers whilst my ex Savoy Hotel friend did likewise for the German dead.

During this job of ours, I saw several German officers approach from their trenches and on reaching where we were grouped, saluted the officers of C Company, then headed by Sir Iain Colquhoun, who returned the salute but did not accept the offer to shake hands.

After I had finished burying some of the dead, I drifted off towards the German front line to check on his barbed wire strength, having been that way some nights previously. Daylight confirmed my night patrol report, ie in strength and in good repair. Time was getting on and sometime between 10 and 11 a.m., news was received that the 9th (Welch) Division on our right of the trenches had orders to commence at 12 noon artillery fire on the ground where the unofficial cease-fire soldiers were still talking together. The news of the artillery fire was passed on to the Germans and a general drift back to their respective trenches then took place.

Clearly, Gordon's memory of the truce is that it lasted far longer than that reported by Colquhoun. Ewart agreed with Gordon that the fraternisation began around 8 a.m., not 9 a.m. as noted by his Commanding Officer, but agrees with Colquhoun that it lasted only a short time. Whatever the exact truth, Sir Iain had permitted a short fraternisation to continue after the burial of the dead, then:

When the time was up, I blew a whistle and both sides returned to their trenches. For the rest of the day the Germans walked about and sat on their parapets and our men did much the same, but remained in their trenches. Not a shot was fired.

That night the Germans put up fairy lights on their parapets, and their trenches were outlined for miles on either side. It was a mild looking night with clouds and a full moon and the prettiest sight I have ever seen. Our machine guns played on them, and the lights were removed.

The Christmas Truce was over, but the ramifications of this fraternisation were about to be felt at divisional headquarters where the festive spirit was in shorter supply. The war history of Scots Guards records that Captain Barne heard about the incident while at battalion headquarters. News came not from the front line but from brigade headquarters that had, in turn, heard from corps headquarters. Barne at once went off to the trenches to put a stop to the fraternisation, but by the time he got there it was all over, and the men were back in the trenches settling down to the day's routine.

Sir Iain records the arrival not of Barne but of a more senior officer. 'The Brigadier (who came round my trenches 10 minutes after my truce was over) didn't mind a bit, but Major General Cavan [Divisional Commander] is furious about it.' Sir Iain was told to leave the trenches the following morning and give an account of what had happened and to explain his conduct. An officer arrived to relieve Captain Barne of his command.

The Scots Guards were taken out of the trenches on 26 December and went in to rest at La Gorgue. The seriousness with which senior officers were taking the meeting in no-man's-land was beginning to make itself apparent, as Private William Gordon realised.

On reaching our farmhouse billets, we were instructed to remain where we were and in no case allowed outside our billets. Immediate action was taken re letter-writing and men warned not to mention any of the Christmas Day happenings. All letters were subject to censorship by company officers, that being the usual rule but in addition the men were informed that the issue of Green envelopes was to cease at once.

Leave to the UK for soldiers serving in France used to take place once in every eight months or so; but as a further general punishment and to block news of the event, all leave was cancelled for six months. In my case I was in France from early October 1915 to late January 1917 before I had my first ten days' leave to the UK, so in a way I did pay for getting friendly with the Bavarians.

Despite the rising brouhaha over his company's participation in a second, strictly forbidden, Christmas Truce, Sir Iain Colquhoun was surprised to be handed a note from the Colonel placing him under arrest for his 'share' in the Christmas Day fraternisation; Captain Miles Barne was also held.

Both men were charged with conduct to the prejudice of good order and military discipline and ordered to attend a court martial hearing set for 17 January. In the event, Miles Barne was acquitted, and exonerated of all blame. When Sir Iain's case was heard, he argued that, as he noted down in his diary, when he arrived in the trenches he discovered 'a very advanced situation', and one 'which I did my best to regularize by having a definite agreement as to how long the situation was to last'. Despite his protestations, Sir Iain was found guilty.

In the end the sentence was light. Sir Iain was to be 'reprimanded', but although General Headquarters chose to quash this sentence, the conviction remained. The court martial sent a warning shot across the collective bow, underlining to all, if they were not already aware, just how seriously the army viewed and would in future view fraternisation with the enemy. As the war became more embittered, the chances of such an instantaneous meeting diminished with each passing year. Incidents of fraternisation continued to occur, but nothing like the truce of 1914 and the much smaller truce of 1915 was ever seen again.

5

Fronting Up

Over on the Western Front something strange was going on in the trenches near Souchez. Gifts were being exchanged with the enemy, but this time it was not a case of illicit fraternisation. On the contrary: orders were being followed, as the War Diary of the 1st Royal Berkshire Regiment made clear.

24 April, 1916

Weather fine. The Brigade sent up three English newspapers with orders that these were to be thrown into the German trenches. This was done by Private Barnes who threw them onto the enemy parapet and retired. A German crawled out and took the papers acknowledging them with a salute . . .

Six days later, at about five in the afternoon, the War Diary recorded that the enemy blew a mine under the British front line, just to the right of the Berkshires' position. No details were given as to casualties but the Germans had followed up the explosion with a 'very heavy bombardment' causing serious damage to the trenches. Fortunately, there was no accompanying infantry attack, allowing the men to make good the destruction. In addition to the clear-up, some small improvements were made to the drainage under the supervision of the Royal Engineers. Then, as though this was perfectly normal, the diary continued: 'By order of the Brigade we sent over several English newspapers and were given 3 copies of the *Hamburger Fremdenblatt*.'

War Diaries vary greatly in detail, and those of three other battalions in the 99th Brigade make no mention of communication with the Germans at this time, nor does the Brigade Diary. However, an intelligence report was sent to Headquarters, 2nd Division, and this does add a few interesting if inconsequential details to the story.

'They [the newspapers] were evidently a popular gift as three German officers were seen standing up this morning, smiling and endeavouring to fraternize – an elderly officer came along and strafed them. When the elderly officer had departed, however, they were again seen smiling across towards our trenches.'

The Germans were clearly expecting these newspapers and Private Barnes must have been confident that he would not be shot on approaching the enemy trenches; he could not have been ordered to attempt an otherwise suicidal task. Similarly, the Germans were ready for the next round of newspapers delivered on 30 April, sending German copies in response. But why did Brigade give such an order and to what end? How were such friendly intentions transmitted to the enemy and why, after a mine explosion and a 'very heavy' bombardment, were newspapers sent across at all?

There appeared to be an 'understanding' of sorts around Souchez at that time. Throughout March, the Germans were observed undertaking trench repairs and building. A close watch had been kept and information logged and passed up the chain of command. 'The Germans can be plainly seen . . . it looks as though a man is pumping or working an air bellows . . . Germans have been seen carrying timber . . . At 6.45 p.m. a peculiar clanging noise – lasting for about ten minutes – was heard.' The enemy's uniforms were noted: '(1) Cap with black band and red piping – figure 9 on shoulder strap. (2) Cap with grey band and red piping – figure 76 on shoulder strap.' These observations were not exceptional; they were carried on up and down the line. What was unusual was that there was never any effort to interrupt activities.

Throughout March when the 1st Royal Berkshire Regiment was in the line, the enemy felt confident enough to appear in full view of British trenches, and, at dusk and dawn, Germans had 'endeavoured to open friendly conversation', wrote the battalion's Adjutant. 'We were not in a position to alter this state of affairs,' he wrote on 11 March. A week later, the same conditions prevailed.

The inability to respond to such carelessness was due to the wretched state of the British parapet and the fact that both German and British trenches could be subjected to enfilade fire, so, the Adjutant continued, it had been 'essential to remain quiet also'. In other words, there appeared to be a mutually agreed stand-off, even though the War Diary continues to record occasional spats.

Had a lull, born out of the inclement conditions, grown into something more interesting and reciprocal? Had officers as high as the Divisional Commander sanctioned the 'truce'? Something was deemed to be of sufficient mutual appeal to permit the trading of newspapers. There was always curiosity in seeing how the enemy's press reported the war, but surely there were easier ways to gain access to enemy newspapers than to risk an exchange across no-man's-land? It is possible that depositing British newspapers in enemy trenches was intended to counter the one-sided view of the war given by the German press to its own soldiers. That might explain British motivation, but not the active German cooperation and not the cordiality between the men of the Royal Berkshire Regiment and the enemy opposite them, the precise reason for which remains opaque.

There was propaganda value in leaving newspapers for the enemy's discomfort. On 9–10 July 1916, parties from the 8th Royal Dublin Fusiliers and 7th Royal Irish Rifles crossed over to leave newspapers in or close to the enemy's trench. The Royal Irish Rifles were first given the task of examining the enemy's wire and then of placing the 'latest war news in German and an English [news]paper on the enemy's wire for his information'.

Nearby, a party of Royal Dublin Fusiliers took three newspapers 'including *The Times* with Sir John Jellicoe's Despatch', which was left in the enemy's trench with an empty bottle of whisky, while more men from the same battalion delivered 'war news attached to a de-detonated grenade'.

Published in *The Times* on 7 July, Jellicoe's Despatch gave the Admiral's full account of the naval battle at Jutland a month earlier, a battle in the aftermath of which both sides claimed victory. With headlines such as 'Enemy Severely Punished' and 'Enemy Vessels Constantly Hit' the Despatch ended with a list of enemy ships sunk or disabled. It gave a very favourable spin to what was, in reality, an inconclusive battle. Whether newspaper reports of this nature undermined morale on either side of the trenches is questionable.

News that could not be given in print form could be posted on notice boards and placed either on the enemy's wire or in no-man's-land. Boards could be used as another form of fraternisation or friendly banter. 'Today is BANK HOLIDAY – TOMMIES. Do not fire – give us a rest' was an appeal stuck up on the German parapet.

Nor was a notice necessarily one-way correspondence. The 48th Infantry Brigade Diary records a patrol of the 9th Royal Munster Fusiliers bringing in a board that had been observed in front of the enemy wire. 'The notice', wrote the Munsters' Adjutant, 'seems to refer to some previous board displayed in our trenches before we took over the line. This would tend to show that the enemy had been unaware that a relief had taken place.' The inscription read 'Request for clearer explication [sic] by written or personally'. The following day, patrols and wiring parties from the 9th Royal Munster Fusiliers were sent out, one retrieving a notice board from the German trenches 'which had evidently been taken by them from our lines before the Battalion took over . . . it was to this notice that the "Explication" of yesterday referred.' The Munsters had relieved the 7th Royal Irish Rifles on the evening of 20 May.

Each side was adept at crowing at the other's strategic misfortune, and notices frequently carried news of some recent catastrophe. The first months of 1916 proved a low point for the British, giving the Germans plenty to write about. 'Interesting war-news of April 29th 1916. Kut-el-Amara has been taken by the Turks, and whole English army therein − 13,000 men − maken prisoners.' And: 'The English Ministre of War and the general kommandre Lord Kitchener is on the trip to Russia with all his generals officers trowened in the east see by a german submerin. Nobody is sowed [saved].'

Most signs were in English, and of variable literacy. One draw-ing, made by Acting Sergeant Herbert Gibson and sent to his sweetheart in Newcastle upon Tyne depicted a board near Mount Sorrel. The Germans had erected it in early March 1916 'to tell us of a big victory at Verdun against the French', wrote Gibson on the back of the card. On this occasion the message was in German and boasted of the prisoners taken so far in the campaign, number-ing 228 officers and 17,370 other ranks.

'Did I ever tell you how eager the Germans are to supply us with news − of their own successes of course?' wrote Lieutenant Melville Hastings in a letter to his family. 'Yesterday a screen raised above the parapet informed us marooned Tommies of the fall of Kut, and last year we were similarly told of the fall of Warsaw' [4 August 1915].

The notice board was a curiosity, and therein lay an obvious trap. 'The Germans stick up a board with writing on such as "What about the *Lusitania*, how many dead?"' wrote one soldier, 'and God help anybody that looks over the parapet at it', the infer-ence being that a sniper was ready for the over-inquisitive. A board was also a provocation and bait. Second Lieutenant Stephen Hewett (14th Warwickshire Regiment), writing to his mother, described why.

I was out wiring the other night with four men for about an hour and a half, and I was tempted to go further out on a little

expedition of my own – to destroy a great notice board which the
Hun has put out in No Man's Land, announcing the fall of Kut-el
Amara: but certainly there must have been a machine gun trained
on to it, and probably by touching it one would have exploded a
bomb, – so it was safer left alone.

It was a sensible decision. Lieutenant Hugh Munro, an impetuous
twenty-two-year-old officer of the 1/8th Argyll and Sutherland
Highlanders, did not resist and went after a German flag draped
on the enemy barbed wire. According to his batman, Munro knew
that the Germans had probably booby-trapped the flag but nevertheless sought to remove it. As he pulled the flag, a bomb exploded,
instantly killing him.

Among the setbacks in early 1916, the situation in Ireland was
of grave concern to the British government. The Easter Rising on
24 April and the bitter fighting that erupted in Dublin was a
cause for German satisfaction. Their attempt to encourage an Irish
Brigade was an abject failure but they could still enjoy posting
barbed messages designed to upset Irishmen fighting for Britain.
On 10 May, just over a week after the Uprising was quelled and
the ringleaders arrested, the Germans raised a notice board above
the parapet that was recovered by an officer of the 8th Royal
Munster Fusiliers.

'Irishmen! Heavy uproar in Ireland. English guns are firing at
your wifes and children! 1st May 1916.'

The Germans knew who occupied the trenches opposite: three
days earlier they hailed the Royal Dublin Fusiliers, asking not
which regiment they were but more specifically which battalion,
8th or 9th. Now, armed with news from Ireland, the Germans
were keen to pass on information that might cause unease among
the Munsters' ranks.

The German attitude towards Sir Roger Casement had darkened long before the Uprising. Casement's failure to achieve
anything worthwhile with the Irish Brigade aggravated the

Germans, who looked to cut him adrift. They cared little for his fate when he was taken by German submarine to Ireland three days prior to the Uprising. Casement was quickly captured. In mid-May a patrol of the Munsters made an effigy labelled 'Sir Roger Casement' and suspended it by the neck from a tree in full view of the enemy. A few days later it was brought in riddled with bullets. 'It appeared to annoy the enemy,' wrote the Adjutant in the Munsters' War Diary.

The Munsters' overwhelmingly Catholic contingent must have known of Casement's arrest, and of the Uprising and its suppression. It also seems likely that news had filtered through of the execution of the rebellion's ringleaders, seven of whom were signatories to their Proclamation of Independence. It was widespread revulsion at the execution of fourteen rebels between 3 and 12 May that caused the British authorities the greatest loss of common support in Ireland rather than the suppression of the Uprising itself, which had proved unpopular among the civilian population. Hoisting Casement's effigy from a tree, the Munsters' attitude and the subsequent German response were very enlightening.

In January 1916, the British government introduced conscription; it really had no alternative. After the great civilian rush to enlist in 1914, the army had seen a remorseless decline in the number of men willing to volunteer, a decline coinciding with a rapidly growing physical and material commitment to the war overseas. The German attacks around Ypres in April and May 1915, followed by the Allies' first combined offensive in September, accentuated the need for more men in steady, predictable numbers. In August 1915, a day of National Registration was held in which every citizen aged between fifteen and sixty-five was obliged by law to supply the government with personal details including nationality, age, marital status and occupation. Although originally intended as a means to utilise efficiently the services of all men and women for the war effort, this information would also be used as preparatory groundwork for military compulsion, ensuring every able-bodied man would play his part, irrespective of background.

Ironically, among one much-maligned group of subjects, the British-born sons of German parentage, loyalty and patriotism had often been demonstrated. Many of these lads decided that their allegiance was to the country of their birth, not the country of their ancestry, and had enlisted into the British Army.

Sergeant Herman Schultz from Liverpool, the son of German-born parents, John and Mary Schultz, served with the Loyal North Lancashire Regiment. He embarked for France in December 1915 and later won both the Distinguished Conduct Medal and Military Medal. George Schumacher, aged seventeen, a lad from Leith in Scotland, was serving with the 1/7th Royal Scots and died in May 1915, in the Quintinshill train disaster on his way to the front. And then there was Alexander Fischer, an undergraduate at Cambridge University and son of a Prussian father. Alexander enlisted on the morning after the outbreak of war, aged eighteen, and was killed serving as a lieutenant in the Devonshire Regiment in May 1916.

Ten common German names, including Hoffmann, Meyer, Wagner and Fischer, contributed well over a thousand recruits to the British Army according to the army's post-war Medal Roll. But how many more men with German ancestry had altered their names both before and during Registration? The Army Council entirely accepted that an unquantifiable number had done so.

It has been brought to the notice of the Council from time to time that a number of British born sons of enemy aliens assumed, when registering themselves, British surnames in lieu of their proper names and, when subsequently called up, were posted to combatant units owing to the fact of their enemy parentage being unknown. The Council can only conclude that the course followed by these men was deliberately undertaken with a view to the avoidance of any suspicion of enemy connection . . .

It is no coincidence that Fischer, one of the most common surnames and the easiest to anglicise, contributed only thirty-three men with the German spelling. It would have been uncomfortable for anyone to serve in the ranks with a German name, and altering or adapting names so as to appear British was the easy solution, allowing volunteers with names such as Lautenberg to become Lawton and Fritsch changing to Fitch.

Not all Germanic names were identifiably foreign. Julius Ring, of Dalston, north London, was forty-two and an internee on the Isle of Wight. He had moved with his wife to Britain in the 1890s and all four of their children were born in England. In October 1915, he received news that his son William had left work as a butcher's boy and joined up, aged just fourteen. In a panic, Julius contacted the Westminster-based Emergency Society of Germans and Austrians in Distress for help. They informed him that his son Willy had been 'overcome with patriotic fervour' and was 'serving his King in the Army'. William had given a false age and address and joined the 1st Royal Fusiliers. He had not been heard of since. Representations were made to the American ambassador in London who made contact with Sir Edward Grey. On 1 July 1916, Private 5024 William Ring was discharged as having 'made a misstatement as to age'.

Such lads may have been keen to do their 'bit' but to their fathers, suffering the indignity of internment, the idea that their sons would fight for the British was, for many, intolerable. In May 1915 William Kunz wrote to the authorities from Knockaloe internment camp on the Isle of Man claiming that his son, William, had been 'forced by his employer' to join the 'English' Army. 'I do not want him to fight against his own flesh and blood. He is consequently the son of an unnaturalised German.' The fact that he was such was actually of no consequence. The father was German, and his British-born wife German by marriage. It might have appeared to William Kunz Senior an anomaly that a child of German parents was legally British, but if that child was born in Britain then he was British until or unless he renounced his citizenship. This he was entitled to do once he had reached the age of majority (twenty-one), but William Junior had not.

Conscription did not alter the legal status of these boys but it did create one unforeseen problem. In January 1916, all men aged between nineteen and forty-one were according to law deemed to have enlisted for General Service. Exemption from service could be granted only if, for example, the army had previously rejected a man on medical grounds. It was all very well the army holding on to lads of German ancestry who had shown their colours by volunteering, but what should the military authorities do with thousands of British-born children of German fathers unpersuaded by patriotism to freely enlist? By rights, these boys could expect to be called up, but with which country did their allegiance lie? If they were ambivalent about serving, could they be relied upon in battle? It was an issue that was without precedent.

In early 1916 the Swiss Legation in London passed on a number of letters to the Foreign Office. They were from Germans interned in Britain, pointing out that, while their children had been called up for service by the British, they, the children, were also pro-German.

Wilhelm Roderwald had lived in Britain since 1890 and his son, Gerald, was born in January 1897. Wilhelm was interned at Alexandra Palace, and he was in no doubt as to where his and his son's allegiance lay. Wilhelm had registered himself again as a German subject at the Imperial German Consulate in 1900, to ensure that he remained unquestionably German, and he therefore believed his son to be German, too. 'My son is entirely German as far as his sympathies are concerned.' Other letters of protest included one from Peter Viel and his sons Johann and Andreas. 'I, the father, most emphatically forbid my sons to serve in any capacity with the British or Allied Forces . . .' while Bartholomus Eid asserted that his son 'would rather be interned than join the British Army'. Was this in fact simply a question of fathers speaking *for* their sons and not on their behalf? It was impossible to know.

In May 1916, Carl Martini objected to the conscription of his sons, Charles and Heinrich, aged twenty-three and nineteen respectively. Both sons had been registered in Germany as of German nationality and were, if anything, he claimed, liable to serve in the German army. Unfortunately, Charles, while old enough to choose his nationality, had made no effort to relinquish his British citizenship at the age of twenty-one and as a result was still liable to serve.

Both sons were called up. In this case they were clearly in sympathy with their father: within days Heinrich was reported absent from his battalion, the 15th (2nd Reserve) battalion of the Middlesex Regiment, followed soon after by his elder brother. Carl Martini was legally obliged to ensure that his sons reported back, as Lieutenant Colonel A. R. Gardiner, the officer commanding the battalion, pointed out to him: 'It is your duty to use every endeavour to induce him [Heinrich] to return immediately to his Battalion. Your attention is drawn to the gravity of the offence of a soldier deserting his regiment while on active service.' Whether or not Carl could have effected his sons' return to the ranks is unclear. Both were recaptured and Charles, though seemingly not Heinrich, served in France with the Army Service Corps.

Fathers like Wilhelm Roderwald and Bartholomus Eid were antagonistic towards the country in which they had chosen to live, but was their aggressively pro-German sympathy in part due to the conditions of their internment, imposed without material evidence of disloyalty? Sons who might otherwise have been willing to serve were shocked at the treatment meted out to their fathers. Harry Steinke, son of Hermann Steinke, locked up on Knockaloe, wrote that he could not be expected to recognise his native country (Britain) or serve when his father, 'an innocent citizen of this country for over 25 years, having always promptly paid rates and taxes, should suffer internment'. He did have a point; the problem was that no one was inclined to listen.

Four months after the introduction of conscription, the Army Council came to a decision on males born in Britain to enemy subjects. An Instruction was issued directing that these men would not be called up under the Military Service Acts, 1916, until they reached the age of twenty-one, at which point they would be given the opportunity to make a declaration of alienage.

There was little political or public sympathy for the position of such lads. Why should they live under the protection afforded by the state and the sacrifices of millions of other British-born men fighting and dying on the Western Front? The children of German-born parents had to play their part in defeating the enemy's manifest tyranny, irrespective of whether they might, in theory, be fighting against their 'flesh and blood'. Internees' claims that, under German law, sons would lay themselves open to penal servitude for life in Germany were they forced to serve in the British Army were discounted. Where there was genuine concern was whether these conscripts, if allowed to serve in the front line, might act as agents provocateurs.

With this in mind, the Army Council issued instruction 1209 on 17 June 1916, authorising the creation of a new battalion of the Middlesex Regiment, the 30th (Works) Battalion, to which such men would be sent on enlistment or transferred from existing units. The following month the battalion was founded in Crawley to be followed in September by a second battalion, the 31st (Works) Battalion, in Mill Hill. While neither unit was destined to serve overseas, they would supply trained but unarmed men to eight 500-strong Infantry Labour Companies (ILCs) that would work behind the lines in 1917 and 1918. As may be imagined, there was no fanfare to herald the establishment of these two units and for a while they filled their ranks without unwarranted attention.

Only in September 1916 did one of the battalions (perhaps in ignorance of the second) become the focus of sarcastic press attention. Headlined 'The Kaiser's Own', the London *Evening Standard* ran an article about the 'Queerest Battalion in the British Army'. The journalist had come across the case of an army defaulter who, on appearing before a magistrate, explained that he had absconded after being sent to a battalion in which 'all the members were more or less directly descended from enemy aliens'.

The journalist continued:

The battalion in question is hardly known at all to the general public. Many soldiers are quite unaware of its existence and even recruiting experts have been known to deny that there is any such body of men.

Yet the Middlesex Regiment knows all about it, for the battalion forms part of itself. Not that the Fighting Middlesex – who have lived up to their regimental nickname ever since the first days of the war – are at all proud of the fact. On the contrary. To them the foreign legion has nothing attractive, and on the rare occasions when they refer to the battalion it is only as the 'Kaiser's Own'.

Until a very few months ago, the problem of what to do with enemy alien Britons seemed beyond the powers of the Army. The enemy alien pure and simple (if such adjectives are not somewhat out of place) could easily be dealt with. He was either interned or allowed to roam about at liberty, explaining in guttural accents that he was really more British than the British.

The journalist went on his merry literary way referring to the attitude of those young men born in Britain to unnaturalised alien enemies. Some lads, he conceded, had tried to volunteer but suspicious recruiting sergeants had rejected their approaches; other boys enlisted under false names.

'However,' he continued, 'it is not to be imagined that all enemy alien Britons are either heroes or aching to die for their Stepmotherland.'

The War Office, it was suggested, could hardly allow these Germans to roam free in British front-line trenches, nor could they be allowed to stay at home and enjoy war wages while 'pure Britons' fought. Hence the Army Council Instruction.

> There are men of every variation of accent, their proximity to the true British standard being more or less judged by the facility with which they manage the letters 'R' and 'W'. The man who can manage 'Around the rugged rocks the ragged rascals ran' three times without sounding like fizzy water is entitled to sergeant's stripes.

No doubt readers smiled at the jocular descriptions, and the writer did conclude by saying that the men were 'stated to be quite loyal', but his scorn was palpable and unfair. The vast majority of these men could speak English as well as any 'pure Briton', and were frequently the children of an English-born mother. Most were born in Britain and had lived all their lives there; they included men such as Charles Kuhr.

In June 1916, Charles was in his mid-thirties. Born and raised in Hull to an English mother and German father, he joined the 1st Volunteer Battalion of the East Yorkshire Regiment in 1899, serving until 1908 when he became part of the Territorial force. A musical man, he played in the regimental band that gave numerous concerts around Yorkshire. After the outbreak of war, his military history remained opaque until he was sent to join the 30th Middlesex Regiment in training near Reading. Once again he joined the battalion band, The Snapshots, of which he was conductor, giving concerts at St Dunstan's Hospital for blinded sailors and soldiers. In 1918, he was sent on a draft for France and one of the Infantry Labour Companies. This was hardly a man of questionable loyalties who would struggle to pronounce the letters 'R' and 'W'.

Another who joined the 'Kaiser's Own' and who hardly fitted the journalist's stereotype was Otto Vollmar. Born in Islington, north London, to German parents, he had found work in the United States where he could have remained in safety working as a stockbroker's clerk in New York. Instead, he returned to Britain in November 1915 to volunteer under the Derby Scheme (allowing men to enlist and, until required, return to their civilian jobs), being called up the following year when he was sent to the 30th Battalion.

In the same battalion was warehouseman Charles Eshborn. In September 1914, the twenty-one-year-old had written an eloquent letter to the *Manchester Guardian* about the pointless banning of German music at public performances. He used a nom de plume, hiding his German heritage for fear, perhaps, that his views would be dismissed as partisan. The son of a German father, Eshborn was reluctant to enlist, having lived for eight years in Germany, but after the introduction of conscription he knew it would only be a matter of time before he was called up.

All men liable for conscription were divided into classes according to year of birth and marital status. Those who were unmarried would, in the normal course of events, be called up before married men. Charles was engaged to a local girl, Janie Puleston, and it is possible that it was with a mind to delaying his call-up that the couple had married in early 1916.

By July, Charles had sought and gained a temporary exemption owing to the fact that his widowed mother was in very poor health, while a younger brother, Bernard, was an invalid; 'both are absolutely dependent on me,' he wrote to the tribunal assessing his case. That exemption was due to run out at the end of August and Charles knew that he was unlikely to be granted an extension or leave to reapply on additional grounds. Nevertheless, he decided to write to the tribunal to ask if they would give the following circumstances their 'kindest consideration'.

Charles was born in Cumbria but had lived in Germany until the death of his father when the family chose to return to England. Indeed, he was eligible to serve in both German and British armies, as he pointed out to the tribunal. 'On the death of an uncle I was to inherit some property [and this] made my father register me in Germany. Had I been in Germany at the outbreak of war, the Germans could have compelled me to serve in their army according to the law.'

Charles assured the tribunal that he would have refused outright to fight against the British but he found the prospect of fighting against the Germans almost as difficult.

> Not only was my father German but I have two brothers who were born in Germany and who are now being educated there by an uncle. Also my grandparents were most kind to my mother at the time of my father's death when our financial circumstances were very precarious . . . I ask in all sincerity is it right that I should actually fight against them in these circumstances? How awful would be my position if I ever fell into their hands. Since I can perhaps hardly be treated as a neutral is there nothing else I can do than fight? I shall be only too willing to undertake anything else – clerical, munitions or Red Cross Work . . .

Charles's exemptions naturally brought him under the umbrella of the two Middlesex battalions, to one of which he was duly sent. A year later he would join the 3rd ILC and leave for the Western Front.

The passing of the Military Service Act in January made British-born children of German parents liable to serve. These parents would be entitled to separation allowances except when in receipt of relief from Germany, as paid through the American

Embassy. In the winter of 1914, the German government had severely restricted those entitled to relief but had continued to provide financial support for German-born women whose German husbands were interned. That support would cease the moment the German government became aware that sons of German-born parents were serving in the British Army, leaving families cut off in an instant without an income. The conscription of a son when he was the principal breadwinner was also a cause for great family anxiety. With the father interned, it was problematic whether the separation allowance alone was enough to keep a family going, without relief, especially when working opportunities were so limited for those with German surnames.

Family finances were uppermost in the mind of Hugo Biskeborn when he was called up. Interestingly, it was not entirely clear whether he should have been serving at all. Hugo was born in Germany in August 1898 to a German father and English mother, Elizabeth, who brought her family to Britain after the death of her husband in 1902. At some point (it is unclear when) Hugo registered himself as an enemy alien at Paddington Green police station but does not appear to have been interned during the war.

In early March 1918, Biskeborn reluctantly enlisted after a visit from the police. He was told, he claimed, that if he refused he would be interned and his mother repatriated to Germany. This was bluster by the policeman, but does suggest that Elizabeth Biskeborn had not reapplied for British citizenship. A visit to the Biskeborn residence was also made by a representative of the Ministry of National Service. Hugo stated that the representative confirmed that on his enlistment Elizabeth would receive 'an adequate allowance'. In the event, and for reasons unknown, his mother did not receive any money and was soon in great difficulty, according to her son. In July, Hugo, now Private Biskeborn, wrote to the authorities requesting that his mother be adequately paid as he was her only support, but he was told that 'nothing could be done' in his case, although a 'paltry sum' was subsequently offered that did not cover even half her rent. Hugo then wrote to the Swiss Legation in London for help, stating the facts as he saw them and adding: 'I wrote to the Captain of this Company, requesting him to do something in the matter or else apply for my release. I received a most insulting and ungentlemanly letter from him, reminding me I am "a German and have no rights whatsoever" and to be "grateful for the consideration" I and my mother had received.'

Private Hugo Biskeborn took a dangerous stance: he went on strike, refusing orders. He was given fourteen days confined to barracks, but as he refused to accept the punishment he was placed in the guard room pending a court martial. He was subsequently sentenced to twenty-eight days' detention. What happened to him is not known although the Armistice may have come to his rescue. His absence from the Medal Roll indicates he was never sent abroad.

The outlook for German-born naturalised Britons was increasingly bleak. Although British, they were despised and mistrusted in their adopted land and interned as enemy aliens in the country of their birth.

Ever since returning from Germany in early 1915, British-born Nellie Fuchs had been attempting to get her naturalised husband released from detention in Germany. Nellie Fuchs's husband, Carl, was the world-renowned cellist whose friends included the elite of Britain's conductors and composers. Sir Edward Elgar had written to the government on his friend's behalf, but Elgar's views were out of step with public opinion. Government policy at home flowed irreversibly against these German-born men, even those with impeccable pedigrees.

In May 1916 an agreement was reached with Germany facilitating the repatriation of alien civilians aged over fifty. Furthermore, those over forty-five could be released if adjudged to be permanently unfit for service in the field. It was shortly after the conclusion of the agreement that the Prussian government unexpectedly proposed to exchange Fuchs for the safe passage home of the German-born painter, novelist and poet Max Dauthendey, marooned on the Dutch East Indies territory of Java since the outbreak of war.

Proposed exchanges frequently floundered owing to mutual suspicion, and it was indicative of the Foreign Office's attitude to Fuchs, and indifference to his standing, that the Prussian request was refused, albeit with an amusing note attached to the Foreign Office file: 'Dauthendey is in Java aged 58. He is accused of being a poet but may be innocent.'

Nellie Fuchs pressed her case, revealing that her husband, like so many men parted from their families, was in poor mental health, but the official dealing with Fuchs's proposed return had no sympathy for the plight of either man.

'I think we can leave Mrs Fuchs to deluge the Home Office with the names of any responsible persons who may be prepared to vouch for her husband' was another sarcastic note attached to the file. 'We should not have Fuchs back now. Apart from objections to him, there is no demand for his return and his job is filled by an Englishman . . . If the Fuchs case is ever raised again we must decline to discuss it further. Enough paper time has now been wasted on this Hun.' 'I agree,' wrote another official. 'The agitation for Fuchs' passport is evidently being run by Manchester Radicals of pro German proclivities, and the longer he is kept away the better!'

Fuchs's job had indeed been taken, by a man named Hatton, and in a report submitted to the Foreign Office by the Manchester Police, Inspector Fisher confirmed that the public in the city would 'hardly tolerate' Fuchs's reinstatement at the 'expense of a British born subject'.

In December 1915, a memo was sent by the then Home Secretary and former barrister Sir John Simon to Sir Edward

Grey at the Foreign Office. It stated that preference would be given in cases of proposed repatriation to 'natural-born' British subjects. Now, over a year later, a decision had been made, seemingly on the hoof, to deny the rights of British citizenship to naturalised subjects of enemy birth, despite cast-iron rights being granted on naturalisation. Fuchs's own certificate, issued in 1899 and quoted by Nellie to the Foreign Office, made matters crystal-clear: '. . . upon taking the Oath of Allegiance, he [Fuchs] shall in the United Kingdom be entitled to all political and other rights, powers and privileges, and be subject to all obligations, to which a natural-born British subject is entitled or subject . . .'

Irrespective of the evidence, the Foreign Office wrote to Nellie Fuchs that the government had determined that 'persons of enemy origin residing in the country of their origin who have previously obtained citizenship through naturalisation [would] not receive British passports', sealing Fuchs's immediate fate. Nellie Fuchs replied, rejecting the idea that her husband was 'residing' in Germany other than at the enforced behest of the Kaiser's government, but her protests were pointless. She was trapped in an impossible predicament. If she, and other women in a similar quandary, did not apply pressure on the government, then nothing whatsoever would happen and their husbands would languish in captivity. But the more they protested, the more they appeared to annoy officials in the Foreign Office who resisted their entreaties.

In Britain, internees were overwhelmingly German subjects, but not exclusively so. Even those who were naturalised British and of German origin could be interned if deemed a risk under the Defence of the Realm Act. Just as the British government was inclined to play hard and fast with the law as it related to 'British' men like Fuchs, so it also justified interning women who were British by marriage but German by birth. Hildegard Burnyeat was interned in 1915 after a U-boat (*U24*) 'bombarded' the Cumbrian town of Whitehaven in the early hours of 16 August 1915. The attack, which caused precious little damage, reportedly slammed a few shells into a railway embankment and killed a dog.

Hildegard's husband was a local barrister and former Liberal MP, William Dalzell Burnyeat, a member of a long-established Whitehaven family. William and Hildegard married in Germany in 1908 but lived in Cumbria in the village of Moresby about a mile from the sea and close to a 'Top Secret' chemical plant at Parton, near Whitehaven. It was the Burnyeats' proximity to these works that was the primary reason for her arrest. It was true that Hildegard was the daughter of a Prussian army officer (one who was, by 1915, at least in his mid-sixties), but that was the extent of her proven 'guilt'. Local sentiment alleged that she was pro-German while claims that her home was spared by the submarine were self-evidently preposterous, as were, in all likelihood, the assertions that 'peculiar lights' were observed near her home at the time of the raid. The Germans were proving to the British that they could mount an attack on the west as well as the east coast, while also searching for the chemical works. They did not require the help of Hildegard Burnyeat to execute their plans, because it was a German company, Koppers, which had constructed the installation before the war. Even with this detailed knowledge, the submarine failed to hit the intended target.

Hildegard Burnyeat was interned at Aylesbury in Buckinghamshire. 'She is one of a nice little lot which we call "14 Bs", which, being interpreted, means persons interned in the interests of the realm under Defence of the Realm Regulation 14 B,' wrote an official to Sir Horace Rumbold at the Foreign Office, in response to German enquiries about Hildegard's whereabouts. Six months later, in May 1916, Hildegard's husband died and she was released from internment and allowed to live with an English family in Harrogate, causing some antagonism in the Yorkshire town. What happened to her subsequently is not clear. She had no children and, after the death of her husband, she may have chosen to be exchanged and returned to Germany; she had precious little reason to stay in Great Britain, irrespective of whether she was pro-German or not.

Regular exchanges of both interned civilians and prisoners of war unfit for further combat continued throughout 1916, with specially selected ships such as the *St Denis* ploughing their way across the sea to Holland. Around 10,000 people, primarily males not of military age, women and children, were repatriated in the twelve months to June 1916, many voluntarily going home. The only group forcibly repatriated was women of less than five years' residency.

There was another spike in anti-German feeling in mid-1916, when Lord Kitchener was drowned on his way to Russia aboard the armoured cruiser HMS *Hampshire*. Casualty lists from the Battle of the Somme hardly tempered feelings and at public meetings during the summer there were again calls to remove from Britain or intern all enemy aliens at liberty, both naturalised and unnaturalised.

Of those Germans repatriated from Britain, the government was eager to rid the country of mentally or physically sick internees, as they posed a particular financial burden on the state. On 8 December 1916, for example, a party of 125 invalid civilians was sent across the North Sea to Holland. Accompanying them was Colonel W. R. Clark, a medical officer appointed to oversee repatriation. The policy was to return these people 'without undue delays, hardships or undesirable incidents' in the interests of Britons making the journey in the other direction. This was not always achieved. A memorandum written by Colonel Clark highlighted how he met with innumerable inefficiencies, 'difficulties and obstructions' in carrying out his task. Furthermore, he had been taken aback in particular by public hostility as the detachment left Stratford for the coast. 'A crowd of hooting and jeering women and children crowded Carpenter's Road and not only shouted and jeered and hissed at the German interned civilians as they emerged from the camp, but also greeted them as they climbed on the tops of the buses with pieces of rotten oranges, cabbage leaves and such like.'

Colonel Clark could 'scarcely believe' what he had seen. 'I am sorry to have to record it. The police ought in future to have strict orders not to allow any gathering of people whatsoever in Carpenter's Road, when the German prisoners are to be repatriated and to repress most strictly any such demonstrations.' The police, if ordered, could control the baying crowds, but, as many internees were discovering, it was officials charged with expediting their removal from Britain who often proved the most refractory.

Diplomatic negotiations between Great Britain and Germany invariably took place with a third party acting as intermediary. Each combatant looked to see if an advantage, however inadvertent, might be handed to the other, closely scrutinising proposals such as exchanges over which joint agreement was required. An offer made by one side alone was normally rejected, at least in the short term, for suspicion lingered that there must be an ulterior motive in play.

There were issues on which consensus was more readily reached, such as the day-to-day welfare of prisoners and the return of property. It seems extraordinary that while war raged on the Western Front, formal but courteous diplomatic transmissions were exchanged, often about matters of a relatively minor nature but which, to the individuals concerned, were no doubt of considerable importance.

In September 1917, the German military authorities allowed the Berlin-based Free Association for the Protection of the Interest of Orthodox Jewry to furnish ritual Passover bread (Mazzoth) to British POWs of the Jewish faith. The German government wanted to know whether German soldiers of the Jewish faith enjoyed similar privileges in British and French prisoner-of-war camps.

On 5 October, a reply was issued through the Prisoner of War Department. The Army Council had received the German memorandum and, in connection with the Jewish celebration of Passover, the army authorities were empowered to 'authorise the issue of a money allowance in lieu of rations for days of observance . . . in order that as far as possible the requirements of the men's religion as to food may be met'.

While British and German armies were engaged at Ypres in one of the most ferocious battles on the Western Front, a note was sent from Berlin to the Swiss for transmission to London. In Germany, British prisoners of war were 'provided with rupture trusses gratis. Excepting in the case of officers, they are also supplied free of charge with spectacles, in so far as they had to wear them before being captured, or if the nature of their work requires them to wear such.' Did the British adopt a similar policy with German prisoners? 'Yes' came the answer a few weeks later from Mr Cubitt of the War Office. 'The regulations regarding these matters would appear therefore, to be practically similar to those obtaining in Germany.' An agreement over the supply of free artificial eyes, false teeth and artificial limbs had been concluded earlier in the war while the issue of inadequate supplies of toilet paper for British prisoners of war was discussed in 1917.

Some diplomatic traffic could be of such minor consequence that it is a wonder communication was countenanced at all. In 1915, the American ambassador in Berlin, James Gerard, contacted his American counterpart in London, Walter Page, about a case of undelivered prismatic field glasses. The essence of the communication was that a Canadian Trade Commissioner, Mr Just, was due to receive a pair of such glasses from Oberleutnant Borcher prior to his leaving Germany for Britain. However, as the

British government confiscated all similar glasses from Germans who had been recently exchanged, so Oberleutnant Borcher felt unable to pass on Mr Just's glasses until repatriated Germans received theirs. Could Mr Hines 'kindly bring this matter to the attention of the British Foreign Office?'

Further examples included those of Hermann Waetjen, Professor of History at the University of Heidelberg, detained, though not interned, in England, who asked whether literary notes required for a book he was writing on the seventeenth-century Dutch colonisation of Pernambuco in Brazil could be sent from Germany; a request from a Mrs Gordon for permission to send the commandant of Blankenburg POW camp, Berlin, an inscribed gold pencil as a mark of appreciation for his kindness to her imprisoned husband, Colonel William Gordon VC; and an enquiry as to whether a dog (a Dachshund) belonging to a prisoner due for exchange, and both held at Lofthouse Park camp, could be repatriated with its master to Holland. Apparently the dog was refused permission to travel on a Red Cross boat and arrangements to have it forwarded by the British Commercial Transport company on a steamer were under way. The request was sent to the Swiss Legation in London dealing with German affairs and presented to the Foreign Office. An official felt that this was one for the Home Office, passing it on with a note: 'What reply?' he asked, perhaps in mild exasperation.

In among this diplomatic traffic was one document of great interest to the family of Henry Hadley, the middle-aged language teacher mortally wounded by a Prussian officer. Henry was attempting to leave Germany on the eve of war with his house-keeper, Mrs Pratley, who was arrested after the shooting and detained for interrogation.

For nearly two years there had been silence as to what had happened to Henry's property and indeed, as far as his family was concerned, what had happened to his body. Miss Henrietta Hadley, his sister, knew only that he had been buried in Gelsenkirchen and that his property, including two trunks and other smaller bags, was missing. Suddenly, at the beginning of 1917, the Germans sparked into life. But the news was not good, as a German note dated 22 January 1917 explained.

'The administrator appointed by the court has sold the property by auction and out of the proceeds of the sale, paid part of the sum owing to the doctor who treated Hadley up to the time of his death.' Among his personal belongings listed were a violin case and violin, one silk hat, one opera hat, fourteen collars and five small pipes. The total raised was just over twenty-seven marks. The British protested that as Henry Hadley had been mortally wounded for no justifiable reason, the idea that he should pay for his own medical treatment was outrageous. In a letter to the Foreign Office, Henrietta Hadley gave details of items of value her brother carried but which had never been returned, including a new greatcoat. In addition, 'the housekeeper [Mrs Pratley] states that before she left Gelsenkirchen a packet of papers was given her of my brother's and that they were taken from her by the police at Münster and not returned when she left'.

Months later, some 'effects' were found in the hands of the Berlin Railway and returned through The Hague, including two trunks of clothes and possibly the missing papers. Property of value reported to have been with Hadley when he was shot was untraceable.

As to what had happened to Henry Hadley himself, Henrietta was 'unofficially told' that his body was buried in a pauper's grave in Gelsenkirchen; a location of 'Zone 11, Division 9' was given, though this meant nothing to her, and she asked the Foreign Office to pursue the matter so that she could find out exactly where he lay. 'What we all feel as a family,' she wrote to the Foreign Office, 'is that Captain Nicolay who shot my brother should be brought to justice.' While Henry Hadley was the first British man killed in the Great War, this dubious distinction would not put him first in the justice queue when the Allies half-heartedly pursued war crimes trials after victory in 1918. Even if Captain Nicolay were still alive, there would be far bigger fish than him who would ultimately remain free and distinctly unfried.

6

Up Close and Personal

For the Allies to win the war, the German army would have to be defeated in the field. In short, and at its most simplistic, this could not be achieved other than by leaving the safety of one's own trenches, crossing no-man's-land, and ejecting the enemy from his.

The trenches were sanctuaries, places of relative safety, temporary homes in which men lived if not cheek by jowl with the enemy, then in close proximity. Was it any wonder that on both sides of the line men could become seduced into maintaining the peace? Most did not champ at the bit to 'get at the Hun'. Trench raids and sniping were useful in breaking up cosy arrangements and gingering up opponents, but nevertheless a sense of stalemate was bound to develop while the men held fast, a situation that would remain until decisive action was taken. If Allied soldiers were going to get to grips with the enemy, it had to be up close and personal.

The net result of fighting thus far had been to establish a war of attrition. The Germans, who had held the initiative in 1914 and 1915, would slowly see the pendulum of ascendancy swing in the Allies' favour as the Battle of the Somme, and later Arras and Third Ypres, eroded the enemy's fighting capabilities and in the end broke his will to resist coherently. The Germans became aware that the tide of war was flowing against them as British, Empire and eventually American forces were committed in ever greater numbers, deploying escalating resources as the Germans' own decayed and diminished. It would take time for the Allies to combine the knowledge learnt, utilise new technology, enjoy the predominance of arms and win the war. In 1916, that knowledge was still over a year away and its decisive deployment closer to two.

Prior to an offensive, the strategic aims were set out by the Commander in Chief. Strategy centred at this time on the idea of the breakout, punching through enemy lines to the green fields beyond, and it was up to his army commanders to plan in detail how this would take place. In turn, it was the junior officers' role to implement tactics on the ground and then to lead their men forward. The other ranks had no idea of strategy or a sense of the bigger picture. They simply had to do as they were ordered.

The significance of the proposed attack would be impressed upon the men. A major breakthrough was expected; by the troops' own actions and example, the war itself might be shortened. There was hyperbole: the imperilled freedom of the world was in their hands; the eyes of the world were on them at this critical moment. This was not a time for failing in one's duty, or for threatening the honour of the regiment. Everyone would be expected to perform to their utmost.

The pep talk went on. The enemy deserved little sympathy; prisoners required feeding and every mouthful of food a prisoner ate would mean one less for the soldiers' families back home. If prisoners were taken, they could not be allowed to hinder the attack in any way. On all sides, troops ready to go into action took their senior officers' nudges and winks as a licence to kill the enemy with little hesitation.

Seasoned soldiers had heard it all before and such talk washed over them; they knew what they had to do. Yet regardless of any misgivings the men might have, the anticipation was such that most simply wanted to get on with the job. As the hours ground down to zero, anxiety grew exponentially. Adrenalin and personal fears of failure or letting mates down allowed few to get any rest, let alone sleep. Each man would be wrapped up in his own thoughts. There was no chance of turning back, no option but to go on and leave fate to decide who lived and who died.

The moment of going over the top, as one soldier wrote, was like plunging into a pool of freezing water. Only as soldiers were on their way, did wretched anxiety dissipate as they were forced to focus on the job ahead. But how to describe the ensuing chaos, as men began to approach the enemy's trench where, for the first time, they might see the grey hue of a German uniform?

Private Bernard Stevenson's terse, staccato description of the fighting on 1 July 1916 gives a good impression. He was serving with the 1/7th Sherwood Foresters, also known as the Robin Hood Rifles.

We go over the top. Lieutenant Wilkins leads five platoon. 'Come on the Robins'. Out of the smoke come bullets. Someone falls dead. On we go. Thro' the German wire and into their front line trench. Our artillery has not stopped and is dropping shells near us. A red light is burned to try and stop them. Wilkins wounded in the arm. Sergeant Buckley slightly wounded, also Berry. Captain Leman sees Germans emerging from the smoke between their first and second lines. Shoots at them with his revolver. Is shot in arm and face. Germans advance with bombs from right and left. Everyone attends to himself. I tumble out of trench and see small trench just behind their wire, about six yards away. Get in this. Germans throw a bomb into it and the dirt half buries me. Lie doggo.

Driven on by fear and aggression, the violence perpetrated by both sides was unspeakable, and the vast majority of soldiers who would talk about the war, write diaries or memoirs, even those willing to impart gruesome details, still glossed over the worst features of hand-to-hand combat. One anonymous account of the aftermath of the fighting around the German stronghold known as the Quadrilateral gave, in a single sentence, some indication of the frenzied fighting that had gone on there. 'I entered their trenches later in the day,' the man wrote, 'and I saw, among the men dead, a German with a Durham pick-axe in his chest from side to side, embedded under his left arm-pit right up to the helve – surely a blow that only a Durham pitman could deal.'

Not many wrote like this but Private Frank Harris, serving with 6th King's Own Yorkshire Light Infantry, was more descriptive than most.

Here the bastards come. There are, however, many Yorkshire Light Infantry, also Durham Light Infantry, who have managed to survive, and, whilst we are famished, parched, unbelievably fatigued, plastered with muck and filth in our eyes and teeth. Whilst we are more or less resigned, light a woodbine if you have one, we accept this bloody challenge, pull our belts in, deploy, spit on our hands, and wait, for Fritz to come a little nearer . . . This lot though, pal, sure hate our guts as we hate theirs. Maybe the equivalent of our Guards, certainly tall and burly enough. They have also, like us, been taught to kill, the creed of war of course.

I was a bloody fool I suppose when I fell on top of a Boche who had just sunk his bayonet into one of my best pals a foot or so away. I lunged myself, missed, parried, then got the 'Squarehead' in the breast, but then, not content with that, followed him to ground, thumbs gouging at his throat until a bloke dragged me away. 'You can only kill the bastards once,' he observed. I shot a glance at my pal, with a penetrated artery, undoubtedly no chance, gave the Boche some boot, and resumed the melee, and what a ghastly bloody business it was.

Clearing trenches was mayhem but it was organised mayhem, and techniques for doing so were developed and perfected: bombs round the next corner of the trench and, following the explosions, a dart round the traverse by the bayonet men to finish off anyone resisting or not. Soldiers would systematically work their way down the line as the enemy fought to the last, attempted to surrender or took flight over the top back to the next line of trenches. The murderous trade of taking and consolidating the trench was assumed by men who, by their training, were automatons in action, temporarily devoid of humanity. They had to be; circumstances demanded it.

Guy Chapman, an officer with the Royal Fusiliers, recalled an incident in which an enemy officer was killed after offering a pair of field glasses to a sergeant as a token of surrender. The sergeant took the glasses, thanked the officer, then shot him through the head, killing him instantly. A fellow officer of Chapman's witnessed the shooting and was at a loss what to do.

'I don't see that you can do anything,' Chapman cautioned the officer. 'He must have been half mad with excitement by the time he got into that trench. I don't suppose he ever thought what he was doing. If you start a man killing, you can't turn him off again like an engine. After all, he is a good man.'

But now and again something would happen that would bring a man to his senses, something completely out of the ordinary. Private Percy Clare of the 7th East Surrey Regiment had waited for the barrage to lift from the German trenches before he and his comrades rose to their feet and advanced with levelled bayonets.

The resistance was greater than one would have expected after such a pounding from our artillery. In the portion of trench that I entered I found two stricken Huns very badly wounded from our shellfire. One was about 48–50 years of age I guessed; the other a mere boy possibly 20 years, bearing a remarkable resemblance to the other. I next noticed that their hands were interlocked as though they had determined to die together. It was easy to see that they were father and son, and deep compassion for them took possession of me. It distressed me to see them in such a case. In spite of the entreaty of our C.O., voicing higher commands, to show no mercy, I felt as sorry for them as I should had they been my own friends instead of my enemies. I would have stayed by them had it been possible to see that they were spared and handed over to our stretcher-bearers.

The faces of those two fellows, so ghastly white, their features livid and quivering, their eyes so full of pain, horror and terror, perhaps each on account of the other. Their breasts were bare showing horrible gaping wounds which without doubt were mortal. One or two of our fellows passing by raised their bayonets as if to thrust them through when their cries for mercy were truly piteous. Plenty of men could be found who never bayoneted any but wounded Germans, and I stood for a few moments restraining any who in the lust of killing, and having in mind our C.O.'s lecture, might thrust them through. Poor fellows, they were doomed. I had to go forward.

The third German trench was some way ahead, and our wave of attackers had dwindled so that reinforcement was necessary. This was effected by combing in half the moppers-up wave behind us. One of these was a man named Bean, a butcher by trade. I discovered from him that he had come across those two poor wounded Huns in mopping up and had thrust them both through the abdomen with his bayonet, not even troubling to see that he had really put an immediate end to their miseries. My indignation consumed me, and friends though we had been I told him what I thought of it and from this moment we had no use for each other. I told him he would never survive this action; that I didn't believe God would suffer so cowardly and cruel a deed to go unpunished. Bean himself was killed on 3 May, and it was I who first discovered his body.

Often the first Germans anyone saw were those who, half stupefied by the bombardment, robbed of all will to fight, surrendered tamely as their trenches were approached. Private Albert Andrews of the 19th Manchester Regiment watched as dozens ran through the advancing Tommies, hands in the air, desperate to reach Allied lines and captivity. Those Germans who stayed to fight, shooting until the last moment before throwing up their hands, were usually given short shrift. There were no rules of war, no rights of the prisoner in these moments. Individuals chose in their own maddened state whether prisoners would be accepted. Private Andrews jumped into the front-line German trench, or, rather, what was left of it.

Just near a dugout door there was a big barrel. As soon as I jumped in, a German leapt from behind the barrel but I was already on my guard and I had my bayonet on his chest. He was trembling and looked half mad with his hands above his head, saying something to me which I did not understand. All I could make out was that he did not want me to kill him! It was here I noticed my bayonet was broken and I couldn't have stuck him with it. Of course, I had 'one up the chimney' as we called it – that is, a bullet in the breech, so that you only have to press your trigger. I pointed to his belt and bayonet. He took these off, and his hat and water bottle as well, emptied his pockets and offered the lot to me. Just then one of my mates was coming up the trench. 'Get out of the way, Andy. Leave him to me. I'll give him one to himself,' he meant he would throw a bomb at him, which would have blown him to pieces. 'Come here,' I said. He was on his knees in front of me now, fairly plead-ing. I said, 'He's an old man', he looked sixty. At the finish I pointed my thumb upwards towards our lines, never taking my bayonet off his chest. He jumped up and with his hands above his head ran out of the trench towards our lines, calling all the time. He was trem-bling from head to foot and frightened to death. I honestly believe he could have done me as I jumped into the trench if he had not been so afraid.

Given the intense nature of trench fighting, soldiers' encoun-ters with the enemy were necessarily brief. An incident might impress itself on the mind, but rarely did individual combat last more than seconds and took longer in the retelling that it did in the event. Private Ginger Byrne was an exception, his one-sided meeting with the enemy lasting most of the day. After going into action near the German-held village of Beaumont Hamel, he had been forced to take refuge in a shell hole close to the enemy wire but, in doing so, was spotted by a German machine-gunner. Byrne lay there with the ammunition boxes he was carrying and just four inches of earth above his head as protection.

> I lay as I fell because I daren't move. I had my legs folded under me and my bloomin' bayonet was on my left-hand side. I was dying to move that bayonet out of the way so I could get my hip down lower. But that Jerry decided he hadn't anything better to do than play his gun across my shell-hole. He knew I wasn't hit. I knew what he was doing. I was a machine gunner myself, wasn't I? He'd be holding the two handles of his gun, then he'd tap, tap so it played right across the top of the hole; then he'd turn the wheel at the bottom to lower the barrel and then he'd tap, tap the other side to bring it back again. He was hitting the dust just above my head and he smashed the bloomin' boxes. Bits of ammo flew about everywhere. In a queer sort of way I was lying there almost admiring what he was doing, as though it wasn't me he was aiming at. He was a fellow machine-gunner, wasn't he? And he certainly knew his job. But he just couldn't get that trajectory low enough.

As it was summertime, Byrne had to wait fourteen hours for darkness as the German machine-gunner kept 'nagging away', firing just over the hole. 'Sometimes he'd stop for a bit and turn the gun on someone else; but he'd got right fond of me. Wasted a lot of ammo on me that Jerry did.' When it was dark, Byrne crawled, then ran, across no-man's-land and escaped the carnage. He was entirely uninjured.

While in action, it was not always easy to discern the ebb and flow of battle. Men saw only what was within instant comprehension; there was no standing about surveying the ground. Normally, shelter was, as in Byrne's example, a shell hole from which observation was limited, or the inside of a trench, in which case the fighting was immediate and the wider context of who was winning or losing of practical irrelevance.

Under such circumstances, it was possible to take prisoners when it was in fact the enemy who was gaining the upper hand. One extraordinary incident took place as a platoon of the 1/6th Seaforth Highlanders was involved in the second assault on Beaumont Hamel, in November 1916. With his platoon, Second Lieutenant George Edwards was given the special job of capturing a battalion headquarters. Despite persistent fog, Edwards worked his way round to the objective, surprising and taking prisoner a large number of the Germans without opposition. The headquarters was in a deep dugout and the men surrendered when told that there were strong reinforcements at hand. These, however, failed to materialise and Edwards's platoon was heavily outnumbered.

The story of what happened next was told by Edwards to General Burn and a fellow officer back at brigade headquarters. Edwards was killed in November 1917 but his story, as related by a fellow officer, was not forgotten.

The German Commanding Officer told him [Edwards] quite nicely and politely that the position was reversed and that he and his men were now the prisoners. There was nothing for it but to submit and Edwards accompanied the C.O. down into the dugout. Here he was given a drink, treated with every consideration and even invited to look through the periscope – a huge affair which gave its owners a commanding view of the surrounding country.

It was then, the fog having lifted somewhat, that Edwards spotted the arrival of the long expected reinforcements. Not to be outdone in courtesy by his German hosts he begged them to consider themselves once more as his prisoners and, as such, to accompany him to the surface. This they did, only to find on arrival that they were called upon to surrender for a third time – on this occasion by a chaplain and a party of Dublin Fusiliers.

Edwards went up to the Chaplain to explain the situation; the Chaplain promptly knocked him down and disappeared in the fog with his captives.

Critical to the process of being taken prisoner was making a connection with the prospective captor and the act of surrender unequivocal. It was vital that the would-be prisoner made himself appear unthreatening, that he was just as much an ordinary family man, sick of war, and not the stereotypical enemy of propaganda. Holding up a crucifix or pictures of wives and children helped, as did removing the paraphernalia of war, such as a helmet, although with so many bits and pieces flying around this was in itself a calculated risk. Conversely, hands in the air but eyes that glistened hatred or aggression was a stance unlikely to gain much other than a bullet, as indeed would shooting until the moment when defence was no longer tenable, then calling out 'Kamerad'.

Emptying pockets, offering gifts, bought time for prisoners during which fever-pitch tension might ease. Chapman's friend was morally shocked at the shooting of the German officer because, in handing over his field glasses, the unspoken transaction of turning a soldier into a prisoner was seemingly cemented. And in just the same way that transactions are completed by the shaking of hands, so it was astute, if possible, to make physical contact too, as Lieutenant Bradford Gordon, of the 9th Kings Own Yorkshire Light Infantry witnessed, when one haggard-looking German surrendered to him.

Several of my men were about to stick him with their bayonets, but he had been badly wounded in the face, and was unarmed, so I stopped them. Seeing this, he tried to shake my hand, and said

'Kamerad'. But I shook him off, and searched him . . . When he understood he was not to be killed, his gratitude was extraordinary. As I would not shake hands, he insisted on shaking hands with a Somerset, who, a few minutes before, had been about to bayonet him.

During the fighting around the Somme village of Lesbœufs, Guardsman Norman Cliff was also approached by a German who offered his hand, though whether Cliff took it is not clear from his memoirs. What helped broker the German's surrender was his excellent English.

As our section advanced across open country with bullets whistling around we sighted a machine gun post, and as we cautiously drew nearer, the German team sprang to their feet, threw up their hands and came forward led by a young officer with an Iron Cross dangling from his chest. Automatically we lowered our rifles and the officer held out his hand, and in English asked us to accept his surrender.

'Where did you learn your English?' I asked.

'In London where I worked,' he replied.

I was struck by his dignity in a desperate situation, and there was no question of butchering them. Realising that he and his team were to be spared, he burst out, addressing me: 'You've been so decent to us I would like to present you with this,' indicating his Iron Cross.

'No! You must have done something fine to get it, and I wouldn't dream of taking it from you.'

Suddenly one of our young officers and a sergeant appeared, and the officer yelled: 'What's going on here? Send those Huns to the rear immediately!' Then, noticing the Iron Cross, he exclaimed: 'Oh, Sergeant, he's got an Iron Cross. I want that!' Whereupon the Sergeant snatched the medal from the German's chest, kicked him in the backside and prodded the group like cattle towards the rear.

I felt ashamed and could not refrain from comparing the disgust-
ing behaviour of this perhaps untypical British gentleman with
the good manners of the 'uncivilized Hun'.

A soldier's status as prisoner was never entirely secure and
making oneself as useful as possible was a good idea. Cliff watched
at Lesboufs how a number of Germans 'surprised and relieved not
to be bayoneted, helped to buttress the captured trenches'. It
was, he claimed, 'one of the few occasions when live Germans
were calculated to be better than dead ones'. Such impressed
work was illegal but who was there to argue? At the fighting at
Gommecourt on 1 July 1916, the Regimental Sergeant Major of
the 1/5th Sherwood Foresters was captured deep in the enemy
lines when Germans unexpectedly emerged from a dugout. He
testified that the Germans set him to work carrying bombs from
a dugout to the Germans in the front line. With self-preservation
in mind, the RSM did as ordered until he seized an opportunity
to jump over the top and make a dash for a shell hole where he
lay until dark before regaining his own lines and telling the story
to the Commanding Officer. More generally, prisoners were ready
to tend or dress enemy wounded, and were quite happy to be
given a stretcher case to carry so that both patient and prisoner
could extricate themselves from the battlefield. Those who stood
on their dignity and refused to help were being foolish in the
extreme.

When Lieutenant Richard Hawkins was badly wounded in the
fighting near Boom Ravine on the Somme, he was removed to a
Advanced Dressing Station where his wounds were dressed. A
number of German prisoners were milling about and three were
ordered by the doctor to take the corners of the stretcher and carry
Lieutenant Hawkins away. As the men went to the stretcher, the
doctor looked around for a fourth man and spotted a young
German officer whom he ordered to help; the officer refused.
Speaking English, the man told the doctor that it was not his job

as an officer to take hold of a stretcher with three private soldiers. This may have been strictly true, but it was not advisable to say so. The doctor ordered the officer again but once more the man refused. Richard Hawkins looked on from his stretcher.

> Doctor Sale was a pretty busy man. He was also a very good rugby three-quarter and he stuck his boot into this fellow's behind and he took off. They started to go round in a very big circle, down in the shell holes, and up the other side, the doctor launching a kick at this officer every few yards and missing practically every time because of the impossible state of the ground. In the end, dear old Sale caught him and kicked his backside several more times, after which the officer decided he would take the end of the stretcher after all.

There was another option for prisoners and that was to curry favour with useful information. Colonel Roger Tempest, commanding the Scots Guards at Flers, in September 1916, recalled taking his four company commanders to a trench on the crest of a low hill to show them the line of advance. Once there, the men met a German officer who willingly pointed out the spire of Lesboufs church, 'and so', wrote Tempest, 'we were able to advance with the definite knowledge that we were advancing in the right direction'. In another example, a German prisoner volunteered to show where the enemy had mined a road along which British troops were about to walk.

And then the prisoners were led away. The greatest threats to their survival were the actions either of a madman (one captured Australian private watched in horror as a German ran up and threw grenades among a party of twenty-five assembled prisoners), or the effects of desultory shelling from either side. Otherwise, with every step away from the trenches, so the chance of survival grew. Prisoners might be verbally assaulted or kicked, but they were rarely attacked.

Battalion stretcher-bearers recovered the wounded. When an assault completely failed, whether a large raid or full-blown attack, the opposing lines remained the same, leaving the wounded in a precarious position in no-man's-land. Rescue was unlikely, or more likely impossible, until dark, and then with the dark came every possibility that stricken men would be overlooked. The wounded might be forced to make their own way back if they were able, but soldiers on both sides, battle-worn and unforgiving, were likely to have a potshot at any movement between opposing trenches.

Just occasionally, temporary truces were organised to give both sides a chance to collect casualties before, at a given time or signal, war recommenced. The Christmas Truce of 1914 began in part so that the dead could be picked up and given proper burial; fraternisation was often a result not a precursor of this cooperation. Since then, there had been other occasions when pity for the wounded overrode any desire by one side to capitalise on a local advantage. After a disastrous night attack by the Germans, one unknown private left an account of how the enemy had been given permission to venture out over the top.

We shouted to the Allemands to come and fetch their wounded. At first they seemed very dubious and would only show their helmets but we promised not to shoot and a man who wore the iron cross advanced boldly to our entanglements and proceeded to assist a wounded man. Another followed and, amidst our cheers, they carried him off. Before going, the first man saluted and said, 'Thank you, gentlemen, one and all. I thank you very much. Good day.' The incident quite upset me for a time and I wished that we might all be friends again.

The costly fighting on the first day of the Battle of the Somme left not hundreds but thousands of wounded caught between opposing lines. Only in one sector, on the southern flank of the advance, did British troops make real progress, allowing relatively easy recovery of casualties. Everywhere else, the lines were much as they had been before the attack. In the north, around the villages of Gommecourt, Serre and Beaumont Hamel, a number of uncoordinated armistices were brokered on the second day, and this time it was the Germans who permitted the retrieval of wounded.

Londoner Harry Siepmann, the young artillery officer of German descent encountered earlier, had arrived on the Somme opposite the enemy-held village of Serre. His battery had been party to a curious unspoken armistice with the Germans in which Serre had been left alone by British artillery, in exchange for German artillery restraint within the British-held village of Colincamps. 'Such an arrangement was easily made by a short period of exact and immediate retaliation [i.e. a brief bombardment]: once made, it was faithfully observed,' wrote Siepmann.

The infantry failure opposite Serre was total, and next morning Siepmann was able to see from his observation post German snipers picking off British wounded held fast in the enemy wire; by this time it was probably a mercy. Then, suddenly, he saw two men climb out of the British front-line trench; they weren't even carrying a white flag.

A stretcher was then passed up to them and they proceeded to carry it ploddingly into no man's land. Hundreds, perhaps thousands, of eyes must have been upon them, and all firing of any sort ceased. Complete, uncanny silence descended like a pall, as the two men trudged steadily on and stopped beside a body lying on the ground. They lifted it onto a stretcher and plodded slowly back, the way they had come. The silence remained unbroken until they were safe, and then the war was resumed.

This singular act of courage relied on the stretcher-bearers' belief, however wishful, that two men on a self-evident mission of mercy would not be attacked. Elsewhere, such pauses in the fighting lasted for many hours as men from both sides ventured out to collect casualties: it was reported by those who took part that there was little or no fraternisation.

At Gommecourt, a couple of miles to the north of Serre, the fighting had been ferocious. British troops had entered the German trenches and fought for most of the day, but in vain. As the Germans brought reinforcements, the British troops were slowly but surely driven back from deep inside enemy lines until the last few were forced to retire to their original trenches. Dead and wounded lay all over the place. Early on 2 July, the Germans raised a large Red Cross flag, and one hour's truce was arranged. German parties were seen to leave the trenches and attend to the wounded in no-man's-land. Stretcher-bearers from the British front line then went out and brought in many more with the assistance of men of the enemy's 2nd Reserve Guards Division.

Immediately to the south of Serre, at Beaumont Hamel, stretcher-bearers from both sides could be seen in no-man's-land. Here, however, a truce was forbidden but had gone ahead in any case. Lieutenant Colonel John Hall, commanding the 16th Middlesex Regiment, had been part of the initial wave that had gone over the top and been badly cut up.

> About 2.30 p.m. the enemy raised a white flag on his front line, and sent over stretcher-bearers to no man's land; in addition to helping our wounded, he no doubt was helping himself to the machine guns, Lewis guns, rifles etc lying about close to his front line. This was reported to the Brigade by telephone, and permission requested to send out our stretcher-bearers to bring in our wounded. Permission was refused (I believe from higher authority), and instead instructions were issued to fire on the enemy's stretcher-bearers. These instructions were not acted on with any

enthusiasm by our riflemen in the front line. Shortly after, our heavy artillery opened fire presumably meant for the enemy's front line . . . Thereafter, whilst daylight lasted the enemy was reported as firing on any wounded man in NML who showed the slightest movement.

Hall's account of the truce is poignant. Scores of men were pinned down, mostly in shell holes. Given the topography of the immediate ground, the Germans were able to look down over the entire position. Rescues were by night, and only wounded men not too enfeebled to call out had any real chance of discovery.

Another who witnessed the truce at Beaumont Hamel was Captain William Carden-Roe, of the 1st Royal Irish Fusiliers, a very British name for an officer who had in fact changed his surname from Liesching, presumably to disguise his German roots. That was in March 1916, by which time he had already won the Military Cross.

Carden-Roe records that a truce took place on 4 July when wounded survivors of that first day's assault still 'dotted' no-man's-land. A bold scheme, he wrote, was the only one that could save them after such a lapse in time.

Accordingly a large Red Cross flag was brought up to the front line trench and then slowly elevated above the parapet, its bearers still remaining under cover. When, after a few minutes, no shots were fired, two Medical Officers scrambled on the parapet on either side of the flag. Still the enemy held their fire, and so after a short pause the two officers advanced across No Man's Land with the bearers of the flag between them. By this time a mass of curious heads appeared above the parapet of the German trench and a German officer wearing a Red Cross brassard and carrying a white handkerchief tied to a walking stick, hastily sprang out of their lines and advanced across to meet the British party.

He was followed closely by several others all presumably of the
Medical Corps. It was an impressive sight. He waited until our
party had come as far as he considered fit, then raised his hand
signalling them to halt. The parties of both sides stiffened to a
ceremonious salute, following which he commenced to point out
all the wounded lying close to our lines. A signal from our two
Medical Officers brought forwards several stretcher parties, who at
once set about their task. At the same time German parties carried
wounded who had been lying close to the parapet of the German
trench as far as the middle of No Man's Land. Here they were
carried off by the British bearers. And so this great work of humanity went on until all that could be found were carried back to their
new chance of life. It was an impressive sight. Throughout the
afternoon, not a word was exchanged between the two great enemy
Nations. At last it all came to an end. The German officers gravely
saluted and turned about; the British officers returned the salute
with a feeling of gratitude.

It is probably this second truce that was photographed by a
German soldier, showing not only that Germans were roaming
around unmolested, but that British troops were, too. In one
photograph, a British soldier can be seen standing unarmed close
to the German lines. Although against orders, this localised truce
ensured that on this occasion common sense prevailed.

After a battle, the temptation to collect souvenirs was often
overwhelming. It was an age-old tradition and in this regard officers were no different from other ranks in their keenness for items of
symbolic value. Seven months before he was wounded, Lieutenant
Richard Hawkins and his battalion, 11th Royal Fusiliers, had done
exceptionally well on the first day of the Battle of the Somme, and
where they had gone over the top success had come quickly and at
relatively little cost. The gains secured, Hawkins and fellow officers went to see what they could find before the Divisional
Commander arrived to congratulate the men.

General Maxse came to see us. 'Morning, gentlemen, damn good show, thank you very much, you did very well. Marvellous. Tell me, where would you expect to find a group of officers congregated together in the middle of the biggest battle there has ever been?' 'Ooh,' we thought, 'now wait a minute.' 'I'll tell you,' he said, 'walking about on the skyline looking for souvenirs! I saw them through my field glasses.' Well, there wasn't anything else to do, all was peace and quietness where we were and I managed to pick up a marvellous German pickelhaube [helmet].

Some men disdained taking personal property from the dead, but not many. Private Stephen Graham believed even the 'best' men in his battalion rarely shied away from taking belongings which might otherwise remain with the dead. As a result of this, items of no value or interest such as pocket books and letters were pulled from the bodies of the dead and thrown to the winds, 'literally to the winds,' wrote Graham, 'for when the wind rose they blew about like dead leaves. There were photographs, too, prints of wife and sweetheart, of mother, or perchance of baby born whilst father was at the war – the priceless, worthless possessions . . .' Graham watched one gunner from a 60-pounder battery 'grubbily but methodically' examining the corpses of German machine-gunners, hoping to find a revolver. 'I watched him examine one without success and he gave the dead body a kick. "The dirty bastard," said he, as if he were accusing the corpse. "Somebody's bin 'ere before me."'

Souveniring was not risk-free. Feigning death was a ploy used by soldiers when their position was overrun, in the expectation either that their own troops might counter-attack and retake the lost ground or that when relative peace was restored they could slip back to their own lines or chance surrendering to the enemy when surrender might be more readily accepted.

Driver Ernest Reader of the Royal Field Artillery was following up the British advance close to High Wood on the Somme. Tanks had been used for the first time in action and, taken by surprise, the Germans had been pushed back over a mile leaving the hitherto lethal ground quiet and passable.

As I stood there holding the horses with the battle getting further and further away, but still plainly visible, and with piles, literally piles, of German dead all around me, a thought occurred. What about a souvenir? Now report had it that the German snipers used to creep out at night over our lines and pinch the cap badge from any of their day's victims, these were subsequently put on their belts as trophies, rather like a Red Indian with his scalp. What a souvenir that would be if only I could get hold of one. I'd never have a better chance. Leading the horses and turning over the dead with my boot, I searched. Then Chunky [a friend] emerged from a German dugout with a box of cigars and a bottle of wine. 'Here, hold these while I look for some more.' With revolver at the ready he again disappeared down a German dugout. I continued my search until I spotted a lone figure, a right Prussian looking bugger he was too, close cropped hair, a pig face and a fat neck. In falling, his tunic had rolled back disclosing a belt fairly loaded with badges. Mine, I thought triumphantly. Wedging the box of cigars under my arm, through which I had also slipped the reins, and putting the wine uneasily in a pocket, I stretched my other hand down and undid the clasp. Then I had to really tug to get it away from his bulk.

Now that perisher had only been shamming dead and was probably aiming to be taken prisoner, but the idea of losing his belt to a mere stripling was too much. He rose, a mighty figure with a roar of rage and made for me. What could I do? One hand and arm holding the reins and cigars and the other his belt. I had no intention of letting either go although it looked as though I might lose the lot with my life thrown in for good measure. It was no time for niceties, anyway I was unarmed, so I kicked him hard in the groin. My boot had a sole over half an inch thick and was steel shod. It doubled him up. I don't know what the follow up might have been had not Chunky arrived at the psychological moment and blown the chap's brains out. 'Have you taken leave of your senses? With all the dead lying around you have to pick out the biggest alive one to search for a souvenir.' That was Chunky, no reference to the fact that he had just saved my life. The German belt had stamped on the buckle 'Gott Mit Uns' so presumably wherever he was bound for he was alright.

By the taking of souvenirs, the body was often robbed of the one piece of information that might afford the remains a decent burial in a named grave. It is understandable that men hardened to the realities of war would not think twice about taking possessions from the dead when life itself was placed at such low value, particularly enemy dead. A valuable ring, an engraved watch would be looted by someone else so, with that knowledge, it was easy to justify getting in there first.

In early 1916, Jenny Felton received a pocket book containing the last will and testament of her dead husband, Corporal Alfred Felton. Felton, the London building contractor serving with the 9th East Surrey Regiment, was reported missing during the attack made at Loos in September 1915, the same attack in which Captain Wilfred Birt had been mortally wounded.

Felton's body had been found by a German soldier named Heine, who took the pocket book. Quite what Heine intended to do with it is an open question. Had he in fact killed Felton and, in the 'time-honoured' tradition of seeking a victor's trophy, simply appropriated the book? Was it a souvenir taken from a body he happened to stumble across or did he intend to return it to the family? Whatever the answer, Heine took it to the grave for he was killed shortly afterwards and his property, including

Felton's pocket book, was sent to his wife, Frau Berta Heine, living in Schönebeck on the River Elbe.

It was Frau Heine who forwarded the last will and testament to Jenny Felton, via the United States Legation, asking for reimbursement of the two marks eighty pfennigs postal charges. These were met from a relief fund with a conveyance of thanks from the Felton family for Frau Heine's 'kindly action'. Did Jenny Felton ever understand that Heine might, in fact, have cost her husband the dignity of a known grave? Felton's body was never identified and he is remembered on the Loos Memorial to the Missing.

The Reverend Montague Bere, a member of the Army's Chaplain Department, was working at a Casualty Clearing Station (CCS) ward when he overheard a heated argument between a man from Exeter and another from Scotland on the 'propriety' of bayoneting prisoners in cold blood.

> The Jock thought that he ought to be allowed to 'do in' all the prisoners and that any interference with this meritorious desire was uncalled for. The Devonian was more soft hearted and maintained that a defenceless man had rights to clemency although he might be a Jerry. I left them to settle the matter remarking that each well-treated prisoner encouraged others to surrender, and that the more surrenders there were the sooner they both would be in Blighty.

The soldiers' diverse social and economic backgrounds and the experience of war each endured, and sometimes enjoyed, affected them in distinctive ways. There were those who lost brothers or close friends and who habitually took revenge, swearing undying hatred for the enemy, never to be reconciled. There were others who were able to be dispassionate: Ginger Byrne, who witnessed the wounded being picked off by German snipers, remained matter-of-fact about his enemy and not embittered. Many soldiers were the same. Private Arthur Wrench, of the 1/4th Seaforth Highlanders, was in the village of Mailly-Maillet, a couple of miles behind the lines at Beaumont Hamel. After the village was taken by his division, the walking wounded began to stream by, including two men who caught Wrench's attention. He saw:

> . . . a wounded kilty of the Argylls walking arm in arm with a wounded German. As they passed the coffee stall there, one man ran out with a cup of coffee which he handed to the Argyll. He in turn handed it to his stricken companion after which they limped on their way together smiling. Enemies an hour ago, but friends in their common troubles. After all, this war is not a personal affair.

The Reverend Bere had arrived in France in March 1916 and had met many wounded soldiers from both sides, including two from the aftermath of a fight in which a British Tommy had 'stuck a knife into the shoulder of a Fritz' during hand-to-hand combat. 'The Tommy was wounded too.' Both men arrived at the Casualty Clearing Station in the same ambulance, 'smoking each other's cigarettes on the way'.

His interest in human nature was well observed and varied. On another occasion he watched 'a curious scene' from the door of his CCS billet.

> Outside one of the wards stands a group of men, walking wounded, English, Scots and Boches. They are on the best of terms and are probably fighting over again the 'stunt' in which some of them took and others were taken prisoner. The 'feld grau' [field grey] predominates over the khaki, and one independent Hun is wandering about the graveyard looking at the inscriptions on the crosses. There is a lightly wounded confectioner from Berlin. He appreciates the white bread and is astounded at his treatment, having

been told by his officers that 'if the English took you, you were "so gut wie todt"' (as good as dead).

Lieutenant Henry Jones, of the Army Service Corps, was intrigued by the absence of malice. In a letter home dated 8 August 1916, he described to his family how, in a village, German prisoners helped shovel refuse into army wagons before taking the refuse to a dump.

> It is a daily occurrence to see a Boche mount up on the box beside the English driver, and off they go – often the Boche can speak English – chatting merrily as if there had never been a war. I have even seen Tommy hand over the reins to his captive, who cheerfully takes them and drives the wagon to its destination, while the real driver sits back with folded arms. This will show you how far the British soldier cultivates the worship of Hate.

It was the nature of a bitterly fought war that most men remained enemies in life and friends only in death, an insight despondently appreciated by soldiers on the Western Front. Guardsman Norman Cliff understood. Passing a large shell hole, he saw two decomposing bodies lying side by side both facing the sky. 'As we passed it became clear that one was a British soldier, the other a German. They lay hand in hand, as though reconciled in mutual agony and in the peace of death. The tragic significance of it plunged me into a whirlwind of conflicting emotions as we marched silently on.'

Scots Guards officer Captain Henry Dundas pondered over the same thoughts in January 1917 as he walked among British graves at Corbie, a cemetery behind the Somme lines. He had seen the grave of Major William La Touche Congreve VC, DSO, MC, one of the most decorated, celebrated and youthful casualties of the war, when his eye was caught by a desolate plot of ground. It 'was a forgotten, uncared for patch beneath which were buried five or six Germans who had died in hospital. Poor Fritz Kolner of the 2nd Grenadier Regiment: I can pity him almost as much as John Macdonald of the Clyde RGA, who lies a few feet off. It is impossible to blame the individual for the sins of the nation, even though the nation is merely a collection of individuals. That is why all wars are so hateful.'

7

Between a Rock and a Hard Place

The Germans truly began to feel the economic squeeze in 1917. British-born Princess Evelyn Blücher, whose private journal captured the public excitement and bravado in the first months of the war, began to note the shortage of necessities in Berlin, from the absence of fuel to the scarcity of food. Bread dough was adulterated with potato and root vegetables such as turnips: later it would be mixed with sawdust. The era of the *Ersatz* (substitute) and *Strecken* (stretch) food had arrived. Coffee, the favourite non-alcoholic drink in Germany, was increasingly made from chicory, grain and acorns, while foliage from trees or bushes was used instead of tea leaves. Milk and beer were watered down.

As early as March 1916, small-scale disturbances had occurred over the bread ration in towns such as Wittenberg, but they had taken place shortly after the opening of the Germans' great Verdun Offensive and well before the Battle of the Somme. It was the cost of these battles that proved ruinous not only to the German army but also to the economy.

In August 1916, the German army's High Command launched its all-out campaign for industrial mobilisation. It was called the Hindenburg Programme to help boost its chances of success, and wooden effigies of the Field Marshal were erected all over the country, and plastered with cheques and cash given by civilians still willing to invest in war bonds. In Berlin, at the top of the Siegesallee, a gigantic wooden statue of the great man was raised on a platform. Contributors to the German Red Cross were permitted to climb some stairs to hammer in nails of gold, silver or iron, the colour of the nail reflecting each individual's generosity: so many were gold that the statue became known as the 'Yellow God'. But, once again, the authorities were ignoring the needs of the wider economy by focusing on the army. The ambition to double industrial output would be at the expense of the civilian population: resources including horses and fuel were withdrawn from agriculture to aid an expansion in munitions. Greater food shortages and higher prices were the result.

The public mood was changing, as Princess Blücher observed. A virulent fungus infected that year's potato harvest, destroying nearly 50 per cent of a crop that was an indispensable part of the German diet, particularly for poorer families. And when the bitterly cold European winter of 1916–17 struck, one of the worst in living memory, she witnessed public morale faltering as hunger and cold took their toll.

> The heroic attitude has entirely disappeared. Now one sees faces like masks, blue with cold and drawn by hunger, with the harassed expression common to all those who are continually speculating as to the possibility of another meal.
>
> All labour resources are being organised for military purposes, which means that every man will be called upon to serve his country in some way, and even those who were passed as physically unfit a few months ago are now being trained for military service.

Government rationing affected everybody, including the Reverend Henry Williams. His food coupons were valid for Berlin only, throwing him on the mercy of civilians once he left the city to visit prisoners of war. 'My prisoner-friends, who usually guessed that I could do with a meal, gave me food wrapped up in newspaper before leaving the camp.' This food he ate in secret as civilians would quickly discern the relative quality of English food and arrest him as a spy.

I can see myself now, as soon as I had left a camp out of sight, looking around me for somewhere to hide, and then sitting in a ditch
or behind a bush or a cow-shed greedily wolfing the contents of
my parcel. It might be only hard biscuit or harder white bread
seamed with green mouldy cracks, and a slice or two of corned
beef; but how good it always tasted . . . It was no wonder that I
began to suffer acutely from indigestion.

In Berlin, Williams was only too grateful to accept a dinner
invitation especially as his host had procured a rabbit, 'a rare
luxury'. Only later did his host ask if he had suspected anything.
'You seemed rather sniffy about that rabbit of mine', she said
before confessing that the rabbit was in fact an old tom-cat.

'Another day I was walking along a main street off
Charlottenburg and passing a baker's shop I noticed a disagreeable
smell coming up through a grating outside the window,' wrote
Williams. 'I thought "I wonder what on earth they are making the
bread of today!" Glancing in the window, my eye fell upon a placard there displayed; it ran "Highest prices paid for
potato-peelings".'

The public's expectation of easy victory had long since evapo-
rated, and now, perhaps, people were beginning to question
whether victory would come at all, and if it did, at what cost. The
population began to blame the government for perceived inade-
quacies in food distribution. Soup kitchens became a common
sight on German city streets and when a nutritionist undertook
that winter to live for six months off the official ration, his weight
plummeted from 76½kg to 57½kg.

One thing that did surprise Princess Blücher was the attitude
of Germans to the British. Since the Battle of the Somme, feelings
had 'veered round', she discovered. 'Men who were scoffing and
railing at England twelve months ago are beginning to express
their admiration, and even dare to display a certain affection and
attachment publicly.' British and German troops had slugged it

out for five months on the Somme, and yet German forces had been driven back. Although retreat was dressed up in the newspapers as an 'elastic bend' in the line, the Princess noted, there was no suppressing the stories brought home by soldiers wounded or on leave. British and Empire troops were in the ascendancy, not least in their use of artillery fire, the weight of which was fearsome and demoralising.

Princess Blücher's opinion was just one individual's view, and from a member of the privileged classes at that. But she was also perceptive. Had she correctly spotted a genuine shift in German attitudes to the war? If so, it was a change that would have profound repercussions for German politicians and the German High Command: it would mean that the ire once directed at the British was turning on them.

In the skies above the Western Front, an air war raged. Portrayed in the press then and since as a chivalrous campaign, such a description, if it were ever true, was by 1917 inaccurate and naive. In reality, chivalry, and its associated traits such as honour and courtesy, was impractical and irrelevant to young men whose survival was tenuous. These officer pilots, fêted as 'knights of the air', were, by force of circumstance, ruthless and gritty killers.

The ultimate aim of fighter pilots was air superiority, preventing the enemy's observation planes from overlooking the battlefield and passing back intelligence on, among other things, troop movements and artillery dispositions. If accurately collected, this information could prove key to inflicting heinous losses on the enemy, even hastening a tactical defeat. This fact was reason enough for an absence of latitude or humanity in combat, and was as strategic a consideration to a pilot as his natural inclination for self-preservation. Fighter ace Captain James McCudden understood this implicitly: his success was not down to flying skill alone. 'One cannot afford to be sentimental when one has to do one's job of killing and going on killing,' he wrote in 1918.

Such single-minded focus had the power to startle even him.

> It seems all very strange to me, but whilst fighting Germans I have always looked upon a German aeroplane as a machine that has got to be destroyed, and at times when I have passed quite close to a Hun machine and have had a good look at the occupant, the thought has often struck me: 'By Jove! There is a man in it.' This may sound queer, but it is quite true.

So close did planes come to each other as they spiralled and twisted in the air that pilots' recollections of combat included remarkably detailed descriptions of the enemy. McCudden recalled one German pilot who, by half-rolling his aircraft, passed a few feet below his own.

> I saw the pilot look upwards; and it struck me that he did not seem the least perturbed, as I should have expected him to be . . . That Hun was a good one, for every time I got behind him he turned upside down and passed out underneath me. I well remember looking at him too. He seemed only a boy.

Aerial killing could never be entirely dispassionate. Down below, in and around the trenches, the war was different inasmuch as artillery and machine-gun fire were responsible for a vastly disproportionate number of deaths in comparison to individually targeted rifle fire and the bayonet. By contrast, aerial combat was as personal as it could be: a one-on-one duel to the death and a likely plummet to earth for the loser.

Pilots flew without parachutes. Not, as is popularly assumed, because it was feared they would jump at the first sign of difficulty, but because parachutes were bulky, heavy and entirely unsuited for tight cockpits. Pilots did everything they could to make their aircraft lighter and faster. Even if parachutes could be worn, deploying one would be tricky at any time and highly problematic from a spinning, burning aircraft. To have any chance, a pilot had to remain with his plane even when it had lost power and was badly damaged. The alternative was to bail out to certain death.

Lieutenant Patrick O'Brien, a pilot with 66 Squadron, Royal Flying Corps (RFC), believed that the worst scenario came once an aircraft was fully alight. Then it took less than a minute for the fabric to burn off the wings, at which point the plane dropped 'like an arrow'. In close combat O'Brien watched, albeit fleetingly, as one German aircraft hurtled past him in flames, and witnessed the look of dread on the pilot's face. 'The Hun was diving at such a sharp angle that both his wings came off.'

Destroying the enemy was all-engrossing and victory elating. And yet on those occasions when a stricken pilot was forced to leap from his falling aircraft, there was a rush of sympathy among pilots for the doomed opponent, and a feeling of sickness as he hit the ground.

'The machine went beyond the vertical and onto its back,' recalled McCudden of the finale of one engagement. 'The enemy gunner either jumped or fell out, and I saw him following the machine down, twirling round and round, all arms and legs, truly a ghastly sight.'

There was something about the lone, tumbling man that evinced sympathy from all sides. Choosing to jump rather than burn to death took guts. Julius Buckler, a German pilot serving with Jasta 17, was aghast when, strafing an aircraft of the RFC, it began to emit smoke, then burst into flames. 'Now came the most horrifying thing I have ever witnessed . . . I saw the pilot stand up – the brave man did not want to burn – preferring to leap to his death from 3,000 metres . . . I cannot describe my emotions as I watched this person plunging into the depths before my eyes.'

The grim spectacle haunted Buckler. 'I could endure

everything again if I had to, but I would not want to experience my thirteenth victory a second time.'

Death was a daily occupational hazard but respect for the vanquished was rarely found wanting. Where a plane was shot down, victorious pilots went to see the defeated pilot whenever possible, regardless of whether that man was alive or dead. One of Captain McCudden's 'kills' in October 1917 included an enemy aircraft brought down over British positions near Mazingarbe. McCudden landed immediately.

> I found the observer shot dead, but the pilot was still breathing, and so I got some Tommies to find a stretcher in order to take him to hospital, but the poor fellow died in a few minutes, for he was badly shot too. I felt very sorry indeed, for shooting a man down where you can see the results of your work . . . It makes one think when one views such an object as I was doing then.

After returning to the Squadron Mess for lunch, McCudden drove back to the crash site with Major Blomfield, the Officer Commanding the squadron. It was the wish of pilots, McCudden acknowledged, to down a German plane over British lines, in order to collect a war trophy and McCudden and his OC were keen to see what they could find. The downed plane was under guard, and as the two men approached, one of the guards handed McCudden a silk cap belonging to the pilot. There was paperwork that showed the German had only recently returned from leave in Berlin. 'We stayed by the Hun for some time, and the O.C. said that it was a pity we could not bring down Huns without this happening – alluding to the dead occupants – and I agreed . . . The Major collected what parts of the machine he wanted and we then came away, as it was getting late.'

After watching a German pilot plummet to his death, Second Lieutenant Patrick O'Brien was in combat again above the Ypres Salient. In this dogfight his squadron was outnumbered two to one. He fully expected a fate similar to that of the pilot he had seen downed in flames but, as he made a desperate sharp turn, he came upon another German plane at point-blank range.

I had the drop on him, and he knew it. His white face and startled eyes I can still see. He knew beyond question that his last moment had come, because his position prevented his taking aim at me, while my gun pointed straight at him. My first tracer-bullet passed within a yard of his head, the second looked as if it hit his shoulder, the third struck him in the neck, and then I let him have the whole works and he went down in a spinning nose dive.

In fighting, your machine is dropping all the time. I glanced at my instruments and my altitude was between eight and nine thousand feet. While I was still looking at the instruments board, a burst of bullets blew it to smithereens, [while] another bullet went through my upper lip.

Any chance of survival for such a pilot depended on the severity of his wounds and his ebbing skills to steer his plane to the ground. Despite the fact that his propeller had also been hit and the petrol tank punctured, O'Brien guided his plane down although he had no memory of landing, and awoke in an enemy artillery officers' headquarters.

A number of captured RFC pilots were so badly injured that they were exchanged, returning to Britain before the war was over. Once home they were interviewed, and related stirring accounts not only of combat but of extraordinary and heart-stopping struggles in fatally damaged aircraft. Lieutenant John Howey, an observer with 6 Squadron, was one such individual. At 10,000 feet he was attacked by two German aircraft and, from below, an anti-aircraft battery.

One of these shells burst within a very few feet of us, killing my pilot instantaneously, and breaking off half the propeller, at the same time making a large hole in the radiator. The machine commenced suddenly to nose-dive steeply to earth, with the engine full on, and vibrating terribly. I looked round and saw the pilot's head hanging over the side, with a large wound on the left of his forehead, quite dead.

As soon as I could get out of my seat, I leant over and switched the engine off (I experienced some difficulty in doing this, as the machine was spiralling as well as nose-diving). I then pushed the joy-stick back and to one side, and managed to get the machine level. I immediately stepped over the partition that divides the pilot's seat from that of the observer, and sat on the pilot's lap, taking over the controls, which were undamaged. The aeroplane then put her nose up, and her tail down, and completely lost her flying speed. She stood thus for a second, or so, and at first I thought she was going over backwards, but she tail-slid instead and managed to right herself. I immediately put her nose down and made a very fast landing.

I must have been pitched out and temporarily stunned, because I know I never climbed out of the machine, but found myself looking at a mounted German officer and several armed soldiers. I was then marched to the village of Ledeghem. A German officer gave me a photo of my machine, which I still have.

Another pilot to leave an exhilirating account of his final dogfight was Captain Francis Don. He had already served at Gallipoli in 1915 with the 1/1st Scottish Horse, and then transferred to the Royal Flying Corps. In early June 1917, he was shot down near Le Cateau.

My engine was hit at about 10,000 feet which compelled me to descend. I was attacked the whole way down. My observer and I were both wounded; one of his fingers was shot away, and he had also a wound in the arm. I was first hit on my right side, which proved a trifling wound and when within about 1,000 feet of the ground I got three or four bullets in my left arm. We landed without accident. The German pilot continued to fire on us making several dives at what was a stationary target. Fortunately we were not hit again.

Rapid improvements were made in aircraft reliability throughout the war and by 1917 planes were much more robust than the flying coffins that took to the air three years earlier. All the same, death and injury as a result of engine malfunction were common and because of this pilots would sometimes take scrunched-up newspaper or a mouthful of chewing gum to plug in-flight oil leaks. Lieutenant Duncan Grinnell-Milne was on a reconnaissance deep over enemy lines. As he and his observer set a course for home, an 'ominous knock' was heard from the engine. 'Suddenly there was a loud explosion; pieces of metal flew past my head and the machine was enveloped in a cloud of blue smoke.' The plane began to descend.

> I find it almost impossible to describe my feelings as it gradually dawned on me that we were certain to come down within enemy lines. I had a sensation of misery, depression and hopelessness, which grew so strong as time went on that I felt almost physically sick. I suppose it was a form of nostalgia – or was it just cowardice? At any rate, I felt unbearably sad at the idea that in all probability I would have to spend that night in a German prison.

Although it was rare to survive an uncontrolled crash, a pilot might walk away from a crash-landing, albeit badly bruised or injured. Escaping the aircraft was a priority in case petrol or petrol fumes ignited. Then, if downed behind enemy lines, relief at survival was soured by the bitter knowledge that capture was inevitable. There was one upside: a stricken pilot could expect his surrender to be routinely accepted, for the enemy converging on a crash site were typically neither pumped up with combat adrenalin nor stressed with battle fatigue.

Yet no surrender was guaranteed. When a German pilot took it upon himself to launch a ground attack, first strafing a lorry to which an observation balloon was tethered and then shooting up some adjacent horse lines, it was probably imperative that he get away. In his case he was immediately brought down. 'Everybody was savage at the machine-gunning, we being so helpless in the wagon lines,' wrote one of the men who chased across open fields towards the fair-haired and youthful pilot. The pilot may have had no inkling of the ill will bearing down on him for a staff car drew up and he was bundled into the back. 'There was an attempt to rush the car, but the sight of senior British officers defending it with their sticks checked us, and the car got away.'

Lieutenant Duncan Grinnell-Milne's aircraft landed in a ploughed field and within minutes the observer had alerted him to the enemy's approach. The two men set light to the aircraft but, as the Germans closed in, a series of loud explosions halted them in their tracks. In the flames the machine gun's bullets began to explode.

> The effect on the enemy was quite extraordinary. Half their number threw themselves flat on their faces while the remainder took refuge in flight. Of those who were lying down I tried a few phrases of my choicest German, informing them that we were quite harmless and would like to surrender. To this they made no reply, merely staring at us wide-eyed. It was a strange position to be in; we begged to be allowed to surrender but our enemies either lay flat on the ground in front of us or ran away. I felt like shrugging my shoulders and walking away in disgust, but presently, when our ammunition had burnt itself out, they plucked up courage and started to return. We were soon surrounded by a large crowd of harmless enough individuals, who stood gaping at us as though we had dropped from Mars. Then some German flying officers arrived and introduced themselves to us with much bowing and saluting as if the war had never existed . . . The German flying officers tried

to engage us in an interesting discussion on aero-dynamics, about which we knew nothing, and we took a last look at our ill-fated craft. A few minutes later we walked away with several German officers and reaching a road where a large Mercedes touring car was waiting we were bowed into the most comfortable seats and driven off at a great speed for a village.

One pilot who received mixed treatment on capture was Captain Harold Rushworth. The thirty-seven-year-old had been badly wounded in the right knee while serving with the infantry at the Battle of Loos. After recovery he joined the RFC. In August 1917, while flying over the Ypres Salient, he was attacked and wounded in the ankle, bullets also smashing the aircraft's rudder bar and perforating the petrol tank. In a spin from 12,000 feet, he regained partial control three-quarters of the way to the ground. Directing his plane into a straight dive, he crash-landed in a potato field, knocking himself unconscious.

I found myself being pulled out from the wreckage by some German private soldiers of a Württemberg Minenwerfer Company. They handled me very gently and at once rendered 'first aid' to the best of their ability. I was particularly struck with the manner in which they removed my boot from my injured foot, keeping a careful watch on my face for any indications of pain. They used two of their own handkerchiefs to form a tourniquet with which to stop the bleeding, and bandaged the wounds with their own field dressings. One of them went off to fetch a stretcher, and soon afterwards a German staff officer of high rank arrived on the scene. He appeared to be extremely angry, and insisted on my standing up in his presence. This I did, but apparently I fainted, and the next I remember is being carried off the field on a stretcher.

Since victorious pilots made a point of visiting the crash sites of downed aircraft, former opponents were commonly brought face to face. Captain Francis Don was shot down by, he discovered, one of the great German aces, Lieutenant Werner Voss (forty-eight victories). Voss's continued attack on Don and his observer after they landed ended only when Voss himself touched down in order to meet the two airmen. 'He hastened to inform me that I was his 34th victim' and was 'perfectly polite'.

Lieutenant John Howey's meeting with the enemy was memorable not least for an unholy row that broke out in his presence. Bethke, the German pilot, claimed victory but was accompanied by a German officer from the anti-aircraft battery who also claimed the 'kill', maintaining his battery had fired the decisive shell.

> The two German officers commenced to have a very heated argument with each other in German, both were very red in the face, and I expected to see them come to blows any moment. Then one of them left and the other turned to me and said in perfect English: 'Excuse me, but were you brought down by a shell from one of our anti-aircraft guns or by one of our aeroplanes?' He then explained to me that he was the pilot of one of the two German machines . . . He insisted on shaking hands with me, and said he was sorry we could not have another fight together.

While the men had striven to bring each other down, there was no animosity. On the contrary, Howey gave Bethke his mother's address and his wristwatch to post home and Bethke assured Howey he would 'do his very best in the matter'. Shortly afterwards an interpreter entered the room and Howey was taken to the town hall in Courtrai for questioning.

Meeting on cordial terms proved useful to stricken RFC pilots eager to let comrades know they were alive. Werner Voss spoke English and, while talking with Captain Don, offered to drop a note over British lines confirming that the officer was a prisoner. 'He asked the number of my squadron and the locality of the aerodrome, this of course, I refused. However, he promised to drop a note anywhere over the trenches, and he took my name and rank and those of my observer.'

In 1916, much the same offer was made to Lieutenant Harvey Frost and his observer, shot down by another ace, Max Immelmann.

> I wrote that I was 'slightly wounded and doing well . . .' The German aviator who had been deputed by Immelmann to drop our note, visited us [in hospital in Courtrai] and told us that he had gone over in a 'Fokker' and dropped it on the aerodrome at Bailleul. He had been chased by two British machines on his return. The observer of the LVG [a two-seater reconnaissance plane] we had been fighting also visited us, and showed us photographs of the wreck of our machine. All the officers of the German Flying Corps that I met in captivity were very chivalrous and anxious to do anything in their power for our comfort.

Immelmann presented Frost with a pipe.

Wherever Royal Flying Corps pilots were taken after capture – and many were made transitory guests at the aerodrome mess – their initial treatment at the hands of the enemy appears, in the main, to have been exemplary, impressing those who received such courtesy.

Grinnell-Milne was taken to an officers' mess in a comfortable chateau where he and his observer chatted with German pilots until four in the afternoon. 'Here we were entertained to a most excellent lunch, accompanied by numerous wines and liqueurs.' Second Lieutenant Patrick O'Brien, taken instead to an artillery officers' headquarters, was given wine and sandwiches before Lieutenant Müller took him to a 'clearing' house for flying officer prisoners.

> I was there two days and was not put under any guard, but Lieutenant Müller slept in the same room. I know no German, but he spoke English very well, and he told me that he had come from

South America on the same boat [from New York] as [Sir Roger] Casement, and that they both came on forged passports. He told me he had translated two books for Casement.

I had my meals in the dining room in an adjoining house, and with the exception of breakfast which I had alone, I had them in company with Lieutenant Müller. I was given three meals a day and tea. I used to get roast meat, potatoes, two kinds of bread and jam. I also had a proper bed to sleep in.

There was an innate affinity between British and German pilots, the vast majority of whom were officers. Combat took place between gentlemen, as they saw it, men who had devised and therefore understood the rules of the 'game' even if those rules were interpreted and executed ruthlessly. The German staff officer who had insisted Captain Rushworth stand in his presence was old-school and did not understand the pilots' etiquette. During Rushworth's careering descent, he had shot down an enemy aircraft inadvertently crossing his path. 'The [non-flying] staff officer considered it an act of treachery,' wrote Rushworth, 'in as much as, in his opinion, the surrender was consummated when my machine was rendered uncontrollable.' It was not a view shared by pilots serving in the victim's squadron: they regarded Rushworth's action as 'perfectly legitimate'.

Cordiality was understandable, but the Germans were the enemy and active war did not end with capture. Regrettably, once-clear distinctions blurred amidst handshakes and liqueurs, the risk that Royal Flying Corps pilots would be seduced by such bonhomie was all too real, as Lieutenant Patrick O'Brien saw when taken to Courtrai. 'There were two British officers who had been there for some time with whom I and the others did not care to associate, as in our opinion they, or rather one in particular, was too familiar with the German commandant, going to tea with him and, I believe, to church. Everyone thought it was going too far.'

The early appearance of Intelligence Officers would alert British pilots to the fact that questions were bound to follow, questions they were not at liberty to answer. These enquiries could be batted away without too much difficulty and might not need to be addressed at all. When Captain Frost was introduced to Max Immelmann, the German ace arrived accompanied by an Intelligence Officer. 'When I refused to answer any of the questions,' recalled Frost, 'Immelmann very considerately requested him to stop worrying me.'

It would have been entirely understandable if British pilots, still experiencing the euphoria of having survived, relaxed. Waving away Intelligence Officers would encourage British pilots to drop their guard as mess wine and good food were served. In such a convivial atmosphere, British tongues might wag, as the Germans well knew.

It is impossible to gauge what chat was mere banter and what constituted 'softening up', or direct efforts to collect intelligence. Lieutenant Geoffrey Parker, taken prisoner in May 1917, recalled meeting a German captain who was 'most interesting'.

> He informed me that his relatives were English and that he was a professor of History at one of the German universities. He asked me one or two questions as to the number of my squadron, where our aerodrome was etc and I replied that I would rather not answer . . .
>
> He could not understand why we had come in [to the war]. I then gave him my reasons. He went on to say that every nation had the right to expand, and that Germany was fighting for expansion. I asked him how he explained Belgium and he said . . .

Such conversation seems innocent enough but did Parker say more than he remembered? Where did the conversation lead? What, if anything, might the captain have been trying to winkle out of his prisoner? It is interesting how many captured pilots made reference to the excellent English spoken by Germans they met, and to the number who claimed either familial ties in Britain or pre-war residency. Were their numbers suspiciously dispropor- tionate, or just representative of the significant influx of Germans into Britain? After speaking to a German interpreter, Lieutenant Howey was approached by a German staff officer whose English, he noted, was superb.

> 'I see you are in the Bedfordshire Yeomanry, I know a few of your officers very well.' He told me he had been educated at Oxford, and was billeting in the town with a friend, who had also been to Oxford, and he would like me to come and dine with him. He explained that I would have to give a verbal promise not to escape, otherwise I would not be allowed to dine with him, but would be placed in a cell for the night, from which there would be no possi- bility of escape. I agreed to this, and he took me round to his billet. His name was Oppenheim. He lent me five pounds, as I had no money at all, and he took me into the town to buy a few things. He gave me a very good dinner of champagne and oysters, and told me he had procured a very comfortable room in the Red Cross hospital, where I could sleep the night. In this hospital I was treated exceedingly well. The next morning I was taken round to Oppenheim's billet again.

If there was a blueprint on how to soften up an enemy officer then surely this was it. Asking Howey to promise on his honour not to escape manifestly led Howey to believe he too was dealing with a man of honour, a man not involved in espionage or intelligence. The German officer's action might seem somewhat unsophisti- cated today, but RFC pilots were untutored in the concepts of subtle interrogation.

How much was gleaned from officers young and junior in rank is, nonetheless, debatable; not much, believed Grinnell-Milne. In unsubtle questioning, he was asked about the disposition of corps and divisions, of which he knew almost nothing. He was then taken from the enemy's aerodrome to Army Headquarters where he and other captured officers were 'pumped' for information; he wrote that 'all kinds of tricks [were] played on us in an attempt to extract important news which, perhaps fortunately, we did not in reality possess.' Grinnell-Milne did not record what those 'tricks' were.

It was tempting for captured officers to turn the tables and feed the enemy utterly useless information. Grinnell-Milne got into conversation with one German officer who astonished him with the name of a new secret British aircraft known as the Crosse and Blackwell, fitted with two new-style engines of great power and made by Huntley – 'I forget the exact name,' remarked the German.

'"Huntley and Palmer," I suggested timidly, suddenly tumbling to the hoax of which this poor man was the victim.'

The yarn may have worked that time although Captain Francis Don was doubtful about the wisdom of playing such games. 'I know that some officers take a very natural delight in stuffing these interpreters with false information. However, they are so clever and plausible in their methods that I venture to suggest that this should be discouraged.' Whether Don was aware or not, those methods included the newly embraced art of bugging.

The idea that one gentleman officer might be party to eaves-dropping on another's conversation was anathema to most British officers, but the Germans saw no contradiction in this pursuance of war by other means. The Germans consequently stole a march on the Allies in developing operations that became common practice in the years ahead. Don arrived in Karlsruhe after a stay in hospital recovering from the wound to his arm. Karlsruhe, as Don came to understand, was another place of 'clearing' for prisoners coming directly from the front or hospital. In the city there was a 'hotel' to which officers were sent prior to leaving for a POW camp. Don believed his experience at the hotel was typical of that of all officers sent there.

> I was first of all locked into a small room alone. Soon a very plausible German interpreter (officer) came and made himself pleasant. He explained that he had to interrogate us simply for form's sake and because 'the camp commandant is rather a fussy old man'. I adopted the attitude which I have always found completely successful, namely, to tell him that I have promised my government only to give my name, rank and regiment (R.F.C). That I am honour bound to give nothing more – 'Do you expect me to break my honour?' This invariably shuts them up. Not finding me communicative, he produced a pocket-book and rather astonished me by informing me of the number of my squadron and of the name of my squadron commander and asked me if it was correct. I, of course, gave a non-committal answer. He then informed me that he thought I had been in the 7th or 9th wing, which was wrong.

The interpreter expressed his sympathy for Don: it must have been difficult to stay in hospital without another Englishman to talk to. To make life easier he was going to place Don in a room with another English officer.

After a few days' stay in the 'hotel', Don was moved to an established prisoner-of-war camp where he was able to compare notes with fellow officers.

> Many of us are strongly of the opinion that it is used as a 'listening post' for Intelligence purposes. Some of the walls of the room have undoubtedly recently been replastered. I may mention that I met four officers at Karlsruhe who had just been captured and who came, I think, from Courtrai. They had spent four days together in a small room, at the end of which time they discovered four microphones fixed in the walls. They tore these out and put them down

the drains. Nothing was said to them on the matter . . . It is the general belief among prisoners of war that the system of microphones is enormously used as a perfectly legitimate means of getting information.

The pampering did not last, and when the Germans felt there was nothing further to be gained from listening in, the prisoners were moved on to camps where the regimes were often harsh and unforgiving. No more oysters and liqueurs. Food in the POW camps was in the main uniformly poor and officers, like other ranks, survived on Red Cross parcels.

Neither Max Immelmann nor Werner Voss survived the war. Immelmann was afforded the utmost respect by British pilots on news of his death when, as an official token of admiration for a great pilot, Lieutenant Long, an RFC observer, dropped a wreath with black bow and message of condolence on to Immelmann's airfield. Werner Voss was shot down in combat in September 1917 but only after an astonishing lone battle against seven British planes. Captain James McCudden, who took part in the engagement, recorded Voss's extraordinary flying skills. 'The German triplane was in the middle of our formation, and its handling was wonderful to behold. The pilot seemed to be firing at all of us simultaneously, and although I got behind him a second time, I could hardly stay there for a second . . .'

Mortally wounded, Voss and his plane smashed into the ground. 'As long as I live,' wrote McCudden, 'I shall never forget my admiration for that German pilot . . . His flying was wonderful, his courage magnificent, and in my opinion he is the bravest German airman who it had been my privilege to see fight.' Lieutenant Rhys-Davids was congratulated in the mess that evening on bringing Voss down but his victory was tinged with regret. 'Oh,' he said to McCudden, 'if I could only have brought him down alive.' His remark, wrote McCudden, was entirely 'in agreement with my own thoughts'.

Such were the short lives of these pilots. Like their German counterparts, neither Arthur Rhys-Davids nor James McCudden lived to see final victory. Rhys-Davids was shot down in October 1917. McCudden, who was awarded the Victoria Cross and became the seventh highest scoring ace of the war, was killed in a mundane flying accident in July 1918.

After the exhilaration of living life so close to the edge, it could be tough for Royal Flying Corps pilots, when made prisoner, to survive, grounded, suffocating behind barbed wire, irrespective of the quality of food, facilities or the attitude of the camp commandant. It was hardly surprising that many officers chose the option of escape, as much as a way of killing time and keeping occupied as in any realistic hope of reaching home. In the meantime, as plans were hatched and tunnels dug, camp life would be stoically borne. Yet no matter how brutal the camp regime became, no officer came close to experiencing the barbaric treatment of one select group of prisoners removed from their camps for a collective punishment for which none was culpable.

The routine policy of reprisals reached its terrible climax in February 1917 when 500 British prisoners of war were sent to the Eastern Front to work in German trenches opposite Russian forces. These prisoners were regular soldiers or Royal Naval Volunteer Reservists (RNVR) from the Royal Naval Division (RND). The vast majority were captured either during or shortly after the Retreat from Mons or at Antwerp, where the RND landed in late September 1914. These men were the 'paid murderers' despised by the Germans in 1914, the men who had frustrated von Kluck's thrust towards Paris and ultimately cost Germany the quick victory promised to the nation. In an act of vengeance, these men were sent to the front in temperatures as low as -35°C and forced to work with little or no food, returning to a camp and a seventy-yard-long tent pitched on a 'frozen swamp'. Not surprisingly many died, with survivors losing toes, fingers, even hands and feet, through severe frostbite and amputation.

'It would be beyond the powers of any man, no matter how able or fluent, to describe, in writing, the impression it left as you gazed upon these human wrecks, starved, frozen and unwashed,' recalled a witness and exchanged prisoner of war, Sergeant James Morrison of the Royal Marine Light Infantry. 'They were simply a frame of bones covered with skin, breathing and looking at you with eyes sunk deep in their sockets, and worst of all, when you spoke to them some of their answers were quite unintelligible.'

The process that led these men to injury or death on the Eastern Front had begun ten months earlier, in March 1916. A seemingly uncontroversial memorandum sent by Sir Edward Grey to Walter Page, the American ambassador in London, declared that the British proposed to lend the French 2,000 German prisoners of war for work in the city of Rouen and at the docks at Le Havre. These men were held in Britain but would be shipped overseas. Page was assured that none would be involved in moving munitions.

Shortly afterwards, Page was informed that 750 prisoners had gone to Le Havre on 5 April 1916, followed by 700 more on 26 April. Another group of 500 would be sent the following month. As part of America's role as neutral intermediary, the information was relayed to the Germans through the American Embassy in Berlin.

It was a decision that should not have caused great consternation, at least not according to the British. Britain's Commander in Chief, Sir Douglas Haig, continually used German prisoners of war within five miles of the fighting line, and saw no problem with that policy so long as prisoners were not exposed to shellfire, although it is unclear how he could guarantee their absolute safety. Prisoners' labour, other than in the direct movement of munitions, was of great importance, he believed, and he resisted suggestions that this distance between them and the fighting line should be increased to twelve miles. Rouen was a good sixty miles, and the docks of Le Havre a hundred miles, from the Somme region.

For this reason alone, the British were not expecting an adverse reaction from Berlin. It was no secret that the Germans continued to use Russian prisoners of war as labour on the Western Front, and very close to the front line. Haig was equally certain that British prisoners were employed on the Western Front, despite the enemy's vigorous denials.

Britain and Germany regarded each other's protestations of fair play with automatic suspicion and, almost as a matter of policy, chose retaliation as the default setting for any move of which they disapproved. In response to the British decision to deploy prisoners, the Germans announced that 2,000 British prisoners of war would be moved from Germany to the Russian Front to be employed under the same conditions as British-held prisoners in France; of these, 500 would be sent to the front line. These men were taken primarily from Döberitz, Friedrichsfeld and Senne POW camps, as Company Sergeant Major Alexander Gibbs of 2nd Argyll and Sutherland Highlanders testified:

> I was the senior 2nd Class Warrant Officer of a party of 1,000 NCOs and men (25% NCOs) who left Döberitz Camp on 8th May 1916 for Russia. We knew nothing at that time of our destination or the reason for the move, and as it was very warm weather we left our warm clothing and half our food to follow. We arrived at Frankfurt an der Oder the same day and by 11th May 1916 another 1,000 NCOs and men from a number of camps in Germany had also come to Frankfurt.

On 11 May 1916, four parties sequentially numbered EK1 (Englische Kommando 1), EK2, EK3 and EK4, consisting of 500 men each, left for the Russian Front; forty men were packed into each cattle truck for an initial three-day journey to Russian Latvia.

One of those sent east was a twenty-year-old Royal Naval Reservist, Cedric Ireland. The sixth son of a Derbyshire vicar, Cedric was sent to a school in Leatherhead, Surrey, founded for the education of the children of impecunious clergy. On the outbreak of war he joined the Royal Navy's Hawke Battalion and the following month was sent with the newly formed Royal Naval Division to assist in the defence of Antwerp. The division was ill-equipped for such a role and was forced to retire; on 9 October, many, including Able Seaman Ireland, were captured. Within weeks he was at Döberitz POW camp, a few miles west of Berlin. In late August 1915 he sent two postcards home to his sister depicting the funeral of a fellow RND seaman, William Malcolm, of the Collingwood Battalion. Malcolm, captured on the same day as Ireland at Antwerp, was killed in a carting accident while at work near the camp. Cedric Ireland almost certainly appears in both photographs and the priest taking the service of committal is the Reverend Henry Williams. The following year Williams would be made aware of the men's departure for Russia. He recalled their loss with sadness. 'These men, most of whom I knew personally at Döberitz and other camps, were splendid fellows, the pick of our "Old Contemptibles" and RNVR in Germany, and included many or most of the heroic survivors of Mons. I was not allowed to visit these men in Russia, though I made every possible effort to do so.'

The men worked very hard but as they were supplied with parcels from home, life remained bearable. For eight months EK4 worked in Libau docks before being sent to Mitau. At that time 'most of the men, on our departure from Libau [to Mitau] were the picture of health and strength,' recalled Corporal Robert Steele, probably an exaggeration but an understandable one, given what was to follow.

Throughout 1916, the Germans remained convinced that the British were contravening the rules of war by using prisoners too close to the front line. By January 1917, they had had enough. In a telegram sent through the American ambassador to Berlin, the Germans claimed information had reached them that His Majesty's Government were 'employing near the immediate front large numbers of German prisoners who are reported to be badly fed and lodged'. Several had been killed and wounded. In short, if the British did not rectify the situation immediately and withdraw these men to a distance greater than thirty kilometres from the front line, British prisoners would be 'given the same treatment as that meted out to German prisoners by the British Military Authorities'. The Germans also demanded assurances as to the conditions under which prisoners were kept. The British were given four days to reply.

The British government was furious. Not only did it consider the conditions under which enemy prisoners worked and lived 'extraordinarily favourable', but believed the 'absurdly short notice' given was being used by the Germans as a pretext to send British prisoners closer to the front line in order to dig trenches. The British refused to meet the ultimatum, although a note sent on 6 February offered a compromise that would remove prisoners on all sides to a point at least twenty kilometres from the trenches. This distance was not acceptable and retribution was now at hand. British prisoners would be informed of their altered circumstances in a note entitled 'Declaration to the English Prisoners of Respite'. This note was distributed or read out to prisoners.

Upon the German request to withdraw the German prisoners of war to a distance of not less than 30 kilometres from the front line, the British Government has not replied. Therefore, it has been decided that *all* [my italics] prisoners of war who are captured in future will be kept as prisoners of respite ie very short of food, bad lodgings, no beds, hard work (also beside the German guns under shell fire) no pay, no soap . . .

The English prisoners of respite are allowed to write to their relatives or persons of influence in England how badly they are treated, and that no alteration will occur until the English Government has consented to the German request . . . You will be supplied with postcards, paper and envelopes, all this correspondence in which you will explain your hardships, will be sent as Express Mail to England.

It seems that the Germans originally intended to send prisoners from Germany back to the Western Front but instead decided to send the men from EK4 to the trenches on the Eastern Front. The wording of the German note seemed to ignore the fact that none of the 2,000 prisoners sent east were anything other than long-term prisoners of war. It is possible that the message read out to the men at Libau was altered to reflect that fact, although the ramifications were identical. At Libau, 500 prisoners were notified that they would be sent to the trenches between Riga and Mitau, where they would remain within range of Russian artillery fire.

According to the Reverend Williams, and as described by one survivor, the men were told their fate in direct and graphic terms.

On arrival at Mitau, they were paraded by a German officer who told them: 'I suppose you know that you have come here to die, and we expect you to die like English gentlemen.'

I know . . . that the German authorities refused to forward any food parcels from home to any of these men on the grounds of 'Reprisals', and indeed I saw thousands of these parcels stacked up and rotting in the camp at Friedrichsfeld. This meant that the men were being practically starved, for men in Germany, the prisoners, could not exist on their rations for very long.

In addition to effective starvation, German guards were instructed to mistreat the prisoners. CSM Gibb claimed to have obtained printed orders stating 'that no mercy was to be shown to us; we were the men who had, every one of us, assisted in stopping the Kaiser's army from going to Paris and they were to think of their comrades who were being brutally treated in France, and be strong.' Gibb claimed the German interpreter encouraged prisoners to write home describing conditions.

At Mitau, the men were forced to clear or dig trenches in the German second and third lines, as well as constructing communication trenches linking them to the front. They were also employed collecting ice from a nearby river. According to Gibb, the men paraded at 5.30 a.m., moving off around 6 a.m. and returning to the camp about 5.30 p.m. They were given no food between these hours and there were only two breaks of twenty minutes during the day. Survivors recalled that Russian shelling injured a number of men and at least one prisoner was shot in the stomach by a sniper.

The lack of food coupled with atrocious weather quickly took its toll. Private Arthur Soder of the 1st Dorsetshire Regiment, for example, was left helpless as his weight dropped from 69kg to 40kg in a little over five weeks and one leg swelled to twice its normal size through the effects of frost.

If Corporal Robert Steele's description of the men's physical condition on leaving Libau was even moderately accurate, there can be no doubt as to the terrible conditions at Mitau where victims died within three weeks of arrival. On 17 March, Private Reuben Wilmott of the Border Regiment died from the effects of cold. According to Soder, 'He was quite stiff through the frost when we found him in the morning. He was lying just by the flap of the tent.' Six days later, Able Seaman Philip Rootham also died. Witnesses stated that he was carried back after a day's work unconscious through exhaustion. He died on the way to hospital. Private Albert Roberts of the King's Own Royal Lancaster Regiment died later the same day and was buried next to Rootham. Private James Brown of the Highland Light Infantry followed soon after, succumbing to the cold on 22 March, and on 23 March Private Mulholland died.

Only those who were dangerously ill were taken to hospital, including those, survivors claimed, who self-mutilated in order to escape their circumstances. Lance Corporal Harold Sugden was detailed to work in the hospital where 200 men from Mitau were taken. He noted that they were in a deplorable state, just 'bags of skin and bone, with frost-bitten feet and mostly suffering from nephritis or kidney complaints, with swollen legs . . .' In hospital more died, including Private Kinsman, Lance Corporal Waterman, and Privates Harvey, Walker, McCulloch and Farmer.

'By the end of March the parties were in a terrible state,' acknowledged Gibb. 'The remainder had to be assisted to their work in the morning, and we had to carry most of them home in the evenings.' Derbyshire vicar's son Able Seaman Cedric Ireland died on 26 March in his comrades' arms on the way back from work.

Ireland had reported sick that morning but was detailed for work nonetheless. Witnesses stated that he had to be helped from the trenches at the end of the day and that he died on the way back from 'weakness, cold and hunger'. His death would be followed by five more in as many days.

By 2 April, only 176 men were left in the camp, just over a third of those who had arrived less than six weeks before. Of these only fifty were fit enough to work although many more were sent out regardless of their physical condition. Four days later, another three men died, although, of all the deaths, that of Private Alan Skett was the only one reported as murder rather than as the result of gratuitous neglect. CSM Gibbs witnessed his comrade's death.

On the 6th April about 10 p.m. Private Skett, Coldstream Guards, was shot at point blank range. Owing to weakness he was a light arbeit [worker], but he had been working all day with a party and had collapsed on the mud. When ordered to proceed with his work he could hardly rise. He got up somehow but could scarcely stand. He could not work or even walk, so he was shot. The body was left out where it fell. It was covered with a piece of corrugated iron. I managed to get him buried somehow on the 9th, quite near the camp.

One witness, Corporal Charles Wright of the 5th Lancers, backed up Gibb's story.

I was outside the tent in which we lived, about 9 p.m., when I heard a shot. About 15 minutes later a party of about seven or eight British prisoners came in. I asked them what the shot was, and they told me that Private Skett, Coldstream Guards, had been shot because he was too weak to walk, and the sentry who was with the party did not want to leave him behind . . . I saw the wound in his chest which had been made by a rifle bullet fired point blank. The jacket round the place where the bullet had entered the body was torn and scratched. On asking for further details I was told by an eyewitness, Private [James] Fudge, [2nd] Manchester Regt, that Private Skett collapsed in a heap, being too weak to walk any further. He could not be placed on the small two-wheeled wagon, which the party was dragging with it, as it was already occupied by a man who had previously collapsed. The sentry ordered him to get up and when Skett replied in German 'I cannot' the sentry stepped back a pace and shot him dead.

In April a further eleven men perished before the weather gradually began to improve.

Survivors of Mitau picked out two Germans for condemnation. One was the camp interpreter, named Logermann, who, it was said, was fond of interpreting a man's answer in such a way as to land him in trouble. The other was the camp commandant, Lieutenant Hermann Prahl of the 1st Jaeger Regiment, 8th Army Corps.

According to witnesses, Prahl spoke fluent English; he had been living in England with his family when war broke out and was interned on the Isle of Man. Corporal Robert Steele, presumably in conversation with Prahl, reported that the officer had been badly treated in England 'and was now going to have his revenge'. Steele claimed that Prahl secured his release from internment with forged documents, but, whatever the truth, there is no doubt that this officer deeply resented the prisoners under his command. Private Charles Brown, 1st West Yorkshire Regiment, recollected that in a moment of anger Prahl declared 'that he had a son in England, and said he would treat us dogs as the English were treating him'.

The Germans hoped that the free passage of letters home would pressure the British government into changing its tune. The ploy worked well. A number of letters, all expressing desperation, were forwarded by parents to the government and Prisoner of War Department, with covering letters pressing for action to help relieve the plight of these men. All prisoners' letters were variations on the same theme and included words to the effect that they were in Mitau purely because of the British government's treatment of German prisoners in France.

In mid-March, Private Frank Barlow, 1st West Yorkshire Regiment, wrote to his father, John Barlow. His letter is typical of those sent home.

I told you in my last letter that we were going to be removed, and so we have, to a worse place than we have ever been in. We have been moved right up behind the firing line, and where we go to work is right in the Fire Zone; where the shells are dropping and it is very dangerous.

The work we do is digging trenches and felling trees; also carrying them, which is very hard. We live in a tent, which is partly heated, but it is very cold. When we wake up in the morning our boots are frozen. The reason we have been sent is that they say our Government have German prisoners doing similar work, and that they have sent them behind the firing line, and the sooner they move their men to a better place, the sooner we shall be moved.

So father will you please show this letter to somebody of higher rank in order that something can be done, because if this goes on much longer, the sooner a bullet or a shell puts us out of our troubles, the better . . . We are behind the Russian and German firing lines, and if you have any idea what a Russian winter is like you will know how things are with us . . . God help us if we have to stop here much longer. [Sentence here crossed out by the German censor] account of frost-bites . . . so please try and do your best, because we can't stick this much longer, as we are all getting weaker every day.

Excuse my writing as I am so cold; perhaps you will hear from me again if I am lucky . . .

His father did not hear from his son again. Private Frank Barlow died on the last day of March, just as his parents received the letter.

Another letter forwarded through the Germans' so-called 'Express Mail' was sent to Kathleen Peploe, living in Southgate, north London. It is not known who she was, other than that she was part of a small charitable organisation sending parcels to prisoners. In two years she received more than three hundred letters and postcards from grateful prisoners, but in early May 1917 she received one from a private in the Middlesex Regiment and this time it was regarding his plight. She forwarded the letter to *The Times*, which published it on 18 May, precisely as the Germans had hoped would happen, albeit a little late in the day. Once again, the letter bemoaned the prisoners' dilemma, which was 'many times worse than in 1914'. The letter also spoke of the atrocious food and asked Kathleen Peploe if she could help by making the facts known 'as we all think it very unfair either to German or English prisoners to be in such a position'.

In the international battle of wills, Germany gained the upper hand. Reports of the suffering reached a wider audience through the press and questions were asked in the House of Commons. Tough-talking MPs such as William Joynson-Hicks suggested taking 1,000 German officers from Donington Hall POW camp and transferring them straight to the front line, but this was not the answer and would only increase pressure on Allied prisoners in German hands.

The British blinked first. On 28 April, the War Cabinet ordered all German prisoners to be withdrawn thirty kilometres from the trenches, Berlin being notified of the decision. On 11 May, the government demanded an assurance that the Germans would withdraw all British prisoners from the firing line on all fronts: that assurance was received on 16 June, six days after the survivors of Mitau had returned to Libau. In response, the British notified the French of their 'urgent desire' to recall the 2,000 loaned German prisoners to Britain. This transfer was completed the following month, at which point the British government felt in a position to request the removal of British prisoners from Russian soil. Those men still at Libau were allowed a month's rest after their ordeal. Accommodation was improved and food parcels previously withheld were distributed. Light work was the order of the day until the men were returned to Germany in November.

The story had come full circle but at great cost to the prisoners of war. CSM Alexander Gibb recorded that of the 500 sent to Mitau only seventy-two survived the rigours of camp life without needing extensive hospital treatment; as many as thirty had died. Today these lie together in Nikolai Cemetery in Mitau in Latvia. Many of the men had suffered grievous physical injury, which the Reverend Williams bore witness to in his diary: 'Of those who survived to return home, many were so physically crippled and broken that one could almost wish they had died.'

Survivors who were exchanged gave statements as to what went on at Mitau, and, while dates and times occasionally contradict each other, the consistency of their stories is compelling. CSM Gibb probably spoke for many when he asked, 'When the war ends, and the reckoning comes, is all this to be passed over in silence?' It was, in fact. It was forgotten. Neither Logermann nor the guard who shot Private Skett was ever sought at the end of the war, never mind prosecuted, for their treatment of British POWs. Lieutenant Hermann Prahl was killed in action in Italy in November 1917.

The aggressive diplomatic petulance exhibited by both sides was typical of the spats that characterised Anglo-German relations in 1917. Concurrent with the reprisal in Russia was another incident in March that was to cause more than normal consternation in Britain, and another round of irritability and non-cooperation. It concerned the death of an able seaman, twenty-four-year-old John Genower, at Brandenburg POW camp.

Reports of deaths in POW camps were commonly exchanged between nations at war but this case was different. Through the American Embassy, the British government was informed that Genower had died 'as a consequence of burns' in a fire at the camp, but further details were not forthcoming. The government was unwilling to accept what they felt was a terse and uninformative response from the Germans. In retaliation, it was decided that the British would respond as evasively when a German POW death warranted the same sort of additional detail.

In May, the British government sent a Memorandum of Communication to the German government concerning the death on 12 April of a German prisoner of war, Adam Ultsch, from gunshot wounds. Ultsch was shot while attempting to escape from a POW enclosure in France – not that the Germans were given this information. Other than announcing Ultsch's death, the Memorandum was deliberately vague.

> The German prisoner of war Adam Ultsch of Theisenort, born on the 24th September 1887, died of a gunshot wound on the 12th April.

It is recognised that the above particulars are insufficient but they correspond with those furnished in the under-mentioned German notes verbales . . . On receipt of a satisfactory reply to the Foreign Office Memorandum, relative to the insufficient particulars furnished by the German Government regarding the violent deaths of British prisoners of war in Germany, further particulars will be furnished in regard to the death of Ultsch.

Only in August did the Germans agree to send full particulars of Genower's death, on receipt of which, in early September, the British government furnished the Germans with details of Ultsch's death.

The German explanation of Genower's death was reasonably detailed. He had been held in secure detention awaiting trial after assaulting a guard. A fire had broken out near the punishment cells and spread so rapidly that, despite the best efforts of the sentry on guard who 'at once gave energetic assistance to the work of rescue', the prisoner could not be saved. Rumours that Genower had been bayoneted as he tried to escape from a window were a 'malicious fabrication'.

The British response was direct. A Foreign Office official appended a note to the German reply: 'I do not believe the Germans' story for a moment – the story which we pieced together is too well founded not to be substantially correct.' As far as the British government was concerned, Genower had been murdered. The case became high-profile enough for a Government White Paper to be published on Genower's death, and questions about the incident were asked in the House of Commons and reported in the press. Once again, the government promised to keep a record of known atrocities for post-war prosecution.

Diplomatic traffic concerning the death of John Genower had passed through the good offices of the American Embassy in Berlin, much as it had done for the previous three years. The United States had always pursued a policy of non-intervention in the war, although the German sinking of RMS *Lusitania* in 1915 had sorely tested their resolve. After the disaster, the USA had demanded an end to attacks on passenger ships, and Germany acquiesced. However, in February 1917, it resumed a policy of unrestricted submarine warfare in an attempt to blockade and starve Britain into submission. Submarines soon attacked and sank several US merchant ships bringing food and materials across the Atlantic. Knowing that America was likely to enter the war on the side of the Allies, the Germans attempted to bring Mexico into the war on their side by promising support for the long-held Mexican dream of recovering the states of Texas, New Mexico and Arizona. The disclosure of this plot, proposed in the so-called Zimmermann Telegram, proved to be the final straw. America declared war on Germany on 6 April 1917.

8

The Crying Game

Enemy alien or prisoner of war: neither was likely to be comfortable when living under the legal 'protection' of an adversary. International law entitled prisoners of war to food, clothing and accommodation, but there was no such guarantee for enemy aliens. At the outbreak of war, British and German governments had given paid support to their own nationals living under the other's jurisdiction. This meant, of course, that the British taxpayer supported the Bavarian *Hausfrau* married to an Englishman and living in Munich and the German taxpayer looked after the Peckham-born-and-bred wife of a Saxon resident in London. Relatively higher German immigration to Britain made this a bad financial arrangement for Berlin and almost inevitably Germany reneged on the arrangement. Financial assistance would be given to German-born nationals in Britain and not those naturalised through marriage; in retaliation, the British followed suit. By their actions, both countries abandoned families to the grudging welfare of the enemy state or, more often, private charitable foundations. Then, as the years passed and the German economy faltered, Berlin looked for further ways to cut expenditure. In 1917 it withdrew all payments to nationals whose sons were conscripted into the British Army, and then stopped all support to German families who had lived in Britain for over ten years, halving their commitment to 687 German families, including 1,240 children.

The work of charitable organisations protecting the welfare of enemy aliens proved vital. The paltry sums awarded by both

British and German governments could not sustain a family and even if an application for aid was entertained, it took many weeks to process. There were a number of charities concerned with the distress of all immigrants in Britain. The Central Council of United Alien Relief Societies had brought under one umbrella representatives of a number of relief organisations concerned with aliens' welfare, although inevitably much of its work was with enemy aliens. Another was the Quakers' Friends Emergency Committee (FEC).

The FEC was staffed by a group of people for whom nationality and national boundaries were of little or no importance. In the teeth of wide public resentment, this relatively small number of British citizens worked tirelessly to support and provide welfare for enemy aliens caught up in the conflict. From a haphazard start in 1914, by 1916 the Friends Emergency Committee had become well organised, with various departments and sub-committees actively working. The activities of the FEC included offering food parcels to British-born women and children who elected to follow their repatriated husbands to Germany, and giving support to internees stuck with all the strains and stresses of interminable captivity.

The tightening of German welfare payments helped channel a further 331 destitute families on to the books of the London FEC, in addition to the 6,200 families that had already come to the Committee's attention in the capital. Outside London, FEC offices in towns and cities such as Manchester, Edinburgh, Liverpool and Bristol dealt with many more equally deserving cases. Fortunately, families who were helped through difficult periods with clothing, accommodation and food often became self-supporting once children became old enough to earn money, simultaneously freeing up mothers to search for work.

The FEC's task went well beyond providing the essentials, as Anna Thomas, a Quaker serving on the Executive Committee wrote in the FEC's Fourth Annual Report in 1916. In helping internees a veritable raft of ancillary duties was undertaken, covering 'every kind of domestic and business difficulty'.

> Would we find out why the wife was not writing; whether she was seriously ill or not; could we help in the discipline of an unruly boy, or with the education of a brilliant one; more common than all, could we not help with food or clothing or work to prevent starvation or illness which inevitably descended on those homes where the slender Government grant was the only income; could we find missing luggage, will or papers; could we pay off landladies, collect debts, redeem pawned goods, trace relatives, send children to Germany, patent inventions, pay wife's fare to camp, arrange a wedding or a funeral, with many other suggestions. And usually, to end with, there was a pathetic belief (no place like an internment camp for false beliefs or rumours) that we had only to interview the Home Secretary in order to get the man released or the whole internment system abolished.

Because the FEC focused on helping enemy aliens, the organisation retained a high public profile, certainly in comparison with other charities. For that reason it was never free from press ridicule. The *Daily Express* ran a headline, 'Aid for the Enemy Only' and the *Evening News* called the FEC 'Hun Coddlers'. But although a threat was made to shoot the FEC's Secretary 'at sight', there appear to have been few, if any, physical attacks on Committee members.

In fairness, one of the biggest 'Hun Coddlers' was the British Army itself. Within its ranks it fed, clothed and accommodated thousands of sons born to German parents, and paid them. The soldiers' Anglo-German ancestry had proved an irritant to the authorities, unsure of what to do with men whose loyalty was in question. Now, eight months after being bundled together into the Middlesex Regiment, these sons of enemy alien parentage were trained and ready for active service.

The idea of sending them overseas did not thrill all MPs, although not necessarily for the same reasons. One who raised the issue was the nonconformist Liberal MP for North Somerset, Joseph King. As a young man, he had studied theology at the University of Giessen in Germany. Unlike most MPs, he appeared to have sympathy for the plight (as he saw it) of Anglo-German soldiers in the Middlesex Regiment. On 21 March 1917, he complained to the House that a pledge made by Lord Kitchener not to send such men overseas was being broken. Replying, the Under Secretary of State for War pointed out that the units had not been raised until after Kitchener's death. King rose again. These battalions, he said, were composed '. . . very largely of men who think in German more than in English, and I am told that their conversation is largely carried on in German. They all have German names, they sing together German songs, and though I believe they are loyal subjects of the King and of our cause, undoubtedly they have strong German associations.'

If these men were entirely loyal, then why would they act in such a way as to appear anything but British and loyal? And why should they not serve their country overseas? Surviving records indicate that between 15 and 20 per cent had British surnames, such as Davenport, Greenwood and Williams, and there is no evidence that anything King suggested was much more than rumour or gossip. King argued that these men were considered German by the Germans and would, on capture, be shot after court martial, but his arguments were unfounded and scatter-gun in their approach. It hardly mattered anyway; these men were going to the Western Front.

Eight Infantry Labour Companies (ILCs) were created from men of the 30th and 31st Middlesex Regiment. In late February and early March, six companies were informed of their imminent departure for France, causing mixed emotions among recruits about to take an active part in the war against Germany, not least those whose German fathers were languishing in internment. The decision by two unnamed men serving with 1st ILC to desert on the eve of the company's departure from Reading for France suggests that not all were enthusiastic. Surviving evidence is patchy, but the action of these two does appear to be exceptional, and, while it would be surprising if every man's allegiance to King and Country was unwavering, the vast majority would show admirable loyalty.

Unlike men of the army's Labour Corps, which was made up predominantly of soldiers unfit for front-line service, the ILCs consisted of individuals in generally good physical health. Their commanding officers were of unquestionably British stock but, by contrast to those under their command, of a lower medical grade. Of the officers belonging to 3rd ILC, the Commanding Officer, Major William Renwick, had been severely shell-shocked and deafened by the explosion of a heavy gas shell in March 1916, and invalided home. A medical board considered him permanently disabled and unfit for overseas service, although that had not prevented his return. A second officer in the 3rd ILC, Second Lieutenant Frederick Ruscoe, was an old soldier. An ex-Regimental Sergeant Major of the Royal Welsh Fusiliers, he enlisted in the army in 1883 and had been in France since December 1915, returning to England for a commission in 1916. His health was also poor and he would be sent home from France in 1918 and died in 1920. In command of 2nd ILC was Captain David Burles, a man in his early fifties. In August 1916, the Board recommended that he should serve at home, or as an officer in a labour battalion overseas. In England, he had been sent to help train men of the 30th Middlesex Regiment and then, in March, ordered to take 2nd ILC overseas.

During March and April, the first six companies embarked for France, to be followed in July and December by the remaining two. The first companies arrived on the Western Front during the bitter winter of 1916–17, beginning work that was severely hampered by snowstorms and a lack of available transport. The issue of transport greatly concerned Captain Burles, who noted down in the unit's War Diary his repeated requests for vehicles of any kind. His unit was under the command of the Deputy Assistant Director of Labour, VII Corps, who promised to rectify the situation, although nothing materialised. On 14 April, four days after the company arrived to undertake work near the French town of Doullens, Burles wrote: 'The Company is still without any transport whatsoever, and great difficulty is experienced hereby in procuring rations.' Two days later he was griping again: 'The supply dump is 15 kilometres distant. [We] have to depend on the kindness of other units to loan motor lorries. Secured one for today and drew three days' rations. All iron rations.' Burles's transport problems did not improve for another ten days.

Is it possible that the issue over transport was an example of institutional prejudice against men of German extraction? These companies had arrived in France just as Britain unleashed its spring offensive near the town of Arras and, inevitably, the great preponderance of resources was sucked towards the battle. VII Corps was part of the Third Army, which was heavily engaged in the opening phases of the battle and, with the Western Front gripped by intense cold, causing both horse-drawn and petrol-driven vehicles to founder in snow and mud, serviceable transport was at a premium. Half a dozen labour companies, new to the front and regardless of their composition or characteristics, were never going to be made a priority at that moment. In the admittedly scant records concerning these ILCs, there is no evidence that they were treated appreciably better or worse than other units of the British Army.

The fact remained, however, that these men were not entirely trusted. They would not be employed at or near a base port nor, in theory, within sixteen kilometres of the trenches. They were unarmed and not supposed to handle ammunition and they were to be kept away from densely populated areas. Sensitive to issues of security, General Headquarters directed that they were not to be employed as mess cooks, barbers, waiters, clerks or orderlies. They were also barred from working in officers' clubs or cinemas, although over time such restrictions were relaxed.

There are only two known incidents in which a soldier's loyalty was questioned, and, ironically, both men had British as opposed to German surnames. The first occurred at the end of April 1917 when an intelligence officer was sent to visit 2nd ILC to investigate a letter written to Private Herman Cook. The letter had been damaged in transit, the contents apparently falling out of the envelope. It was found to contain, wrote the Commanding Officer, 'many coarse insulting phrases and [was] evidently pro German'. The letter had been addressed to Reading and forwarded to France. There is no record that Cook approved of or in any way solicited the contents of the letter. The second incident occurred a few months later when Private Harold Guest, serving with the 1st ILC, was sent back to England as a result of proceedings taken against him by his Commanding Officer on account of his 'pro German agitation'. How many more felt the same way can never be known, although General Edward Wace, in a Report on Labour, estimated that less than 5 per cent had pro-German sympathies and that these men were known to the Commanding Officers.

The men of the ILCs were used piecemeal, rarely if ever working as a complete unit. By and large they were broken up into small groups and sent wherever they were needed and to whoever asked for help, being employed on what was known as the 'task system', giving men a distinct challenge to complete.

In the first six weeks overseas, 3rd ILC helped lay over fifty miles of light railway track behind the lines, as well as maintaining the existing line in running order. The officer commanding the Second Army's Light Railways was undoubtedly pleased with the work, sending a memo to be read to all ranks employed: 'I wish to express my personal thanks to each of your officers and men for the work which they have done and are still doing . . .

throughout the worst conditions of shell fire. Every man's best efforts are wanted, and I am sure that we shall have them.'

Much of the ILC's work was repetitive and physically demanding. There was work in forestry, cutting down trees and, in quarries, digging sand. Parties of men worked on farms and in brickworks. They were sent to load lorries at Royal Engineer stores, or to help construct Nissan huts, even, on one occasion, to build a compound for German POWs. At least some of the 3rd ILC's time was spent in the menial but important job of salvage from abandoned or overrun battlefields, scouring the ground and disused trenches for everything that could be reused or melted down, including rum jars, biscuit tins, oil drums, petrol cans, rubber and shrapnel helmets, all of which would be taken to the Company Dump. Salvage work was dangerous. Private Albert Wenninger, of the 3rd ILC, a butcher from Shepherds Bush in London, was accidentally killed when a 4½-inch shell exploded while he was helping to dump old ammunition into craters. The explosion set off dozens of other shells, wounding a further eighteen men.

In May, Private Woolf Adler, aged twenty-eight, died at the 10th Casualty Clearing Station (CCS) of shrapnel wounds to his back and left hip after the Company's billets were shelled. One other man was wounded. Adler, the son of German parents, and a former stockbroker from West Hampstead, had volunteered in December 1915 and was working in munitions when posted in February 1917 to the 31st Middlesex Regiment. He had been in France just ten weeks and was one of four men serving with the 3rd ILC who died overseas. His widowed mother, Regine, was notified that her son had died for his country.

Woolf Adler was buried in Lijssenthoek Military Cemetery, seven miles west of Ypres. He is one of 9,901 British and Empire troops almost all of whom died as a result of their wounds at a nearby CCS. For this reason, more than 99 per cent have known graves. Inadvertently, the cemetery creates the impression that the majority of men did not simply disappear, never to be seen again. Tragically, however, around half of those killed in the Great War have no known grave.

Receiving news of a loved one's disappearance released a trap-door through which families fell into a pit of instantaneous fear and despair, leaving the majority of those affected with nothing to do but wait. The army would forward further details, if any were ever received.

Hope was not extinguished altogether; there was a reasonable chance that a loved one had been taken prisoner, but as time passed the silence on all fronts became too much to bear. If the Germans did not notify the Red Cross within a month that a man was a prisoner then, in all likelihood, that man was still on the battle-field. With shellfire churning up the ground over which attacks were made, the chances were poor that a body would remain iden-tifiable for long. Families might get word from a comrade of the missing man, but all too often it was to confirm their darkest fears; it was not a kindness to hold out flickering hope.

'The missing' were an egalitarian group among whom there was no distinction between rich and poor. In desperation, those who could afford it could pay for additional private searches that invariably confirmed what the family already knew, that the man was untraceable. Pre-war contacts were called upon: German governesses who had returned home at the outbreak of war were asked through third parties to place appeals for information in the press and to circulate names of missing officers. But to what end? Leaving no stone unturned may have proved ultimately cathartic for some but searching could also lead to a pointless fixation on the missing, and the purgatory of forlorn hope. Hard as it may have seemed, stoically waiting for news was probably the best option for families and, just occasionally, it was enemy soldiers who provided the answers.

On 25 July 1915 the 1/6th Sherwood Foresters were holding front-line trenches near Sanctuary Wood, just outside Ypres. The battalion War Diary's otherwise sparse entries that day noted one item of interest: a German aeroplane had been shot down, and the observer had fallen 'in rear of our trenches'. A great many men on the ground witnessed the incident. The German plane, raked by machine-gun fire, had burst into flames. Eyewitnesses reported that the observer fell as the plane turned upside down, others that he jumped; either way, a man was seen to fall well before the plane crashed. In the history of the 1/5th Sherwood Foresters, a neighbouring battalion in the line that day, this account was given. 'It was an interesting sight for those who saw the event – the first burst of smoke, the observer throwing himself out, falling the greater part of the way like a partly deflated balloon (his trench coat held the air), the bump when he struck the ground.'

The 'observer' was identified as thirty-nine-year-old Captain Hans Roser, and from his body were taken various 'decorations' including a 'flight badge'. The 1/6th Sherwood Foresters' Commanding Officer, Lieutenant Colonel Godfrey Goodman, felt the belongings were of enough sentimental value to be returned to Roser's family. After some understandable delay, these were sent to Danzig in November after which a reply was received from Mrs Roser thanking Colonel Goodman for his kindness.

This should have been the end of the matter but news of Goodman's actions reached Captain Roser's nephew, an artillery officer by the name of Reinhardt, who, mindful that one good turn deserved another, penned this remarkable letter 'in the field', in May 1916.

My family have received correspondence which passed between Lieutenant Colonel G D Goodman and the German Foreign Office through the intermediary of the American Embassy at Berlin. According to the statement of this officer, who commands the 6th Sherwood Foresters, Captain Roser, my mother's younger brother, was shot down in his aeroplane behind the British lines east of

Ypres on July 25th 1915, and was buried with full military honours by the orders of Colonel Goodman who saw the machine fall. The decorations found on his body have also been forwarded to us through the same channels together with detailed information about the position of his grave. It is through the exertions of Colonel Goodman that my family received the first certain news of my relative's death, as he was previously certified as missing.

Having been appraised by this means of the possibility of communicating with the relatives of enemy officers through the American Diplomatic Representatives, I am now anxious to convey news of a fallen English comrade in arms in a similar manner to his widow who has probably remained in complete ignorance of his fate since 1914. The officer in question is Captain [Henry Telford] Maffett of B Company, 2nd Leinster Regiment who fell in the field of honour on October 23rd 1914, under German artillery and machine gun fire together with the greater part of his battalion (he was with the centre company but seems to have been leading the battalion). His death was caused by a shell splinter and must have been quick and painless, as he still had a pencil and half written despatch in his hand. His grave, dug by my men, is 600 paces north-west of height 42, west of Lille, on the slope of a little fort, immediately at the corner of a ditch lined with willows which runs there. The grave was at the time marked with a cross and bore his cap and epaulettes. Some of his men and one or two officers were buried by his side or in the British trenches near by.

I have this officer's wrist compass and two despatches, one apparently addressed to his regiment, the other to a subordinate company commander. In the former he describes his position and asks for artillery support; in the second he gives brief fighting orders. I had in my possession also an empty envelope addressed to his wife, Mrs Maffett, but I have unfortunately lost it . . . I will forward the things I have to Mrs Maffett as soon as it is certain that this endeavour to get in touch with her is successful.

I should be glad if a translation of the contents of this letter could be communicated to Captain Maffett's widow through diplomatic channels so that I may be able to make a return for the chivalrous service rendered to my family by Colonel Goodman.

Reinhardt, Lieutenant, Battery Commander

Reinhardt's letter was sent to Captain Maffett's sister, Emilie Harmsworth (sister-in-law of the great newspaper proprietors Viscounts Northcliffe and Rothermere), who asked that a message of appreciation be conveyed to Lieutenant Reinhardt.

Viscount Grey will be much obliged if the US Ambassador at Berlin can be informed that the sister of the deceased officer is anxious that the expression of her grateful thanks may be conveyed to Lieutenant Reinhardt for the particulars which he has thus kindly communicated to the family, as well as for the details in regard to Captain Maffett's burial and the care bestowed upon the preservation of his effects.

Through the recovery of personal possessions belonging to Roser and Maffett, both families were informed of the circumstances in which their loved ones had died. In time they discovered where they were buried, too. Captain Roser's grave is notable as the only German casualty buried in the CWGC cemetery at Sanctuary Wood, while Captain Henry Maffett lies in Houplines Communal Cemetery Extension.

The family of Private Charles Mole was in a state of limbo, similar in circumstances to those experienced by the families of Roser and Maffett. Their son was missing near the town of Cambrai and nothing further was heard of him, until the family received a letter from a German missionary, Immanuel Genahr, and his English wife, Constance. Immanuel Genahr had received a letter from the battlefields from a German soldier and fellow Christian named Weingartner who had found Charles Mole lying in a shell hole with shrapnel wounds to his legs and hands. Weingartner had dressed Private Mole's wounds and brought him a cup of tea, after which Mole was carried to the main road where he would be picked up and taken to hospital. Weingartner's letter was detailed.

> He had two letters with him, which he [Mole] handed to me. These letters I am sending you with this. Whether they ever will reach you I do not know. Mr Genahr will know how to deal with these letters, which I presume are written to your son ... We could not make ourselves understood, he talking English and we German. He tried also to speak some French. From what I understand, he had been lying there for two days. As the place was some distance from the main road, no one had noticed him. So I went again to see my poor friend late in the night and found him still lying there ... I was glad to find him still alive. I had some tea and water with me and allowed him to choose what he preferred and tucked him up as well and as warm as I could. Before I left him I knelt down at his side and prayed with him. Though he may not have understood me he well knew that I was praying with him and for him. I was moved to tears to see how grateful your son looked at my little services.

The next morning Weingartner returned but Private Mole was already in a field hospital. 'My sincere and fervent wish is that this letter will safely reach you, especially in case your son should succumb to his wounds and no news about him should ever reach you.' Nineteen-year-old Charles Mole died a day after reaching hospital and a day before Weingartner wrote his letter. He was buried in Cambrai East Military Cemetery, a plot begun by the Germans for war dead irrespective of nationality. It was designed with great care and attention, and included monuments to German, French, British and Empire dead and in the centre a memorial stone with the words inscribed: 'The Sword divides, but the cross unites'. In September 1918, Cambrai was captured by the Allies, when the cemetery too fell into Allied hands.

Weingartner's letter reached Charles and Emily Mole probably before confirmation of their son's death. While the letter must have offered hope that he had survived, the knowledge that someone had cared for him, and had shown him extraordinary humanity, must have been of enormous comfort in the difficult years to come. The fact, too, that Weingartner had been instrumental in helping their son find a known resting place instead of joining the ranks of the missing must also have been of consolation.

In May 1915, the parents of Lieutenant James 'Jack' Brewster were desperately worried about their son, serving with the 3rd Royal Fusiliers. He had gone missing during an attack in the Ypres Salient and soon afterwards the Brewsters received a letter from Captain James Laird, an officer in the battalion. He apologised for not writing: he was 'trying to find out definitely' what had happened to their son but had 'no news of him'. Laird described the situation further.

> Lieutenant Brewster was ordered to support an attack which was being made. The regiment on his right had attacked and had been repulsed, and one of their men, seeing his own bad plight, yelled out 'Fusiliers, attack'. Poor Jack, who was waiting for his orders to attack at any minute, did not stay to question who the order was from, got up and rushed forward with his men before the Fusiliers were quite ready. He consequently got no support and was last seen rushing towards the German trenches.

Captain Laird asked Lieutenant Brewster's parents whether *they* had heard anything of their son. He was Laird's 'greatest friend' and he was 'desperately anxious to know something definite about him'.

The prognosis was not good and the likelihood high that nothing more would be heard of Lieutenant Brewster. Then, out of the blue, a letter arrived from Denmark. Jack Brewster had been found, not by his own men, but by a German soldier, Sergeant Egbert Wagner.

Brewster was extremely fortunate to be alive. He had got within fifteen yards of the enemy trench when a bullet passed through his thigh, splintering his femur. Pulling himself into a small pond to avoid enemy fire, he lay there binding his broken leg to the good one, using bayonets taken from the dead to act as splints. He then proceeded to drag himself back across the shell holes, past the wounded and dead. By the following morning he had covered around 200 yards when he fell into a narrow ditch. Exhausted, and caught between the fire of both sides, he fell into a deep sleep, so deep that he was unaware that the Germans had attacked and taken the British trenches so that, when he awoke, he found himself behind German lines. The next day he was discovered by Sergeant Wagner, serving with the 25th Jaeger Regiment.

Sergeant Wagner's letter to Brewster's parents was written nine days after the fateful attack.

Dear Sir

On 11th of this month, through God's gracious guiding hand, I was led to discover your son, Lieutenant JA Brender [sic], 3rd Royal Fusiliers, in a shell hole, where he had been lying for two [three] days with a gun shot wound in the upper part of his thigh. Acting on the command of our Lord Jesus 'Love your Enemies' I bandaged him with the permission of our officer, and provided him with bread and wine. I had a lot of conversation with your dear son, whose condition visibly improved by evening. With eight of our brave Riflemen I arranged to get him conveyed, with the assistance of some medical staff, back from our front line position to the collecting centre for wounded. There I handed over your dear son to the care of best and competent hands, and now carry out my promise given to your son, when we were lying so happily together in the shell-hole, in spite of the rain of bullets,

that I would communicate his deliverance to his dear father. I offer
you my earnest wish for peace and await your reply via Denmark.
     Sergeant Egbert Wagner

The letter was sent to Wagner's friend Axel Backhausen for
forwarding to England with the request that his friend send any
reply back to him in the trenches. Three weeks later a letter arrived
in Denmark. The family assured Backhausen of their 'great relief'.
Sergeant Wagner 'must be a very good man', wrote Lieutenant
Brewster's father, asking Backhausen to send or convey the
contents of his reply to Wagner. 'We trust he may live to do other
good work in the world for such men are badly needed in these
terrible times.' The Brewsters' letter thanked Sergeant Wagner
profoundly, telling him that friends had requested the contents of
his correspondence. 'I hope you will forgive me for granting their
requests. I believe, in some cases, it will be used as a text for
sermons next Sunday,' wrote Mr Brewster in closing.

     Lieutenant Brewster was taken to hospital and into captivity.
His injury was severe enough to ensure that he would not see
active service again and the Germans agreed to send him into
internment in Switzerland. In September 1917, he returned to
Britain and gave an account to the military authorities of the incidents that had led to his capture. In his declaration he wrote of
Sergeant Wagner, of the bread and wine brought to his shell hole,
and of his rescue. Sergeant Wagner's letter to John and Eliza
Brewster 'is still in the possession of my father', he added.

     A bond of sincere friendship was cemented. In 1918, the tables
would be turned when Sergeant Wagner's brother was badly
wounded and captured by the British.

The future for pilots such as Captains Rushworth and Don, and
Lieutenants O'Brien and Grinnell-Milne, was both obvious and
yet unclear. Obvious, in that they would languish in a POW
camp, unclear as to how long they might have to remain there

before hostilities ceased. Some officers were content to see the war out, others not. Many Royal Flying Corps pilots, imbued with the thrill of flying, would not wait, and focused instead on a new set of thrilling challenges provided by their desire to escape. In seeking to get away, they improvised, relying on anything they could lay their hands on and adapting it to their advantage.

Weilburg camp was located forty miles east of the Rhine and occupied mainly by Russian and French prisoners with a smattering of British officers including Lieutenant Grinnell-Milne. These British officers had conspired to escape from the start of their incarceration, digging a shallow fifteen-yard tunnel that was discovered after a German guard, stumbling, stamped down hard on the ground, causing a collapse. The British officers were paraded before the commandant and told that if they tried to escape again they would be shot. It was back to the drawing board for the prisoners.

In his memoirs, Grinnell-Milne maintained that owing to chronic shortages in Germany there was 'in practically every camp at least one German whom one could bribe with such luxuries as chocolate or white bread'. He conceded that there was 'great risk attached to this proceeding', but that through the guards, civilian clothing, maps and even a compass were obtained, if at exorbitant cost.

Officers were periodically allowed to leave camp for one or two hours' exercise. Brokered by neutral countries, this privilege was granted to those who gave their word they would not try to escape. Although escorted by guards, officers were still able to pick up items, natural or otherwise, that could be used in a later escape, while walks also kept men physically fitter than might otherwise have been the case.

One man who unwittingly helped these officers escape was none other than the Reverend Henry Williams. In his desire to minister to POWs, he travelled the length and breadth of the country visiting as many camps as he could gain access to, including Weilburg. The success of any breakout plan was dependent on forging passports and travel permits. The only hitch was that no one had any idea what these looked like until, to Grinnell-Milne's delight, the Reverend Williams turned up.

> Some of us, I am afraid, needed personal freedom more than the consolations of the Church and when the parson came to Weilburg, we turned his visit to a more practical end. While he was holding a short service, we examined a small black bag he had incautiously left in our room. The first thing we saw was a brand new railway timetable, containing a small-scale map of Germany and the various frontiers. Furthermore, on looking through a bundle of papers, we found a large number of passes signed by various highly placed German military officers. These passes, authorizing the holder to travel from one end of Germany to the other, were just what we needed. We had obviously no right to touch any of the parson's belongings, but, after debating the matter for some minutes, we decided that for once the end would justify the means. Replacing the majority of the passes, we retained three or four as well as the timetable. The parson left shortly afterwards without apparently noticing anything.
>
> I still feel that I owe him an apology, but as a matter of fact his papers were of inestimable value to us and formed the basis of a large number of forged passes, many of which were successfully used by escaping prisoners.

The Reverend Henry Williams was not quite the innocent he appeared. To gain the high-level consent required to visit POW camps freely, Williams used the good offices of the American Embassy to negotiate with the Germans. John Jackson, an American official in Berlin, acted as intermediary with the German War Ministry and obtained the necessary permission. In return, Williams promised that he would not aid or abet any escape attempts.

Now remember, padre, I trust you not to abuse this privilege in any way. Should you, for instance, even smuggle any letter or paper into or out of a camp, and it comes to my knowledge, I will accept no excuses but will immediately report it to the German authorities, and then you must be prepared to take the consequences.

This warning Williams took to mean playing an active rather than a passive part, as he revealed post-war in his memoirs.

A few of those who wished to make such [escape] attempts may have found my visits of some slight use to them. The most indispensible thing that I always carried about with me on my journeys was a Reichkursbuch [a railway timetable]. This I naturally left in my bag while conducting a service, and it did occasionally happen that after the service I would silently notice that my railways-guide was missing. Then of course my feeling would be 'Gone again? Well, good luck!'

Many years ago, when I was listening to an ex-prisoner of war in Germany describing some of his experiences there on the wireless, I heard him say: 'The English padre who visited us little knew how useful some of his belongings sometimes were . . .' Well, perhaps I 'little knew', but I sometimes guessed.

Only once did Williams break the promise made to Jackson. Visiting a camp in early 1917, he was given a letter smuggled from the Russian Front containing the names, addresses and other particulars of thirty-five men taken from the camp to Libau/Mitau. The position of these men 'was so desperate that their lives were actually in danger [and] on this occasion I did feel justified in putting that letter in my pocket . . .'

At Weilburg, the prisoners' plans to escape were augmented by sometimes risible security. One idea to escape in laundry baskets was scotched only because the baskets were too small. This discovery was made when one of the British officers had the 'good fortune' to get hold of the key, allowing a midnight inspection of facilities. On another occasion, when disguise was deemed necessary for a successful getaway, a bottle of hair dye was simply pocketed from the canteen.

And it was not just security at Weilburg that was found wanting. In what seems the most extraordinary example, an iron-bound box was stolen from a commandant's office in a camp known as Fort 9 near Ingolstadt in Bavaria. This box contained useful items such as cameras, compasses and maps, all of which had been confiscated from prisoners after previous failed escapes. German efficiency was such that every prisoner was given a receipt for his property and the item ticketed with the owner's name. The box was kept at a depot outside the camp but when a prisoner was transferred, the box was brought into the commandant's office. Any belongings of the prisoner were checked out and handed over to the senior NCO in charge of the escort. He would pass on the confiscated items at the next camp. Knowing that two Russian prisoners were to be sent away and that the box would make an appearance, a party of French prisoners agreed to parade in the commandant's office to orchestrate a distracting row. Captain Alfred Evans takes up the story:

> As the row became more and more heated, other Frenchmen and Russians crowded into the bureau. A fearful scrimmage and a great deal of shouting ensued, in the midst of which a party specially detailed for the purpose carried the box unobserved out of the bureau and into our 'reading room,' which was only a few doors away. There men were waiting with hammers and other instruments. The lid was wrenched off and the contents turned out on to the floor.

Once the items had been carefully hidden in pre-prepared hiding places, the box was smashed. 'The Germans discovered their loss.

The bells went and we were all ordered to our rooms. Then, amid shouts of laughter from every room, two rather sullen and shame-faced Germans searched vainly for an enormous box which had only been stolen five minutes before and for which there was no possible hiding-place in any of the rooms.'

Such spectacular opportunism did not provide would-be escapees with the means to escape the camp itself but, rather, items useful for the subsequent journey. To while away time, prisoners thought of endless and often unrealistic plans, but it was usually the tunnel that offered the best means of getting away, though not always.

Fort Zorndorf was an ugly and forbidding complex, more secure than other camps, to which officers who had attempted to escape were sent as punishment. Lieutenant Grinnell-Milne was transferred there at the end of 1916 and met several British officers, some of whom had undertaken multiple escapes. The Germans told Grinnell-Milne that escape was impossible, which, as he discovered, was not strictly true as two Russian officers were still on the loose after using the camp laundry baskets to get away (baskets evidently larger than those at Weilburg). Another ambitious escape attempt had only just been foiled when Grinnell-Milne arrived at Zorndorf. It was a tunnel and a great feat of engineering, for its proposed length of 150 metres was more than two-thirds completed when it was detected.

The camp commandant at Zorndorf, described as a fat, benevolent-looking Prussian, lived outside the camp in a cottage on the fringe of a wood. According to Grinnell-Milne, this man was extremely lazy and if he wished to see any prisoners he did not bother to go into the camp but sent for the men to be brought to his cottage. Guards taking the prisoners numbered no more than two and by early 1917 this escort had dwindled to one, carrying a bayonet. When the prisoner reached the house, the guard knocked, entered, leaving his charge outside. Fifteen yards away was the wood, and five seconds was all a man required to run, jump over a fence and dash into the undergrowth. A sprint followed by a steady jog for several miles would take him, Grinnell-Milne calculated, 'clear from all immediate pursuit'.

What need for elaborate tunnels when prisoners could make a dash for freedom? Grinnell-Milne and two other officers, Lieutenant John Breen, a fellow RFC pilot, and Lieutenant Jocelyn Hardy, decided that such an opportunity was too good to pass up. Hardy was a veteran of multiple escape attempts. He had been one of two travelling companions of the late Major Charles Yate when all three officers were taken to Torgau, in August 1914, shortly before Yate's own failed bid for freedom and his shocking suicide.

Of the three men, Hardy and Grinnell-Milne spoke excellent German. Grinnell-Milne was yet another officer who had studied in Germany, in this case thirteen months at a language school in Freiburg under the direct tuition of a Professor Bauer. He was being prepared as a candidate for the Foreign Office's Diplomatic Service and was, according to Bauer, an exceptional student. Grinnell-Milne could plausibly pass as German.

On the pretence of enquiring whether a camp cinema might be permitted, Grinnell-Milne, Breen and Hardy were given an audience with the commandant. Dressed in civilian clothes beneath their prisoner uniforms, and with pockets stuffed with biscuits and chocolate, maps and compasses, the three men were marched under escort to the house. No one noticed that the prisoners looked decidedly chubby.

'Our escort went inside the house according to plan,' recalled Grinnell-Milne. 'There was not a moment to be lost, as he [the guard] would be out again in less than a minute. We tiptoed away from the door, rounded the corner of the house, and broke into a run.'

All three entered the wood but quickly split up once into the trees. With this in mind, each had an escape map, travelling passes and compass. Grinnell-Milne soon stopped to catch his breath and to remove his prisoner's uniform before carrying on, skirting houses where German labourers were working. By chance he ran into Hardy again and the pair continued together. By the following morning both men were bitterly cold but had covered a considerable distance, stopping for coffee and biscuits in a shop.

Grinnell-Milne's talent for languages came to the fore when he spied an 'unpleasant-looking individual, sallow-faced and with a Kaiser moustache' coming from the back of the store. The German appeared suspicious.

'Have you come a long way?' said the man, eyeing our clothing.

'A fair distance.'

'You seem to have been out all night; you are very wet.'

'Yes, we had to start last night to catch the train here this morning.'

'Are you travelling a long way?'

'As far as Berlin. This is my cousin,' I said, pointing to Hardy, 'who is going with me. You see my mother has just died and we are going to the funeral.'

This silenced him for a time. The story of the 'dead mother' is always useful, and, if told with proper pathos, generally most effective.

Presently our friend got inquisitive again and asked where we had come from. I hurriedly thought of the name of some village which we had passed in the night.

'Güstebiese.'

'Who is your employer there?'

'Herr Ebenstein,' I answered.

He could not say much to that, as he obviously did not know the village, and could not possibly know Herr Ebenstein because he did not exist. This about ended our cross-examination, and we went on with our coffee.

Unbeknown to Grinnell-Milne and Hardy, Breen had been recaptured. The map he was carrying was used to calculate where the other two prisoners were likely to be and, after boarding a train, Grinnell-Milne and Hardy were arrested at gunpoint.

> A man came into the carriage who instantly recognized Hardy, drew a revolver and shouted 'Hands up' at the top of his voice. Then seeing me next to Hardy, he repeated his yell with various epithets of abuse. Several women in the carriage shrieked, the men got up and waved their arms at us, and some officials outside joined in the chorus. It was awe-inspiring, but I think we would have been more impressed if we had not noticed that the aged revolver levelled at us was unloaded and did not even possess a breach.

Returning to Zorndorf, all three men were sentenced to a week's solitary confinement, 'about the most lenient punishment any of us ever received in Germany, and far less than we had expected', wrote Grinnell-Milne. Breen had been recaptured quickly and was knocked about by the pursuing guards, whose 'blood', Grinnell-Milne speculated, was probably near 'boiling-point'.

Hardy and Grinnell-Milne were not assaulted in any way. Both men were bundled off the train, but there was no baying crowd and no jostling. In fact, the men were treated well, given the trouble they had put the German authorities to, and the light custodial sentence again pointed to a change in atmosphere in Germany from that reported by both officers and men in 1914. Such leniency was by no means typical of all POW camps but, where it existed, the impression is given that some commandants, especially those drawn from civilian life, no longer had the stomach for prosecuting the war to the fullest extent, if they ever had. They might even have had one eye on the aftermath of defeat.

The German people had more pressing issues to worry about than Boy's Own escapes by British officers. A multitude of hardships were concentrating civilian minds on daily survival, as continued economic mismanagement and a blinkered focus on the

A British BE2c aircraft brought down over German-held ground. The Royal Flying Corps pilot seems unhurt and is talking to a German officer while, behind, a number of Germans look on intently.

Verwund. engl. Flieger 9/III .16.

Lieutenant Leo Heywood and, looking away, the observer, 17-year-old Second Lieutenant Douglas Gayforth, are driven away in the back of a Mercedes. Many Royal Flying Corps officers enjoyed a visit to their opponents' Squadron Mess, frequently staying for dinner and wine. However, such gracious hospitality often came at a price.

Reading, March 1917: 'The Kaiser's Own' or British soldiers of German heritage await transfer to the Western Front. Eight Infantry Labour Companies (ILCs), of 500 men each, served overseas but behind the lines in the British Army.

Major William Renwick (centre) with the officers of 3rd ILC. Most of the officers attached to these labour companies were no longer fit for front-line service. Renwick had been shell-shocked in March 1916.

Winter 1916: as a punishment, a British prisoner is tied to a post and left out in the snow. The photograph was taken on a secret camera owned by a sergeant in the Lincolnshire Regiment at Hesepe POW Camp.

Hinter der englischen Front im Westen.
Eine Gruppe deutscher Gefangener bei Landarbeiten hinter der Front.

Zensiert
Paul Hoffmann & Co.
Berlin-Schöneberg.

The British employment of prisoners within twelve kilometres of the firing line caused outrage in Germany. The Germans demanded that prisoners should be no closer than 30 kilometres, a demand ignored by the British.

British prisoners labouring behind the lines in France. Although none are pictured carrying the artillery shells seen in the foreground, some POWs were employed in moving munitions, against international law.

A funeral at Doberitz camp presided over by Reverend Henry Williams. In the foreground are men of the Royal Naval Division. Many of these men were sent to work on the Russian Front in February 1917 as a German reprisal for the alleged ill-treatment of prisoners.

This postcard (the reverse of the picture above) was sent home by Able Seaman Cedric Ireland, who is probably one of the men in the foreground of the photograph. Ireland was sent to Russia where he would die in his comrades' arms while working in atrocious sub-zero conditions.

An exceptionally rare photograph showing British POWs at work in the German support trenches on the Russian Front. These men are almost certainly among those sent to Mitau, where dozens died of cold and neglect.

German guards watch prisoners distribute Red Cross parcels. As the Allied blockade on Germany intensified, such parcels saved POWs from virtual starvation.

Cassel POW camp, November 1918: the parcel hut with all the records goes up in flames. There was suspicion among some POWs that comrades running the hut were taking items to sell to German guards.

March 1918: British prisoners remove the personal possessions of dead enemy soldiers killed in the opening days of the German spring offensive. A German soldier makes a note of the items retrieved.

A Red Cross boat carrying exchanged British POWs sails up the estuary towards Boston Harbour. The crowds on the riverbank cheer the arrival of the men. An hour earlier, the same civilians roundly booed German internees on their way home.

1914 - 19 ?
DON'T WAKE US
WE'RE DREAMING
ABOUT THE
EXCHANGE

Dreaming of exchange: this humorous image obscures the fact that many men were suffering severe mental stress or 'barbed wire disease' after being cooped up for years.

Private Bill Easton, seated on the barrel, with his German friend Charley Feldner. Bill agreed to stay on behind enemy lines to help clear the wounded. Given his front-line experience, he was given the honorary rank of Acting Sergeant so that he could give orders to the Germans. On the extreme right stands Sub-Lieutenant Lindemann.

May 1918: the day after capture, Brigadier General Rees meets the Kaiser behind the Chemin des Dames battlefield. Rees recorded the event in his diary, noting how the Kaiser appeared reflective and downbeat.

November 1918: an effigy of the Kaiser is strung up in a British street. The public were assured that the Kaiser would be brought to justice but little diplomatic effort was expended in forcing the Dutch to hand over their 'guest'. He remained in Holland until his death in 1941.

10 November 1918: the Kaiser quietly slips across the border into Holland. It was 24 hours since the verger of St George's Church had watched him visit the neighbouring Hohenzollern Museum. As he left, he took a last look at the Church and then walked away into exile.

The Hohestrasse, Cologne, 1919: British and Empire soldiers walk amongst German civilians. The order not to fraternise was soon ignored by soldiers keen to enjoy the delights of an unspoilt urban metropolis after the devastated battlefields of the Somme and Ypres Salient.

Tired German soldiers withdrawing through Cologne, cross over the river Rhine. Throughout the city banners exalting the courageous efforts of these men were raised by the nervous civilian population and then quickly taken down as Allied troops approached.

British infantry pass German soldiers packing up to go home. The 'pomp and polish order' given to British troops ensured that Allied troops looked in near-immaculate condition as they crossed into Germany, bringing home to Germans the reality of defeat.

Men of the 23rd Royal Fusiliers pose for a picture with the German family on whom they were billeted. Despite complaints about ruined carpets and cigarette burns, most British soldiers got on remarkably well with the civilian population during the seven-year occupation of Cologne.

A lifelong friendship. In the 1950s, former artillery driver Alfred Henn and his wife (right) pose with the family of a German soldier with whom he became friends during the occupation. They remained in contact until the late 1990s.

The author's grandmother, Margarethe van Emden, née Berndt (centre), studying at Leipzig University around 1924. Behind her stands Ernst Jünger, the highly decorated former German infantry officer and author of *Storm of Steel*. Margarethe moved to England in the 1930s where she remained for the rest of her life.

needs of the forces exacerbated problems at home. When, for example, the bread ration was cut in mid-1917, there was much public anger in Berlin and an outbreak of rioting looked likely. When food controllers offered cheap meat to assuage the anger, large numbers of cows were slaughtered as a short-term fix, but then came an inevitable milk shortage and renewed discontent.

'There is a decided inclination to a milder form of revolt, and riots and disturbances do now and then take place, though they are hushed up. The Germans are such a patient and long-suffering race that they do not as yet realize their own power,' wrote Princess Blücher.

By the autumn the shortages were acute. There was almost no petrol or methylated spirits for home lighting, and the electricity supply was erratic. In the morning darkness, long queues formed in every town waiting for vegetables and fruit to be brought from the countryside, with supply never enough to meet demand. All clothes had to be bought with official vouchers. If the German people were showing a distinct lack of interest in prisoner escapes that summer, Private George Allen found that by winter they could not care less.

Allen had been a prisoner since August 1914 when, serving with the 1st Rifle Brigade, he was captured at Mons. In early 1917, he was one of those unfortunate men selected for reprisals and sent to Mitau. In November 1917, Allen escaped from Schwarzkollm camp. During the day he slept rough in woods and at night continued his journey in the general direction of Berlin. Armed with nothing more than indifferent German, he stopped on several occasions in an attempt to buy coffee and food.

Allen's experiences were recorded after repatriation in 1918. The examiner believed the witness credible, answering questions 'fully, frankly and without hesitation'. The examiner believed that he was also a man of 'considerable coolness'. Allen's testimony is interesting not so much for what he did as for the Germans' response to this palpable foreigner.

Nobody asked me who or what I was except on one occasion when I took out (in a café) a tin of bully beef and opened it. A waitress saw me doing this, and came and sat down beside me. I understood enough German to know that she asked me where I had bought the beef, and when she saw I could not tell her she said I was not a German. I tried to say I was. She then asked if I had any meat I could sell her, and I told her no. She then helped herself [to Allen's food] saying she was hungry. She asked me various things in German that I did not understand, and at last I told her I was an escaped English prisoner. She appeared to sympathise with me and got me some more coffee, which I paid for. She asked me how I was going to get away, and I asked her if she could help me. She said she would try. I then went out and returned there in the evening. I tried to get into conversation with the waitress again but failed as the café was too full of customers. I therefore left, and went into another part of the city . . .

On a bridge over the Spree I got into conversation with a man. He said, 'Good day' and asked me what I was doing. I thought he was a detective and I was going to give myself up, being very hungry. He could tell by my bad German that I was a foreigner, and spoke to me in English. I told him I was an escaped prisoner, and he said he felt very sorry for me and gave me a packet of cigarettes. We talked for a long time about the war – he said things in Germany were very bad, and that they must win before long or else they would all be starved . . . he told me he was a socialist and was sympathetic towards prisoners of war. I asked him to help me to escape, and he said it was impossible, as I could not succeed in getting out of the country. He said he hoped I would be successful in getting away.

The next day Allen approached a policeman and gave himself up. He had not eaten for two days. Allen was taken to a police station and then to Döberitz POW camp. He was given fourteen days in dark cells, and released back into camp just before Christmas 1917.

The examiner finished his brief report on Allen:

> His statement to his opening a tin of bully beef in a café seems to show both utter recklessness as to the consequences on his part, and a singular amount of either dullness or indifference on the part of the customers of the café who saw him do so, as the fact of a man being in possession of a tin of meat must, under the circumstances, have been, to say the least of it, unusual, considering the probable scarcity of meat in Berlin.

And that was the key point: German indifference. George Allen did not feel threatened. Was it a coincidence that his apathy towards his own security and anonymity coincided perfectly with the apparent civilian lack of interest in who or what he was? Probably not, and that should have told British Intelligence much about the state of Germany as the war entered its fifth and final year.

9

Biting the Bullet

A general exchange of civilian prisoners would have made sense for the British were it not for the fact that the majority of German internees were of military age. Such an exchange would hugely favour the Central Powers who could and would call up those who were released. A House of Commons debate on the issue in March 1917 concluded that a policy of general exchange would prove to be a mistake. The problem was hypothetical in any case, as no one was going anywhere after the German reintroduction of unrestricted submarine warfare the previous month, forcing a temporary halt to all repatriation and exchanges.

The halt was yet another blow to internees. In May 1917 a letter sent from Islington internment camp claimed that the men were at breaking point. 'Mental depression bordering on desperation' was the internees' description of their plight in the letter sent to the President of London's Swiss Legation (German Division). Although the internees did not complain of ill treatment, their desolation was evident, exacerbated by constant talk of exchanges that 'came to naught'. There were 'cases' that had ended in 'deplorable results'. Almost all the men were married to British-born wives and the pressure on their families was so intense that spouses had suffered breakdowns – 'mental derangements' and 'attempts at suicide'.

The Swiss Legation wrote to the British Foreign Office but the reply was depressingly predictable. The British government had made special arrangements to return a large number of civilians over the age of forty-five but the German government, by 'announcing its intention of sinking all vessels in the neighbour-hood of the British Isles', had scuppered arrangements. 'I'm afraid that the German Government must accept the whole responsibil-ity towards their nationals for their continued detention in this country.'

Deteriorating mental health issues were not peculiar to German internment camps, of course, for what was happening in Britain mirrored events in Germany at POW camps and at Ruhleben. Melancholia, as it was known, was the cause of a number of suicides. In Silesia, where a small number of British prisoners were held, one young officer leapt to his death from the roof of the prison house and at Crefeld, close to the Dutch border, forty-two-year-old Major Arthur Nicholson, of the 1st Cameron Highlanders, committed suicide; again, melancholia was the cause. In his case, wrote the Reverend Henry Williams who presided at the funeral, the major 'had fallen under the delusion that he had not done his duty and therefore did not wish to return home. But he had been careful to exonerate the German authorities from all blame for his actions by leaving a written statement.'

The outward manifestations of melancholia might vary but the root cause was almost always the same: time. Time enough to think, time enough to worry, time enough to feel hemmed in and claustrophobic. In a letter written on 9 June 1917 by an anony-mous Cambridge graduate, a story emerges of men living on the mental edge. 'Everybody's nerves are getting worse . . . these circumstances [of internment] deaden the mind and induce a kind of hopeless apathy and indifference to life outside . . .'

It was in no one's interest to let this situation continue. In 1916, James Gerard, the US ambassador in Berlin, warned that British civilians interned at Ruhleben camp were seriously depressed and no longer complained about conditions. 'There was abundant evidence that many of the prisoners, especially among the older men, had become insane; and as regards the younger men there must be a limit to their endurance.'

In June 1917, the British Cabinet agreed to send three representatives to a conference at The Hague, called to address the issue of prisoners of war and internees and chaired by a Dutch diplomat. The Germans sent three delegates. On 2 July an agreement was reached. Not only would there be a resumption of repatriation, but the Netherlands agreed to intern 1,600 invalid prisoners of war from Britain and 400 from Germany. Three steamers, clearly identified as hospital ships, would criss-cross the North Sea between Rotterdam and the Lincolnshire port of Boston to facilitate repatriation. Exchanges began in October 1917 and as, naturally, there was public enthusiasm for ridding Britain of enemy aliens, the British government expanded the operation to the exchange of German and Austrian internees for wounded and sick British POWs.

At his camp in London, Richard Noschke had first applied for repatriation in the autumn of 1916. He had been interviewed but nothing further was heard. Then, in January 1918, he discovered that further batches of civilian prisoners were being permitted to leave and he immediately put his name forward. 'All of a sudden on 14 February 1918 a list was put up and I found my name amongst them, great was the excitement to be free once more. We had to give up our heavy luggage next morning and leave Alexandra Palace at 6 a.m., on the 16th.'

The men who were due to leave were allowed to make a special application to see their families one last time. 'It was a sad day for all of us as no one knew if we shall ever see them again, it was a very sad farewell but at the same time the thought of freedom overshadowed everything.'

It said something of the mental state of these men that freedom seemed to take priority over ever seeing their wives and children again. For prisoners held for three years, saving their sanity was often akin to saving their lives. The Hague agreement made specific provision for the repatriation of 'suitable subjects' among combatants who had been eighteen months in captivity and were now suffering from serious and clear mental deterioration, or, as it was called, 'barbed-wire disease'. Interned civilians were as likely to suffer as soldiers. Men like Richard Noschke *had* to get away.

On the morning of 16 February, 185 men rose early for a quick breakfast consisting of tea and two potatoes each before leaving Alexandra Palace for King's Cross station. Accompanied by a strong military escort with bayonets fixed, the men were locked into carriages before the train left for Spalding, on the Lincolnshire coast. There, under the hostile gaze of civilians, they filed into an old workhouse-turned-makeshift camp. Twenty-one men were allocated to each filthy room, with access to a small garden for exercise. Meanwhile, detectives from London were sent to carefully examine all private baggage destined for Germany, confiscating anything deemed government property. All books and paperwork were removed apart from personal documents, while money amounting to more than £10 was confiscated. The luggage was then sealed and thorough body searches made of all those due to be deported.

A week later the men, Noschke included, were transferred by train to Boston to await a ship to take them home:

> We remained on the train for nearly an hour as all our luggage was thrown out of the different luggage vans and so fearfully handled by those in charge of it; we only looked on from the train. They broke most of the boxes, and smashed them against each other in such a blind fury as was never experienced before, actually played football with the lighter articles, the officials and also the officers who had escorted us looked silent on, several of our men protested, but it was of no use. Many articles were by this time hanging out of their boxes and trunks, but they were all mercilessly thrown down a slipway on to the waiting tug. At last we were let out of our train one by one; everyone had to go before the Port Deportation official, give his name and number once more and then was allowed to pass on to the waiting steam tug. After all were on, off we

started through the Dock gates into the long creek leading to Boston Wash.

As soon as our steam tug left the dockside, up went a lot of flags and bunting all over the Dock sheds and harbour. We first wondered what was up, but we soon realised that the Red Cross ships which were going to take us home, had also brought some British prisoners home, and a welcome had been prepared for them, but as our train came in first, all the flags had been removed, only to be put up again after we had left. As soon as we got outside the dock there was the other tug waiting ready to come in, full of British wounded prisoners and civilians, some shouting at us, some booing, others gesticulating. As we passed close by, it seemed to give the impression as if all these people thought that we were to blame for all their trouble, thousands of men and women and children were standing all round the surrounding meadows looking on, some taking up a threatening attitude against us.

An hour later the tug left the creek and entered open sea. A few miles away lay three Red Cross ships, the SS *Königin Regentes*, the *Sindora* and the *Zeeland*. Other parties of men were expected from the Isle of Man and Sleaford, so the ships waited until everyone was on board before heading off. All in all, the journey from Alexandra Palace to Germany took fourteen days.

Anger at the treatment to which detainees were subjected led to a series of complaints from the German authorities throughout the spring and summer. Written statements were presented to the British government in which returning internees and prisoners complained of the wanton pilfering of their possessions as they were checked through at the docks. There were complaints that items as small as soap, razors and family photographs had been taken. Personal belongings, from leather suitcases to trumpets, gold watches to boots, were missing, and the damage to property, including bags casually slashed open, had been widespread and apparently sanctioned. There were reports that soldiers were seen with their hands and pockets full of stolen property, indeed, according to one witness, these soldiers boasted in front of detainees of their 'souvenirs'. One German named Manntz, nineteen years a resident in Britain, wrote to bemoan the fact that his group had been robbed and he had lost a leather suitcase.

After investigations the British responded, 'emphatically denying' that theft had taken place. It was entirely possible, they said, that the thefts had taken place in Holland as bags were being unloaded. The prisoners and detainees had unfettered access to the property; in other words, they stole from each other. Counter-accusations flew back and forth: those being repatriated had hidden gold coins in soap, hence its confiscation; the agreed limit of 100lb of baggage per person had been wilfully exceeded, therefore property had had to be left behind, though always, it was claimed, 'any prisoner is given the option of removing what he wishes'. These articles were forwarded to the Prisoner of War Information Bureau for 'safe custody'. Certain items such as photographs, new woollens and leather were banned from export and these had been legally confiscated. In a direct reply to Manntz, the Prisoner of War Department wrote: 'It is understood that the bag in question was undoubtedly new but that Manntz had smeared it over with mud shortly before the inspection of luggage in order to make it appear that the bag had been long in use.'

Rarely in diplomatic exchanges did one side concede a point to the other. Through third parties, both Britain and Germany complained vociferously about scores of different issues, not in the expectation that the other would admit fault and cave in, for both were equally belligerent, but in the hope that behind the scenes action would perhaps be taken to ameliorate an individual's plight.

The repatriation of prisoners took place against a backdrop of severe Allied anxiety on the Western Front. Germany was preparing for an all-out offensive to break the deadlock of trench warfare and force a decision in France and Belgium before the Americans arrived in enough numbers to tip the balance irretrievably against the Central Powers.

After the Russian Revolution of October 1917, and Russia's effective exit from the war in December, Germany had been able to transfer one million battle-hardened men from the Eastern to the Western Front. These men would be used to spearhead an assault against the British, using the modern combat tactics of a carefully targeted and short bombardment and the fast infiltration of front and support lines. Storm troopers, tough and motivated soldiers, would lead the assault, bypassing pockets of resistance to penetrate as far as possible, sowing chaos and confusion as they went. The German army had concentrated its artillery and stock-piled supplies, as the Allies, well aware of their preparations, worked on their own plan of defence. All indications were that the offensive would begin during the second half of March. By the third week of the month, German prisoners were indicating that an assault was imminent.

In Berlin, Princess Evelyn Blücher was torn by emotional ties both to the country of her birth and to the German society of which she was such a notable part. On the evening of 21 March, the Princess was due to hold a large reception at her home but, as the afternoon passed, several of the army officers invited made their apologies: they would not be attending. That evening other officers left early and hurried back to their regiments. At 1 a.m., after the last guests had departed, the Princess sadly contemplated how many of these young men she might never see again.

'The great offensive has begun, and the newspaper headlines all speak of a great German victory. The whole town is being flagged and the bells are ringing.'

The Princess stood at a window and looked sorrowfully out on to the city's most famous public park, the Tiergarten. In the morning sunshine, she noted the first green shoots of spring:

This morning I feel fascinated by the seemingly cheery life going on out there, and stand rooted to the window, trying to escape my own sad thoughts. There are the freshly equipped troops marching away staidly and soberly enough, with the small pathetic following of white-faced women trying to keep pace with their swift march. How many of them will ever see the Brandenburger Tor again?

There is a newspaper-man shouting out the news in a voice that almost makes one believe that the Germans have crossed the Channel. There is the flower-girl offering her small first bunches of violets and snowdrops to women who have no thoughts of flowers, but hurry by with anxious pale faces all in one direction, and I know where, to the Kriegsministerium where the fresh lists of casualties appear daily . . .

My husband enters the room full of the latest news just received straight from the General Staff. They have informed him that a success is certain, but that it seems to be of a local nature, and not so great as the papers make it out to be, and by no means important enough to make those in authority confident of a great ultimate victory.

A thick fog that cut visibility to a few yards aided the opening hours of the offensive. The German army's forward units quickly crossed no-man's-land with few casualties, crashing into the British trenches almost before anyone knew they were coming. Only as the morning progressed did visibility improve, but for many British battalions in the line that was all too late: they were already surrounded.

Private Jack Rogers, serving with the 1/7th Sherwood Foresters, had been due to go on leave on 20 March but because of the emergency his pass had been cancelled. Instead, he found himself in a slit trench from which he and a few other chosen men would try to hold out and inflict as many casualties on the enemy as possible. The German dawn barrage had plastered the ground to the left and right, leaving 'lanes' through which the enemy poured. The plan had worked perfectly and, six hours later, the Germans were sending out mopping-up parties to deal with pockets of resistance.

As they closed on Jack's short section of trench, they began shouting and throwing stick grenades. Then into the trench they came and up went the hands of those still unwounded men defending their position, including Jack, who watched horrified as a German came straight for him, bayonet fixed.

> At that moment I said 'goodbye' – there was to be no more of me. I expected the bayonet. Strangely enough, when he got right up to where I was, and I swear the point of his bayonet was nearly touching me, he stopped, stood down his gun, looked at me and said 'Cigaretten Kamerad?' I nearly dropped to the ground in surprise. Of all the things anybody could ask for. I wondered if I'd heard him correctly but I felt in my jacket pocket where I carried a little tin of cigarettes I used to roll each morning and said 'Yes' and he took some and put them in his pocket, then pointed to my equipment and said 'los'.

In a sap located in a quarry, and directly in the line of the enemy advance, were five signallers of the 16th Manchester Regiment. Their job was to send messages, but, with the fog appearing to hamper enemy troop movement, there had been nothing definite to report. One man was left on top of the sap to keep a lookout and, as the fog began to lift, he reported what he could see, as Lance Corporal Harry Hopthrow recalled: 'He came down and said, "My word we're doing well today, there's a lot of prisoners gone by!" This didn't quite ring true, so one of us went up to look and we found that the "prisoners" were all carrying bayonets, in other words they were the German main force.'

Hopthrow and his mates remained undetected until a white dog, which had appeared out of nowhere, ran towards them,

drawing the attention of two or three Germans who followed suit.
A quick decision had to be made to destroy all the signalling
equipment before the Germans arrived. Surrender was a
formality.

> The Germans came and took over, came down the sap and sat
> down with us – very little communication, because we hadn't each
> other's language. There was no question of resistance; there were
> five of us and battalions of Germans going by. We offered them
> some spare food and cigarettes. Those three chaps were on to a
> very good thing – they were getting out of the war, they'd got a
> bunch of prisoners, they could always say that was why they were
> down there!

Both friend and foe remained in the dugout for much of the
day, being joined by other isolated British soldiers. The ground
shook and reverberated with shellfire, Hopthrow suggesting the
fire was German, the Germans that it was British. When a small
counter-attack organised by some men of the 17th Manchester
Regiment brought British troops back to the quarry, the tables
appeared to have been turned. 'As soon as they realised our troops
were on top the Germans threw their arms on the table. We didn't
bother about them, it was getting dusk and I decided it was time
we were getting out. I led the four of us, none of the others came;
we made a dash for it.' Hopthrow and his mates escaped, but most
men were not so lucky.

Nineteen-year-old stretcher-bearer Private Bill Easton was an
experienced soldier for his age. He had enlisted in 1915 at sixteen
and went to France the following year, serving eighteen months
on the Western Front. On 21 March he was sent forward from his
unit, the 77th Field Ambulance, to an aid post to help with
expected casualties; in the confusion he got mixed up with around
forty infantrymen uncertain what to do and short of food. At one
point Bill had gone off to an abandoned trench in search of rations,

returning almost as the Germans arrived. He was taken prisoner and joined the throng of men being sent to the rear.

We marched from four that afternoon until late that evening and it rained like the devil. It was cold, dark, and as we walked along, there were hundreds of us, I suppose, and if one man fell down you had to leave him, they wouldn't let you pick him up. Eventually we were taken to a field, where some workers came and put barbed wire around us and we lay down.

At four in the morning, I heard a voice ask, 'Any Field Ambulance men who would like to do their comrades a good turn, come to the wire.' I went, and this German said, 'We have got a lot of wounded in the church and we can't look after them because we haven't got enough men and we've got our own people to look at.' I went with a friendly sergeant who could speak English. He took me to the church in which there were a few candles flickering, and a couple of poor hurricane lamps burning. He said, 'You'll find a good supply of water here, and I'll see you in the morning' . . .

In the morning, the main doors of the church flew open and a German came in. He'd got an escort of four soldiers who passed, about turned, banged their rifles on the floor, then shouldered them. After a lot of ritual stamping, the man saluted me. I thought, 'That's a funny thing, saluting a prisoner'. Then he said, 'I'm speaking on behalf of my colonel, who wishes to thank you very much. With our job we can't afford to be bitter enemies. Do you feel my bitter enemy?' I told him that I had no personal animosity against him. We shook hands and he told me not to think of him as an enemy; he couldn't have been nicer.

Over the next few days, Bill Easton helped evacuate the wounded on lorries.

I was given permission to accompany the last of the wounded down to the railhead, but when I got there and the wounded were unloaded, I was ignored. Everyone carried on and I was left standing there until a German came up and I was taken to a canteen for some food. After a while, I was approached by a German sergeant named Charley Feldner. 'I have a request. If you agree, we are allowed to keep POWs close to the front to help with the wounded.' The German medical service's motto was 'The wounded always come first', they used to quote it to me, and they needed as much help as they could get. There was a hospital being opened about four miles from the line, and I consented to stop and help. On the 25 March I wrote in Sergeant Feldner's diary: 'This is to certify that I, William Easton, do quite voluntarily proceed within thirty kilometres of the front with the 625th Sanitäts Komp.'

Given the earlier furore over the employment of prisoners close to the front line, the decision to ask Bill Easton formally to stay and help with the wounded was administratively correct if a little surprising.

There were no ambulances so a miniature train was brought up to take the wounded away. It was driven by a little petrol motor and manned by what were known as Freiwillige, under-age boys who could volunteer for service but were not allowed closer than 10 miles from the front. I'd wanted some other prisoners to help me load the wounded onto the train but Sergeant Feldner came back to say he'd spoken to four men who came from the Midlands and that they were not willing to help. Two of them said they might but this other fellow, a big chap, he swore and told them they would be shot for helping. I was asked if I would have a word with them.

I went and asked what they had against helping to evacuate the wounded. However, this big fellow said, 'We're not all German lovers, you can go and help them but you won't get any help from us.' There was a hell of a row, and he swore at me, calling me everything but a Christian. I told them that the job I had got was really nothing to do with Germans and that I only wanted a bit of help to get those fellows away. I told them I would come back in half an hour. When I returned two of them were wavering and I mentioned that the Germans were picking men out for labour camps and if they didn't help me 'you'll go and lord help you if you do'. In the end I bulldozed them into helping.

I was nicknamed the Kleiner Englander, the little Englishman, and I worked at this hospital under Sergeant Feldner. He was very good to me and called me William and spoke to me in beautiful English, having lived in America for some time. A lot of the men in the company came from Hamburg and pre-war there had been a sea link between Hamburg and Kings Lynn, my home. Several had visited my town and could speak English well. A lot of Germans had the idea that we were fighting the wrong country and that we should have turned on the French instead.

There was a sergeant major, Sub-Lieutenant Lindemann, and he was a brute to his own men but he treated me marvellously. Every morning, about 11 o'clock, he'd shout at the top of his voice, 'Wilhelm, Kommen Sie mit,' so we'd go to the canteen and he'd order a flagon of beer. After a drink he'd get up and throw a note on the counter and he'd say, 'Wilhelm, pfennige', and the change would rattle on the counter and that was a sign for me to pick them up.

There was a fine line between helping the Germans in a human-itarian capacity and being seen to be pro-German. As noted earlier, plenty of accusations were made in interviews given by repatri-ated prisoners that a small number of British soldiers had gone beyond the boundaries of civility and actively sided with the enemy. One or two had even received honorary German ranks, which roused the indignation of fellow prisoners. Such POWs were never called to justify their actions or to give their side of the story. Bill Easton, charged by another POW of being a 'German lover', was in a rather different position from other accused. He remained within range of artillery fire to help the wounded and, because of his knowledge drawn from serving eighteen months on the Western Front, he was valued by his captors above other inexperienced German soldiers.

Honestly, we were friends and I worked among the Germans quite willingly. I had been working there for a while when Sergeant Feldner, he seemed to run the show, came up and said, 'I have an invitation for you. It's not right that you should be here giving orders to men and you're not a sergeant, so while you're with us you'll be an acting sergeant.' This meant I could ask one of these German orderlies to do something and they'd do it. He then told me, 'As a mark of respect, you'll be the guest of honour at our party.' The party was held in what seemed to be an old schoolroom. The Germans managed to get together free casks of beer, and I was asked along where this whole company toasted my health. I was offered a beer but I never drank, because I was a teetotaller, but they wanted to have a photo taken so there I was with a pint of beer in my hand – just for show – and with Sergeant Charley Feldner with his arm on my shoulder.

I worked like a free man. I went into the Mess as a sergeant, and slept in the same room as them. By that time I'd come to respect the Germans, individually I mean, because they were so friendly. Eventually I got dysentery, and that put an end to my work near the front line. The Germans were frightened of anything infectious and so I was put on a lorry straight away – no argument – and that was the last time I saw them.

It might have been the last Bill saw of the German company, but he heard at least once more from Charley Feldner. In May 1919, Feldner wrote a letter from Hamburg which he handed to a British officer whose ship had docked in the port. The officer promised to forward the letter. Sergeant Feldner praised Bill

Easton as a 'courageous and brave boy', and he hoped he had been reunited with his dear ones at home. He hoped, too, that Bill would write back and ended the letter, 'In the meantime a warm handshake and the heartiest greetings from your Charley Feldner'. Bill did write back but the two men never met again.

The process of being taken prisoner was frightening because a soldier gave up all his weapons to throw himself on the mercy of a well-armed and excited enemy. If their surrender was accepted, captives felt an initial euphoria, quickly followed by a tidal wave of depression. With no knowledge of where and in what conditions he would be kept, the prisoner faced the knowledge that his confinement was entirely open-ended. Yet in one respect the prisoners taken in the spring and early summer of 1918 had an advantage. They were buoyed up by the obviously dilapidated state of the German army.

Private George Gadsby was captured on the morning of 23 March after a two-day fighting retreat from Cambrai with the 1/18th London Regiment. After Gadsby's platoon officer had failed to appreciate the need to withdraw once again, his men were surrounded and forced to surrender, Gadsby receiving a friendly whack on the back from a German who said in French, 'Ah oui, la victoire'. It was a victory of sorts but George Gadbsy saw that it was one built on sand.

We had not been on the march long when we realized what a terrible state Germany was in. The roads were blocked with transport, two and three motor cars were lashed together and pulled by the power of the front one, and vehicles (not much better than orange boxes on wheels) were packed so heavily that they creaked under the weight. The Germans' transport reminded us of a travelling circus. Behind each cart generally followed a cow, whilst on the top of the loads could be seen a box of rabbits or fowls. What a pandemonium! Now and then a troop of dusky cavalry mounted on bony ponies passed us on the way, whilst battalions of infantry led by martial music (which did not sound much better than the noise made by a youngster kicking a tin along the road) advanced to the front with stooping heads looking particularly fed up and worn out. Although we realized what privations confronted us, we could not but raise a smile as we marched along.

The seeds of German failure were being sown. They could see, as one of their men noted wryly, 'how magnificently equipped' British soldiers were, with leather jerkins, quality puttees and boots. The contrast with the Germans' own threadbare existence was pronounced, and soldiers began wearing items of captured British kit.

'Our men are hardly to be distinguished from English soldiers,' wrote German officer Rudolph Binding.

Everyone wears at least a leather jerkin, a waterproof [cape] either short or long, English boots or some other beautiful thing . . . Today [27 March] I was mildly hit, so mildly that it only raised a weal. A rifle bullet went through two coats which I was wearing in the early morning on account of the cold and struck my thigh like a blow from a hammer. I was wearing a pair of riding-breeches of English cloth, against which the English bullet stopped respectfully, and fell to earth. I picked it up almost like a friendly greeting . . .

The Germans overran field canteens and depots in which astonishing quantities of food and other provisions were piled high. As men filled their empty stomachs, halted to scoop up cigarettes, or knelt down to smother their boots with British dubbin, it became increasingly difficult for officers to stop a serious and concomitant loss of momentum.

Within days, the Germans captured the town of Albert and, in doing so, passed out of the annihilated Somme battlefield of 1916 and into almost pristine territory. With farms and villages intact, food was in abundance, and chickens, cows and pigeons were taken from civilians as soldiers gorged themselves. 'There is no doubt the army is looting with zest,' wrote Binding. And therein lay the problem. In Albert, thousands of German troops of a Marine Division showed no interest in advancing, to the intense frustration of their officers. They knew that retiring British forces must be harried at all times and not allowed to gain a fresh footing. The strategically vital Allied city of Amiens lay a few miles down the road, but the advance was already stalling.

On 29 March, Binding was billeted in a British artillery repair shop. Around him lay new guns of the latest type and gun parts made of brass. There were also cables, axles, wheels and gun carriages in colossal qualities, amazing Binding, who felt as though he were a visitor at an exhibition.

> Under normal conditions wealth does not attract such attention, but when even the rottenest hut has brass hinges and latches, when every electric-light switch is entirely composed of brass, when one sees depots of thousands of pairs of rubber trench-boots, piles of rubber tyres, a pyramid of iron nails of every sort, when one sees bath-houses with enormous rubber baths and so on, then one realizes the difference between poverty and privations and wealth.

In the distance, Binding could clearly see the spire of Amiens cathedral but neither he nor any other German troops would set foot in the city. Brilliant and tenacious Allied defensive actions helped to save Amiens, and by unintentionally advertising to the enemy the sheer extent of the Allied material advantage, a critical blow was also delivered to German morale.

As the Germans strove to secure a decisive breakthrough, they switched the thrust of their attacks from one region to the next, tactics that led to the inexorable dissipation and degradation of

their forces. From the Somme region, they tried their hand further
north at Armentières, then in May they switched to the area
north-east of Paris, and the Chemin des Dames. On each occasion,
early success was thwarted as supply lines became stretched and
Allied resistance stiffened. During May, the Germans managed to
secure themselves the prize of a well-regarded and experienced
British officer, Brigadier General Hubert Rees, commanding
150th Brigade, 50th Division. Rees's memoirs describe how
quickly the Germans launched their attack, forcing him to withdraw with whoever was to hand from village to village and always
with the impression that the Germans were already to his rear. At
one point his only chance of escape was to hide in a wood until it
was dark, then try to swim across the River Aisne in the hope of
catching up with retreating British forces.

> After dark, we set off and reached the Aisne about 11 p.m. After
> some consideration, we decided that we had better get a log to
> help to ferry the party across and set off downstream to find one,
> or an unguarded bridge. Unfortunately, in crossing a road we were
> seen by a man on horseback, who trotted up, shouting to us to
> halt. We ran into a barbed wire entanglement and struggled
> through it, whilst the man on the horse emptied his pistol at us,
> without effect. Running away on the other side, I thought we had
> come off rather well, but almost at once, we ran into a line of
> transport carts, right across our front. There was nothing left to be
> done then except ask the nearest man where his officer was.

Rees was taken to the headquarters of the 231st German Division,
which, by pure coincidence, had been his headquarters three
weeks earlier. Here his personal possessions were taken away,
including notebooks that, he was pleased to record, contained
little of military value. That night he was reunited with one of his
officers, Captain Edgar Laverack, whom he had last seen in a
village a few hours before capture.

At eleven o'clock the following morning, Rees, Laverack and a third British officer were ordered into a car that took them to the nearby town of Craonne. Here they were directed to the top of a plateau. Rees was angry.

> I imagined that we were being taken to see some corps commander and thought it was deliberately humiliating. I made a remark to Captain Laverack to this effect. The German staff officer with us overheard it and said, 'When you reach the top, you will see His Imperial Majesty the Kaiser, who wishes to speak to you.' When we approached, the Kaiser was apparently having lunch but stepped forward onto a bank and told me to come and speak to him.

In the short but telling interview, Rees spoke to the Kaiser who was in a reflective, almost weary, mood that, with the benefit of historical hindsight, appears to suggest he was aware of the gravity of Germany's military position.

> He asked me numerous questions with regard to my personal history and having discovered I was a Welshman said 'Then you are a kinsman of Lloyd George.' He asked no questions which I could not answer without giving away information and made no indirect attempts to secure information of this character either. Presently, he said, 'Your country and mine ought not to be fighting against each other, we ought to be fighting together against a third. I had no idea that you would fight me. I was very friendly with your royal family, with whom I am related. That, of course, has now all changed and this war drags on with its terrible misery and bloodshed for which I am not responsible.' He added some further comments on the intense hatred of Germany shown by the French and then asked, 'Does England wish for peace?' 'Everyone wishes for peace,' I replied. He then after a pause said, 'My troops made a successful attack yesterday. I saw some of your men, who

have been taken prisoner; they looked as if they had been through a bad hour. Many of them were very young.' I then said that I hoped my troops had fought well against him. He said, 'The English always fight well' and bowed to intimate that the interview was at an end. I withdrew. He talked English with practically no accent.

I rejoined Laverack and the GSO3 of the 25th Division who had stood some distance away whilst I talked to the Kaiser and we went down the hill again to the car. Just as we got into the car, I saw Hindenburg coming up the road on foot, followed by a large staff. He was unmistakably like his caricatures. The German staff officer with us said rather excitedly, 'Here is von Hindenburg,' and as I made no comment, he said in explanation, 'He is our generalissimo, the same as your Foch,' as if I had never heard of the man. I was rather amused.

In ten weeks from the launch of the German March offensive, the British Army reported that nearly 111,000 men were missing, a far higher figure than during the last German offensive against the British in April and May 1915, when 9,100 men were reported missing in six weeks' fighting. The vast majority of the men missing in the spring of 1918 were prisoners and they were taken precisely at a time when Germany was least capable of looking after them. For some, capture was only the start of a living nightmare.

At one camp near St Quentin conditions were beyond appalling and, according to survivors, the behaviour of the commandant and erstwhile civilian barrister, Captain Emil Müller, was atrocious. The camp was called Flavy-le-Martel and, in the immediate aftermath of the German assault in March, prisoners were corralled there in excessive numbers. These men were to be kept where they were and used as labour behind the lines.

The camp consisted of three large huts built for no more than 400 men. Into these huts around 1,200 were squashed, forcing many to sleep outside: no beds or blankets were provided. There were no washing facilities and drinking water was tipped into a wooden trough. Rations consisted of one slice of bread and acorn 'coffee', and a very unpalatable soup made with dried vegetables and sauerkraut. Within weeks dysentery had broken out and it spread quickly among prisoners who were, regardless of their physical condition, expected to work carrying ammunition (illegal under international law), mending roads and building light railways. According to eyewitnesses, the men were frequently struck by Müller or by one of the guards using a rifle butt. Gunner Nathan Sacof, of the Royal Field Artillery, captured on 21 March 1918, acted as an interpreter for the commandant and witnessed how sick men were sent out to work, many collapsing on the road.

Up to seventy prisoners were said to have died in the camp by June, after which a new regime was introduced and conditions improved. At no time did the Red Cross know of the prisoners' whereabouts and no parcels, upon which prisoners in general depended, arrived at the camp.

In interviews conducted at the end of the war, which were used in the first international effort to conduct war crimes trials, a number of soldiers gave damning evidence of the camp's conditions and its notorious commandant, Captain Müller.

In Germany, reports of success on the Western Front were soon tempered by the news that no decisive breakthrough had occurred. In her journal, Princess Evelyn Blücher recorded the darkening mood that summer.

Through news gleaned from friends and from my husband, who is continually meeting military men, I learn that the offensive has not been successful enough to justify the confidence proclaimed in the newspapers. Everything has been staked on their breaking through the enemy's lines, and they have not done so, although they have driven the enemy back. Indeed, I hear the German troops are even being scattered and separated . . . We hear universally that the pluck shown by the English was almost superhuman.

In late April, the Princess received news of the death of her English nephew, Osmund, a nineteen-year-old officer and only son of her eldest brother, Frederick Bretherton-Stapleton. He had been serving with the 9th Lancers and was killed on the second day of the offensive. Poignantly, news of Osmund's death arrived just as nineteen-year-old Norbert, a German nephew and an officer in the German army, was visiting his aunt.

He is on leave, after having been through the whole of the Western offensive. His descriptions of it are terrible. For six days and nights, he says, they lay in the front trenches, with nothing to eat but what they found in the English trenches on the first day. From these they obtained a perfect banquet, such food as none in Germany is accustomed to any longer, with cigarettes and other luxuries. He described to me the friendly manner with which they discussed the war with English officers who were taken prisoner. One Englishman, on being asked when peace would be, answered: 'Well, I suppose it will take two years more before you are really beaten.'

He told that the Americans are daily becoming a more serious asset to the enemy, as each day more troops are pouring in, all fresh and well equipped, a contrast to the tired-out troops opposing them.

In Germany, rumours persisted of peace proposals but they were merely 'ghostly birds of despair', as the Princess described them. The Germans hoped conferences at The Hague, which discussed issues such as prisoner exchanges, would turn into peace congresses; such wishful thinking was brought on by war-weariness and fears for the future. The poor summer weather dangerously affected the potato crop and in the towns and cities people were down to one pound of potatoes a week. By July, it was clear that, while some might hope to scrape by in the summer, the winter held out great horror. The Princess noticed how shabbily people were dressed, wearing wooden clogs instead of shoes, 'the unwilling fashion of the hour', while children ran about barefoot. A friend who managed to track down a pair of boots for her child found that they cracked and split in a dozen places. The boots were not leather, as presumed, but cotton, covered with a thin veneer of polish.

Living in Berlin, the Reverend Williams could see the precipitous decline in morale. He watched with alarm the rise in dishonesty and theft, and the growth of the black market. On one occasion he overheard a distinguished German lawyer negotiating over the telephone for an illicit supply of meat. The lawyer turned down the offer of meat as he had yet to sell on all that he had bought before.

> Everything of value that could be taken away was stolen; not only stair-carpets but brass stair-rods disappeared from the main staircases leading to flats. More than once I had to get up at night to prevent the brass knocker and plate on my front door from being removed. Railway carriages were stripped of their upholstery which occasionally reappeared unmistakable in small boys' nethergarments. A thieves' market was set up in the Rosenheimer Strasse, under the very nose of the Police Presidency, where stolen goods of every description from valuable jewels to household utensils were offered for sale.

Given his high-profile position and the relatively small size of the British community in Berlin, Williams had spoken to Princess Blücher on many occasions and often visited her. He believed the Germans were desperate for the war to end but some still clung to the belief that Germany might ultimately prevail: Princess Blücher disagreed.

> I notice a great change in the people here from what they were last year. They are all 'tired of suffering,' as they express it. 'We want our sons and husbands back, and we want food,' is all they say. And the priests and clergymen too say how difficult it is to hold them in now. Any moment they fear them breaking all control. A man whose business it is, as he puts it, to go round begging for the new war loan, told us that it is very difficult now to persuade people to subscribe, not that they have got any money, for they have more than they know what to do with; but 'patriotism' is dead, it does not 'catch on' any longer, and he can only get them to subscribe by exerting real pressure, and telling them that if they do not do so they will lose everything they have already invested . . .

By the end of July, Germany was talking of defeat. There was even speculation that the Kaiser would choose to die at the head of his troops rather than return with a beaten army. According to Princess Blücher, others said openly that if 'he only had the courage to abdicate now, he might save his whole country from the terrible fate impending . . .'

German newspapers could no longer disguise the seriousness of the position. Stories of the Germans shortening their lines were now taken by the public as an admission of loss and retreat, while at home the constant military and political merry-go-round of sackings and hasty appointments gave the impression that an implosion was nigh. The fear of spreading Bolshevism grew daily. Stories abounded of a nascent rebellion in the army and of wounded men refusing operations for fear that successful treatment would hasten their return to action.

'It is sadly tragical to look on and see the slow fate of Germany overtaking her,' wrote the Princess. 'I, who have watched the people struggling, and seen their unheard-of sacrifices and stolid resignation, cannot but pity them from my heart.'

The public were tired in Britain, too: tired of shortages of food and ever-increasing state control over their lives; tired and bitter at the losses incurred at the front. The German offensive, and the national anxiety at the idea of defeat after such sacrifice, chipped away at public resolve. In their exhaustion civilians were too willing to be swayed by any rabble-rousers who once more returned to the threat offered by uninterned Germans at home. Why, they asked, should they be tolerated and not *all* be sent home?

The desire to repatriate uninterned Germans grew throughout 1917 and 1918 and in the press there were constant reappraisals of the numbers interned and at large. For some, the figures were always too high, whatever they were, and were used to berate the government. During the war there had been two peaks of Germanophobia: October 1914 and May 1915. In July 1918 there was a third and final surge.

After The Hague agreement of July 1917, some MPs had asked why all enemy aliens could not be sent back in one great exchange. Yet their wish to exchange 'All for All' civilian prisoners hit the intractable problem that the British held far more Germans of combat age. The point was conceded and an agreement was made to allow men aged over forty-five to leave, regardless of numbers, even if it meant ten Germans being exchanged for every Briton. In the Lords, questions were put as to whether the government would reconsider sending back Germans of military age, perhaps to a neutral country for continued internment. If nothing else, Britain would be relieved of the expense of looking after these aliens, while returning these Germans would also release an estimated 2,500 men charged with guarding them.

The repetitive nature of the debate made some weary of the whole question. Speaking in the House of Lords, the Archbishop of

Canterbury, Randall Davidson, voiced his growing boredom: 'Anyone who had tried to follow the long-drawn story of talk on this subject [of repatriation] would be surprised by the extraordinary monotony and sameness of every discussion which had taken place.'

The problem was never resolved. No neutral country would take 20,000 internees, and the British government would not countenance the appearance on the Western Front of a new German army division formed from the repatriated. Equally, there was no appetite within the Cabinet to out-Prussian the Prussians as Lord Newton, speaking for the government, pointed out in the Lords in March 1918. 'It would require a double dose of German brutality to send away some of the Germans who have lived in this country for practically all their lives, have married British women, and have sons fighting in the British Army.'

It was precisely for the reasons given by Newton that, despite the hardships of incarceration, many enemy aliens did not want to leave Britain. Newton stressed in his speech that he had just heard of two interned Germans who had committed suicide after receiving repatriation orders, their deaths highlighting again the desperate mental fragility of men in long-term captivity.

Newton explained that, while hundreds of Germans were being repatriated every few weeks, at least a third of those interned would wish to stay owing to family circumstances. 'The presence of a number of Germans in this country will have to be tolerated,' he insisted.

Nevertheless, in July, the Commons listened to a second reading of the government's British Nationality and Status of Aliens Bill, the main purpose of which was to widen the powers required to revoke certificates of naturalisation. The Home Secretary, Sir George Cave, addressing the House, emphasised that hitherto the state revoked certificates only when they had been obtained by false representation or fraud. 'We have all come to the conclusion, mainly owing to experiences arising out of the war, that that power ought to be extended.' 'Hear, hear,' cried MPs.

Cave reassured the House that the government was not looking for arbitrary powers to revoke certificates and that it should be remembered that an individual who gained British nationality generally lost his nationality in the country of his birth. Nevertheless, it was the government's intention to revoke an individual's right to citizenship where it was proven he or she was disloyal or of bad character. If it was no longer in the public interest for a naturalised British subject to remain a citizen, he or she could be judicially stripped of that nationality. A proposal was made to amend the Bill so that certificates awarded since the outbreak of war would be subject to review, although this would not apply to British-born persons.

This last remark sounded contradictory but Cave was referring to British-born women who married Germans and acquired through marriage their husband's nationality. When these German men applied for naturalisation so, by default, had their wives, who were issued with their own certificates of naturalisation. In a case where an individual was to be deprived of his naturalisation, his return to 'alien' status would not be followed by those of his wife and children; they would be given six months to make a declaration of alienage should they wish to cease being British citizens.

The proposals of the Bill met with cross-party agreement, although one or two MPs wished the Bill to be a wartime measure only. Other MPs foresaw that the only danger to the Bill's passage into law would be public insistence that the new rights did not go far enough.

Plenty of civilians were swayed by the arguments of parliamentarians, among them Brigadier General Page Croft MP, who mercilessly played to the public gallery. Naturalised Germans, he said, were to be more feared than unnaturalised ones, as they gained privileges with citizenship while paying only lip service to loyalty. 'They [the government] could tie a peacock's tail to an elephant but that did not make the elephant a peacock,' he told a crowded public meeting in Manchester on 23 July, as the government's Bill reached its last stages. Page Croft told the audience that Germans had been sent to Britain before the war to gain positions of responsibility, becoming naturalised and making themselves indispensible to the country. It was all part and parcel of Germany's scheme for world domination, he said enlighteningly.

Page Croft was doing what other MPs did with apparent impunity: making wild claims without evidence; insisting that both he and other MPs knew of instances of potentially dangerous enemy aliens running free in Britain without sanction.

As predicted, the main objection to the government's Bill was that it did not go far enough, although one press demand that naturalised Germans should be deprived of their citizenship by class and not just on an individual basis was dismissed out of hand by MPs.

The Bill received Royal Assent on 9 August. The legal basis for stripping citizenship from alien-born British subjects was passed and almost no one demurred. An Advisory Committee officially known as the Certificates of Naturalisation (Revocation) Committee was set up and began reviewing cases presented before it, notifying the Home Secretary who should have their certificate of naturalisation revoked. The Committee, composed of three judges, did not have to give reasons for its recommendations and, as reported by *The Times*, 'was not bound by the strict rules of evidence'. The policy of the government, as publicly stated, would be to deport those stripped.

On 7 October, the Committee met for the first time in the Grand Committee Room of Westminster Hall to deliberate in private over an initial tranche of 190 cases. Three weeks later, the press reported that Udo Willmore-Wittner, granted naturalisation in January 1913, had had his certificate revoked for an unspecified crime committed in May 1917, for which he had been imprisoned for one year. The Home Secretary ruled that 'the continuance of the certificate [in this case] was not conducive to the public good'. This case was followed by half a dozen more: all the individuals whose cases were examined were similarly stripped, one on a nebulous charge of showing himself disloyal to His Majesty.

One case of revocation in particular underlined the unchallenged authority of the Advisory Committee. It concerned Caroline Hanemann, a British citizen since October 1914, a trained nurse and a long-term maidservant to Katherine Graham-Smith, the sister of Margot Asquith, wife of the Prime Minister. Caroline Hanemann had served her mistress faithfully since 1890, for Katherine was in very poor health and an invalid by the outbreak of the Great War.

Horatio Bottomley, the ultra-patriotic and rabble-rousing MP for Hackney South, was one MP who prided himself on finding out through endless parliamentary questions just how many Germans had been ejected from the country and how many had had their certificates of naturalisation revoked. Why, Bottomley asked, when it was the policy of His Majesty's Government to deport all Germans stripped of British citizenship, was Caroline Hanemann apparently exempt from such a rule?

The Home Secretary, Edward Shortt, replied that he never asked the Advisory Committee for their reasons for revoking the certificate of naturalisation 'but I do know there was no question of disaffection, disloyalty, or any danger to this country involved', although, since he never asked the Advisory Committee to account for their decisions, how did he know this? Shortt told the House that he had no intention of deporting a woman who, he said, had been in faithful employment since 1890 and was 'entirely inoffensive'.

Mr Bottomley: Then the denaturalization was purely a fantastic act on the part of the Committee?
Mr Shortt: The hon. Member will form his own view.
Mr Bottomley: I have.

If Caroline Hanemann was someone not worthy to hold British citizenship, Bottomley asked, why was she allowed to accompany Katherine Graham-Smith to 10 Downing Street on several occasions during the war? Shortt stonewalled. The reasons for revoking Caroline's citizenship remained obscure, as they no doubt did to Caroline herself. She was not deported and, given the length of her unstinting and faithful service, it is to be hoped she kept her job.

10

All Fall Down

By early autumn, the combined effects of economic mismanagement and the Allied naval blockade had tipped Germany into terminal crisis. British and Empire prisoners in Germany, particularly those sent on working Kommandos, became familiar with the signs. In October 1917, on the seventieth birthday of Chancellor Paul von Hindenburg, Germany had been festooned with flags and portraits of the Field Marshal. His once undeniable popularity was no more. Private George Wash, a prisoner for more than three years, passed through Münster after the celebrations. The flags and pictures had been systematically attacked. 'Every one of them were torn, the eyes scratched out, or defaced. The war loan placards were treated in the same way.'

Exchanged Allied prisoners reported the decline, too. In interviews, they were adamant that whereas food served to prisoners in 1915 had been intentionally substandard, as the Germans then had plenty, by 1918 meals were inadequate simply because the Germans had no more to give. Private Henry Webb of the Royal Army Medical Corps recalled that, during his exchange in September 1918, the train passed through Aachen. Knowing that better food would shortly be theirs, the prisoners threw away their meagre bread rations and watched as German soldiers scrambled for the scraps. Private James Whiteside reported that troops travelling on the same train conversed openly with prisoners. 'They said everything was "kaput", and that they had no bread or meat and no cigarettes worth smoking. They liked the cigarettes we gave them and threw their own away.'

Private Ernest Hart, captured in April 1915, was repatriated in October 1918. On his release, he testified how, on the journey home, he was taken from Heilsburg camp in East Prussia to Berlin.

> I was in the charge of a German soldier, a man about 50 years of age or more. He kept a greengrocer's shop in Berlin. He took me to his home and gave me some dinner, but we only had potatoes. His wife said it was only England that kept the war going. 'Why did they not give us peace?' I told her to write and ask Mr Lloyd George. The husband said that if they do not get peace by Christmas the German soldiers would throw it in.

Just as the escaped POW Private George Allen had walked freely around Berlin, chatting without trepidation to civilians, so, it would appear, Private Ernest Hart was at liberty to see the capital without fear of attack or insult. Hart testified that after his meal the guard took him for a tram ride in what amounted to a sight-seeing tour. During the trip Hart was confident enough to speak to a number of civilians.

> They were all fed up with the war. The newspapers said that the new Government would bring peace by Christmas and the people seemed to have faith in it. The people seemed interested in me and not hostile. They looked thin and pale, though the children did not seem very thin. One lady asked me if I would give her a piece of soap. She was very friendly. She said that when I got home I was to ask England to hurry up and finish the war. The people treated me with great respect. They were as nice to me as anything. Very different to what it was when I was there in 1916 when people spat at me and called me swine. They said that the

war was now left with Lloyd George, who was carrying it on for the capitalists.

At Berlin there was nothing in the shops, and lines of people waiting outside the shops and stalls. The soldier guard told me that he did not want to go to the front, but if he did go, he would make his home in France or England.

I saw notices posted in Berlin with instructions what to do in case of air raids. Also some big posters showing Zeppelins and aeroplanes setting English towns on fire. These had been put up quite recently. There are also illustrations showing the amount of shipping sunk by submarines. The Berlin people, and also the guards at the camps, thought the submarine campaign a wash-out. They cannot understand how we can get so much food if so many ships have been sunk. What surprises them is to see the contents of the [Red Cross] parcels, especially tins bearing American labels, as they are told that the Atlantic trade is stopped.

The German offensive was thoroughly spent by mid-July, and for a few weeks that summer all sides took time to recuperate. The Germans were exhausted; the great optimism of March had been shattered, to be replaced by a deepening malaise. The last German attacks were spasmodic and little short of a disaster, as Rudolf Binding witnessed. 'I know that we are finished. My thoughts oppress me,' he wrote on 19 July. All Germans could hope for was to hold firm, to maintain their positions, but to what end? A negotiated peace would be ideal, but the Allies were in no mood to sit down and talk. On 8 August the Allies, utilising tanks, aircraft, artillery and infantry in an all-arms assault, made spec-tacular gains. The enemy reeled and fell back. It was the begin-ning of a hundred-day campaign in which German troops were harried and chased across the old battlefields and into hitherto untouched countryside.

Frederick Hodges was a nineteen-year-old sergeant involved in mopping-up operations with the Australians on the day after the initial Allied assault.

> We were amazed and thrilled at the depth of penetration, five miles deep in the German line. This had previously been unheard of. When eventually we came to some German field guns, we swarmed round them, laughing and talking excitedly to one another. Scrawled on them in chalk were the words 'captured by the 1st AIF' [Australian Imperial Force]. We were delighted and said 'Good old Aussies!'

Ernst Jünger, a twenty-three-year-old German officer fortified with courage and resilience and four years' war service, knew the war was lost. The advances showed the Allies' strength, 'supplemented by drafts from every corner of the earth', he wrote in his memoirs.

'We had fewer men to set against them, many were little more than boys, and we were short of equipment and training. It was all we could do to plug gaps with our bodies as the tide flooded in.' There was no longer the wherewithal for the heavy counter-attacks of the past. With every enemy attack, Jünger acknowledged, their 'blows were swifter and more devastating'.

In early September, Jünger led his men in one final and localised counter-attack. The men moved off in two lines, but Jünger was struck early on and fell into a trench. Unconscious at first, he came round to hear the ebb and flow of battle. He listened to the noise with rising alarm and the realisation that it was the enemy who were advancing: shouts indicated that British soldiers had broken through on the left. Struggling to his feet, he became aware of German soldiers with their hands raised in surrender.

> There were now loud yells: 'It's no use! Put your guns down! Don't shoot comrades!'

I looked at the two officers who were standing in the trench with me. They smiled back, shrugged, and dropped their belts on the ground.

There was only the choice between captivity and a bullet. I crept out of the trench . . . The only thing in my favour was perhaps the utter confusion, in which some were already exchanging cigarettes, while others were still butchering each other. Two Englishmen, who were leading back a troop of prisoners from the 99th, confronted me. I aimed my pistol at the nearer of the two, and pulled the trigger. The other blazed his rifle at me and missed.

Ernst Jünger and one or two others escaped, but for Jünger himself, badly wounded as he was, there would be no opportunity to fight another day. He was the old guard, an enthusiast of 1914, and one of the few left from the battles of 1915 and 1916, such was the level of attrition when 40 per cent of a battalion's strength could be lost in a single attack.

More than 200,000 German prisoners were captured by British forces in 1918, of whom nearly 187,000 were taken in the three months prior to the Armistice. Corporal Fred Hodges marvelled at the British barrages that autumn, believing them 'the most intense and concentrated I experienced; the crash and thud of multiple explosions was continuous'. In the last dozen days of September, when the Hindenburg Line was broken, as many Germans surrendered as during the entire five-month Somme campaign two years before.

And when the barrage ceased, 'something almost miraculous happened', wrote Hodges. 'We saw grey clad figures emerging from the long pall of black smoke in front of us and as they got nearer we could hear them coughing as they groped their way through the acrid smoke. They stumbled towards us with their hands up; some wounded and all of them completely dazed. How had they possibly survived?'

Captain Arthur Pick, serving with the 1/4th Leicestershire Regiment, was present at the taking of the Hindenburg Line.

There was a dense fog hanging over the low-lying ground round the canal; some of it probably true fog and some of it smoke shells. One could not see many yards ahead and the company became split up. It took several minutes to collect together again before attempting to cross the canal. The fog lifted gradually. The canal here was in a fairly deep cutting. The bank down which we picked our way was a mass of undergrowth, which concealed barbed wire, and which was very difficult to negotiate. We were lucky enough to find a plank bridge to cross by. The far end had been destroyed but the water was only about knee deep. On the far side, on the towpath, three or four Staffords were drinking tea with an equal number of German prisoners. We met a Stafford major with quite a number of men. They had not reached their objective, but seemed determined not to advance any further. The Stafford major had the wind up badly – when two unarmed Germans advanced through the lifting fog, he ordered his troops to line the canal bank! Our morale would have been affected had we stayed near him, so we left him to capture the two willing prisoners. Actually, I doubt if any Staffords advanced any further than this in our immediate vicinity. On the slope up from the canal we saw in a trench a lot of arms waving above the parapet. On reaching the trench we found the occupants unarmed, all their belongings packed up and ready to be marched back. One ancient officer's servant was deemed sufficient escort for them.

The Hindenburg Line was significant as it was the German army's last prepared defensive position. Once it was crossed, the war continued in more or less open countryside, with Germans engaged in a fighting retreat, destroying bridges and crossroads, flooding ground to halt the progress of tanks, booby-trapping houses and barns. Determined and brave German snipers and machine-gunners fought lone battles to slow the Allies' pace of advance. And, when required, the German infantry could still put up a tenacious defence, but the Allies' predominance in almost every aspect of arms was marked, and in artillery the Germans were hopelessly outgunned.

Andrew Bowie, a lance corporal in the Cameron Highlanders, recalled one incident that brought home to him the tragic and, from the German perspective, futile nature of the last weeks of fighting.

> We took a young prisoner. The Germans had pulled back and had had to leave him. I was assisting the intelligence officer, and they brought this boy to the officer; he was only about sixteen and the area just above his hip had been shot away by shrapnel. It was a bad wound, and bleeding a lot at the back. This poor child could speak a little English and said his mother had told him that at the first opportunity he was to give himself up to the English, they would look after him. He was a nice-looking boy, a healthy-looking lad with a big face. The fellows came in to have a look at him, about a dozen of us, and they were giving him chocolate. He could eat a little. They felt he was their own brother, there was an atmosphere of love, he wasn't the enemy then.

The Allies continued to press the Germans psychologically as well as physically. Allied aircraft leafleted the retiring Germans, drawing their attention to the number of their comrades taken prisoner in recent fighting, at 100,000 an accurate enough figure. The leaflets also highlighted monthly reinforcements of 300,000 'fresh American troops'. Any German reading these leaflets could not scoff at such claims as in his heart he knew they were true.

The Germans leafleted in reply. Gone were bellicose claims, or taunts. If any Allied soldier needed proof that the Germans were on their knees, this was it.

We are of the firm conviction that all belligerents owe to mankind
to examine in common whether it is not possible to put an end to
this frightful struggle now, after so many years of costly but unde-
cided fighting whose whole course points towards an understanding. The Imperial and Royal Government therefore propose to the
Government of all the belligerent states to send delegates in the
near future to a place of a neutral country . . . with a view to a
confidential and most binding conference on the main principles
of a treaty of peace.

The outcome was not in doubt: when and where the war would
end, in France or on German soil, in 1918 or in 1919, were the
only subjects under speculation. In early October, reports reached
Sapper Jack Martin that the Germans were asking for an armistice
and he passed these on to the men of his unit; some of them
laughed in derision, accusing Martin of being over-optimistic.

I doubt if anything tangible will result from the request (even if it
be true). I look on it more as a sign of the beginning of the end,
but how long it will be before the end of the end arrives it is
impossible to say. I only hope that Germany will realize her doom
is sealed and accept the fact very quickly. The march today was
twenty miles.

Twenty miles: this was not an advance of twenty miles, but,
regardless of the winding route the men had been forced to take
that day, it still gave some indication of the pressure German
forces were under and evidence of the ground they were being
forced to concede.

The Allied troops, out of the relative safety of trenches and
exposed in the open, suffered dreadful casualties as a rolling offensive snapped at the heels of the German army. The decision to
allow the enemy no respite was eminently sensible when their
morale was at an all-time low and Allied morale correspondingly

high, but inevitably there were incidents where a well-sited German machine gun on a crossroads or on the edge of a small copse caused brief, if localised, havoc.

Nevertheless, as enemy prisoners were marshalled, British soldiers saw how many Germans were marked out by their age: either very old or very young. Too many were intent on saving their lives, giving up without a fight and appearing docile, willing to allow those who were ready to fight to stand their ground.

In the last days of fighting, Corporal Fred Hodges was ordered to take a batch of prisoners back to a POW cage. The men were waiting at a farm as Hodges arrived.

> As I led this untidy looking double line of prisoners out through the gateway, I could hear the Regimental Sergeant Major's rasping voice counting them out, 'Two-four-six-eight-ten—'. When I was about fifty yards from the farm, I stepped to one side, motioned them to keep going, and looked back to see what I had got. I estimated that I had about forty prisoners, and at the rear, one Lancashire Fusilier. Seeing, about sixty yards away, another Fusilier driving another half a dozen Germans before him, I shouted across to him to join us. A few minutes later we were also joined by another small group, which to my great surprise included a German officer.

With the aid of this English-speaker, Hodges turned the straggling group into a column of men marching in fours. The walk was a considerable distance and had to pass through an area saturated with German gas. It was soon evident that enemy gas masks were of a quality much inferior to the Allied ones, and the Germans coughed and spat their way through the affected area.

Several high-explosive shells burst uncomfortably close until the column reached the POW cage, where they met yet more troops going up to the front.

As these fresh troops passed us on the road, they shouted insults at the Germans, and one of them, seeing the German officer at my side, shouted as he passed, 'Make that bloody bastard Boche carry your pack!' I made no reply, and reflected that the nearer one is to the battle, the less hate there is. Some of these boy soldiers going up to the front had probably not been in action. I felt a certain strange kinship with my prisoners.

When Hodges finally handed the men over, he was surprised to be given a receipt.

The receipt was for one German officer and fifty-eight other ranks. I noticed that they detached the German officer from the rest, led him off into a building and expertly sorted the other ranks by regiment, penning them like sheep. They were only too ready to lie down on the straw in the cattle pens. For them the war was over.

Privately, the German High Command conceded defeat on 29 September, the day the Allies broke through the Hindenburg Line and a day after the capitulation of Bulgaria, a Central Powers ally of Germany. On 3 October, the High Command handed back executive power to the Reichstag so that politicians rather than the army would be responsible for negotiating peace. Politicians accepted the offer in order to try to re-establish control over collapsing civil order, and to diminish the growing threat from Bolshevik-inspired radicals. A new chancellor was appointed, the moderate Prince Max von Baden, who would oversee the conclusion of peace with the Allies. He would quickly discover that he had been placed in an almost impossible situation, with socialists demanding the abdication of the Kaiser on one hand, and the political right steadfastly refusing to accept such a move on the other. A few days later, Germany signalled to the United States that she was willing to take part in a negotiated peace agreement. The message, decoded by the French, served only to reassure the Allies that Germany was finished and therefore that negotiation was not an option. It was almost certainly this rumour that Sapper Martin had heard.

On 28 October, an attempt by senior naval officers to launch the German High Seas Fleet in a suicidal attack on the Royal Navy was resisted by naval ratings who mutinied. These men linked up with disgruntled and radicalised industrial workers to quickly establish councils to demand immediate peace and political reform. The revolt rapidly spread from the naval port of Kiel across northern Germany. On 7 November, the 45,000-strong garrison in Cologne rose up and formed a revolutionary council while across the country workers' and soldiers' councils were formed along the structural lines of Russian Soviets. Two days later, Prince Max von Baden resigned and a socialist, Friedrich Ebert, was handed the reigns of power, and announced that Germany was a republic. Within hours the Kaiser bowed to the inevitable and abdicated both as German Emperor and King of Prussia.

In her journal, Princess Evelyn Blücher vividly described her own feelings in contrast to those of the Germans round about her. The war, on which so much had been gambled, was lost, and the fate of the Kaiser had become little more than an opportunity for a brief moment of relief.

I must confess that I myself feel shocked and surprised at the universal rejoicing manifested at the abdication of the Kaiser. They could not be more jubilant if they had won the war! He may deserve his fate, but it seems very hard and cruel to throw stones at him at such a moment, when he must be enduring untold anguish and sorrow.

I never felt so deeply for the German people as I do now, when I see them bravely and persistently trying to redress the wrongs of the war, for which they were in truth never responsible. The greater part of them were men fighting blindly to guard an ideal, the 'Heimat', some patch of mother earth . . . they were told was in danger, and this they went to save.

Amongst the aristocracy, the grief at the breakdown of their country, more than at the personal fall of the Kaiser, is quite heart-rending to see. I have seen some of our friends, strong men, sit down and sob at the news, while others seemed to shrink to half their size and were struck dumb with pain . . .

On that day, 9 November, the verger at St George's Church in Berlin spotted a visitor entering the Monbijou Gardens. It was none other than Kaiser Wilhelm, accompanied by an adjutant carrying a bag. They passed the chapel and entered the neighbouring museum where Hohenzollern treasures were on public display, among them a scarlet gown worn by the Kaiser in 1907 when Oxford University conferred on him an honorary Doctorate of Civil Law. He remained at the museum for half an hour before he left: 'No doubt with the objects that His Majesty did not wish to leave behind, safely tucked away in the bag,' wrote Reverend Williams. 'Then, as the verger looked on, Kaiser Wilhelm stopped and looked in sadness at his mother's church for a minute or two, before leaving the garden.' Although neither the verger nor Williams had any inkling, the Kaiser, a man once so full of self-importance and grandeur, was preparing meekly to slip over the border into exile in Holland. He would never return to Germany.

The next day, Sunday 10 November, Kaiser Wilhelm crossed into Holland. That morning in Berlin, the Reverend Williams was making his way to church to take the first service of the day. There were reports of sporadic fighting in the capital between revolutionaries and the army, but Williams had as yet seen nothing. As he passed through the Monbijou Gardens, there was a sudden exchange of machine-gun and rifle fire between soldiers in the Guards' barracks on one side of the River Spree and officers firing from rooftops on the other.

'Bullets crackled through the bushes close beside me. It was all over in a minute or two, but might re-commence at any moment.' Aware that parishioners for the eleven o'clock service might well walk into the line of fire, Williams positioned himself in front of the large open gates at the entrance to the garden, directing people to go round another way.

I must have looked so unclerical in my grey flannels that a revolutionary sentinel, a young soldier I had noticed with his belt full of hand-grenades, evidently mistook me for a German officer in disguise and immediately reported what he had seen [to fellow revolutionaries].

I had returned to the vestry to robe for the service when the verger appeared, looking frightened. 'They've come!' he gasped. At the same moment I heard a tramp, tramp, tramp in the church and a sharp word of command. The next moment a revolutionary officer appeared in the doorway. With him were half-a-dozen soldiers with fixed bayonets and a machine gun. They had come to arrest me and had been informed that a number of anti-revolutionary officers were in hiding in the church. I assured the officer that he was mistaken – I was the British chaplain and no German, and could give my word of honour that there were no officers hiding in the church. If he would be good enough to search it, I was at his service.

We went round together and looked in every corner. He then said quite courteously, 'I accept your word for it, Herr Kaplan, that we have made a mistake and beg you to accept our apologies, but should there be any deception, you will of course be held responsible. I shall leave two of my men on guard here and withdraw the rest. I bid you good-day,' clicked his heels and saluted. I smiled and held out my hand. He smiled too, grasped it warmly, saluted again and turned on his heel. A nice fellow.

Half-an-hour later we were half-way through the service when, just as we were singing the hymn 'Peace, perfect peace', there was a sudden outburst of artillery and machine gun fire from the barracks outside. It did not disturb us but seemed a curious accompaniment to the words we were singing.

The next day, 11 November, the Armistice came into force.

During the last months of the war, thousands of British prisoners were kept working behind the lines in France and Belgium. Moved from place to place, they were dependent on food the Germans scraped together that was never enough to sustain them for any length of time. These men rarely, if ever, received Red Cross parcels and as the Germans retired that autumn they were forcibly marched from pillar to post, exhausted and weak.

With news of the Armistice, the Germans abandoned their captives. Private George Gadsby of the 1/18th London Regiment was with a batch of prisoners near Namur. The Germans initially wanted these men to continue with them to Cologne, but the prisoners refused and eventually the Germans marched off, leaving George and his mates to 'enjoy the pleasure of watching the defeated German Army retire'.

The wounded were thrown on the top of heavily laden wagons: men were cursing, and all the German soldiers wore strands of red ribbon proclaiming revolution against the Kaiser. Some of them, as they came out of the estaminets drunk, were singing the 'Marseillaise'. The Germans raided several stores and barges, most of them containing wine and spirits.

Another prisoner who had been captured during the March offensive was Private Walter Humphreys of the 1/15th London Regiment. He was in a poor state, trudging ahead of the retiring

Germans. Along with dozens of other prisoners, Humphreys had spent weeks sleeping by the side of the road or on the floors of empty buildings. They were all desperately hungry, too, but still the enemy kept them captive until one afternoon a German officer walked into the farmyard where they were resting and spoke to the men.

'As the Armistice has been signed, you can do as you like as we have no food for you. You are free. We are going back to Germany.' And he walked out and left us there. Everybody scrabbled out to make sure they were free. Where the men intended to go when it was nearly dark, I don't know.

In Germany, news of the Armistice was usually given to prisoners by the camp commandant. After months of poor treatment and frequent abuse, the prisoners were amused at the craven way commandants who had hitherto referred to prisoners as 'Schweinehunde' now addressed them respectfully, as Private Jack Rogers witnessed.

The commandant spoke to his interpreter and the first word this little man said was 'Gentlemen'. You can just imagine the roar that went up when he said that, cheering, shouting, he couldn't keep us quiet.

At Munster railway station, there had accumulated hundreds of small Red Cross parcels that were supposed to have been delivered to prisoners. They were no good to us but we were still extremely cross and did not want German soldiers to have them. So we had a chat amongst ourselves and said that if the authorities could arrange for all the poor people in the village to come to the station, we prisoners would be there to hand them each a parcel. We knew they'd had very little food and a rough time, so wouldn't it be a grand gesture before we went? The next day there were queues of people all lined up, waiting, and we all had the privilege of giving a parcel and you ought to have seen them, the looks on their faces.

The best policy for prisoners weakened by poor treatment was to stay where they were until Allied troops could arrange their safe extraction. This did not mean that prisoners remained confined behind barbed wire and, where there were nearby towns and villages, they took the opportunity to look around them. They found a crestfallen population whose citizens would step from the pavement to walk in the gutter, allowing prisoners the right of way.

For prisoners fortunate enough to have worked on the land, news that they were free depended entirely on fellow farmhands. Alf Bastin, captured in October 1914 with the Royal Naval Division, had been made an assistant gardener on a big estate north of Berlin. When a local man brought a newspaper with the headlines announcing that the war was over, Alf immediately packed up work. 'We had a conversation. He said, "Terrible isn't it? For years and years we've been singing *Deutschland, Deutschland über alles,*" Germany, Germany above all, "and I'll have to change that now to *Deutschland, Deutschland alles über*", Germany, Germany, all is over.'

The signs of revolution were everywhere. Prisoners in France and Germany witnessed guards ripping off army insignia, removing shoulder straps and tying red ribbons to their tunics. At Namur, George Gadsby saw German soldiers threatening to throw their sergeant into the canal; officers who tried to maintain discipline were attacked. At Minden camp, the commandant, a symbol of the old regime and a man who had made it his business to swagger, now became congenial and asked politely if the prisoners had any red handkerchiefs. He intended to make a flag that could be flown over the military section of the camp, although ultimately this flag did not save him from being badly beaten up by revolutionaries. At Birkenmoor camp, a satellite of Gustrow camp, the guards returned singing from a meeting with red flags tied to their bayonets. Prisoners were shocked to see the commandant thrown into prison, sergeants and corporals stripped of rank and rifles, and a private named Hoffmann seizing authority. Civilians, caught up in the revolutionary spirit, tore down the barbed wire surrounding the camp. 'We are free to go wherever we like, and of course we do not miss the chance,' wrote an anonymous prisoner at the camp.

> At first it is not safe to go alone so we have a guide (one of the guards) who carries firearms for his and our protection and if he meets any person not wearing the red in the buttonhole he takes the law into his own hands. After several visits to Kiel and various places, we find it quite safe to go alone . . . the people treat us with every respect and we can obtain plenty of beer and other drinks at their expense.

Officers' camps were no less susceptible to the revolutionary spirit, as Brigadier General Rees saw.

> A rather miserable looking committee wearing red armlets labelled Worker and Soldiers Organisation (Arbeiter-Soldaten Rat) invaded the camp, kicked out the Commandant, pulled down the German flag and substituted two red handkerchiefs which one of the camp orderlies had given to a Fraulein who had made them into underclothes. As no other red bunting was available, she was made to sacrifice her knickers for the good of the cause.
>
> The camp interpreter became commandant and the prisoners were all paraded to hear a speech from him (and see the aforesaid flag go up) in which he eulogized the revolution and said that the war being now over, Englishmen and Germans could live in friendship forever.

As prisoners were about to leave, a short letter printed and distributed by the new German government was handed out. It was brazen in its appeal to let bygones be bygones, and many prisoners discarded the leaflet; their suffering had been great, that was acknowledged, but it was now time to be friends again especially with this new republican state. That was all well and good, but the Germans had lost and it was now for them to be obsequious in defeat.

> The war is over! A little while – and you will see your native land again, your homes, your loved ones, your friends. You will once more take up your accustomed work . . . Your situation has been a difficult one. Our own has been desperate . . . Under the circumstances we did our best to lessen the hardships of your lot, to ensure your comfort, to provide you with pastime, employment, mental and bodily recreation . . . We know that errors have been committed and that there have been hardships for which the former system was to blame. There have been wrongs and evils on both sides. We hope that you will always think of that – and be just.
>
> You entered the old empire of Germany; you leave the new Republic . . . We are sorry that you saw so little of what we were proud of in the former Germany . . . But these things will remain part of New Germany . . . A barbed wire enclosure is not the proper point of view from which to survey or judge a great nation.
>
> The war has blinded all nations. But if a true and just peace will result in opening the eyes of the peoples to the fact, that their interests are common – that no difference in flags, governments, speech or nationality can alter the great truth of the fraternity of all men, this war will not have been fought in vain. If the peoples at last realize that it is not each other who are their enemies, but the ruthless forces of Imperialism and Capitalism, of Militarism of all sorts, of jingo journalism that sows falsehoods, hatred and suspicion, then this war will not have been fought in vain.

We hope that every one of you will go home carrying a message of good will, of conciliation, of enlightenment . . . we bid you farewell.

Few prisoners were ready to be soft-soaped by an appeal to understanding and justice. More significantly, the British government was unlikely to share any lingering sympathies these prisoners might have had for the German people. Politicians had spent the war and would now spend the immediate peace bowing to political realities by threatening tough retribution against the German state. It mattered little that the German government had changed and that the Kaiser had gone. The Germans had hardly shown such benevolence to France after the war of 1870, and, if nothing else, the French would make sure that a hardline stance would be taken in peace negotiations. A great swathe of northern France and Belgium had been laid waste by war and Germany had been barely touched. No one was going to forget that fact.

It was eminently sensible for prisoners held in camps east of the Rhine to wait until trains were sent to extricate them. Prisoners held in France and Belgium could march west, if they were able, until they bumped into the Allied advance guard; prisoners held in German camps near towns or cities such as Aachen or Cologne could try to get across the Dutch, Belgian or French border.

Private Ernie Stevens of the 20th Middlesex Regiment had spent the week following the Armistice waiting around. He had been working at a soda factory twenty miles from the Dutch frontier and had once attempted to escape, only to be recaptured. As the men waited for repatriation, the board of the factory gave them some marks to spend. Then, suddenly, they were ordered to prepare to join a train that would take them to – but not across – the border. On reaching the frontier, the men disembarked and walked into Holland where

they were picked up by private cars and taken to the town of
Roermond. After a night's rest they would be taken by train to
Rotterdam.

The next morning the men assembled at the station.

At Roermond Station we were told to wait at the rear of the train,
just forty of us, when an officer of the Dutch army who spoke
excellent English came up and called us to attention. He told us
to be quiet and to listen carefully, as very soon a number of high-
ranking German officers would be coming on to the platform
towards the far end of the train and that on no account were we to
make any noise whatsoever. We mustn't whistle, mustn't sing,
shout, comment, nothing. After a few minutes we saw some
German officers looking like Christmas trees, all plastered with
colours and shiny boots. Then almost at the end of the group came
a guy I'd seen caricatures of in magazines and newspapers in
Britain. It was Prince Wilhelm, the Crown Prince of Germany.
Ugly looking guy. They weren't interested in us at all but this
crowd travelled on the same train as ourselves, although I never
saw them get off.

After months, and in many cases years, of confinement, the
desire to get home ran deep. Days turned into weeks as the Allies
struggled to get serviceable ambulance trains on to the German
rail network to pick up men from camps spread all over the
country. Too often, prisoners fed up with waiting took it upon
themselves to begin the long journey home. It was a risky policy
and, although the civilian population appeared benign, not all
returning German soldiers could be relied upon to be as
easy-going.

Private Robert Nisbet of the Northumberland Fusiliers left his
POW camp in Mainz with a party of men, intending to travel
down the Rhine to Holland. The November nights were freezing
and they had no blankets. On reaching Cologne, the men decided

to get off the boat and take a room in the Dom Hotel, close to the
river, paying with what little money they had. That evening
Nisbet and his friends went for a stroll to look in the shop
windows. 'This was nearly our undoing. We were spotted by a
crowd of German "Fritzes" most of them fighting drunk – they
gave a blood curdling yell and drew their trench daggers and
made to set on us.' Nisbet and his comrades took off and sprinted
for their hotel as fast as they could, and arrived just ahead of their
pursuers.

> Horrors! The great wood door was tight shut. We hammered on it
> for dear life. Thank God it was opened just before the crowd
> reached us – we were let in – the big door was bolted again and we
> had the satisfaction of hearing the angry rabble, baulked of their
> prey, hammering on the stout oak panels.
>
> The next morning we rejoined our steamer. On the 'Konig
> Wilhelm' bridge above us the first contingents of the German
> Army were marching across – they looked indeed a broken
> army – only the officers marched in a soldierly manner.
> Hundreds of them broke ranks and hurled their rifles over the
> parapet into the Rhine.
>
> That night we tied up at Wesel Quay. We could find no hotel
> but came across a German railway official who introduced us to
> the stationmaster, a typical Prussian with rolls of skin at the back
> of his neck. He not only made us up beds in the first class waiting
> room but treated us to a magnificent meal, and only after we had
> finished did he inform us that the steak we had enjoyed was
> elephant from Cologne zoo.

Since meeting the Kaiser on the battlefield, Brigadier General
Rees had been held in Bad Coburg camp. The officers received a
regular supply of food parcels through the Swedish Red Cross but,
after the Armistice and the breakdown of normal order, this food
supply was cut off. After waiting three weeks for relief, Rees

decided he would go to Berlin to see about getting the officers repatriated. One hundred marks, hidden as an escape slush fund, was given to a German NCO who organised a railway ticket to the capital.

> I may remark that we were treated courteously all the time we were in Berlin and were often saluted by soldiers in the street. This seemed rather remarkable as all officers were being turned out of barracks and being replaced by red committees.
>
> That the war was over and that they [the Germans] had lost it was axiomatic and the real question agitating Berlin was when the Allies would send them food . . . We arrived at the Esplanade practically starving and dined there. The dinner was instructive. The dining hall looked like any other first class restaurant at first sight. There was a good band playing, waiters in white shirts, etc. The glitter of silver and glass, the spotless white of the table cloths, the general air of a first class restaurant ready to provide two famished wayfarers with the world's best . . .

The spotless 'linen' was made of paper, as were the waiters' shirts. The meagre scraps of food served also failed to take the edge off Rees's hunger.

> Our dinner consisted of soup and one piece of black bread baked very thin in an oven. A couple of mouthfuls of goose with two small potatoes and some macaroni. Paté de fois the size of a half crown and not much thicker. A cup of coffee made I believe out of acorns. We staggered out still starving and badly shaken.

The Reverend Henry Williams was hungry too. He was astonished at the events unfolding about him and strolled around Berlin with an air of detached interest. So much had changed that it was as if he was in another country. Walking down the broad boulevard of the Siegesallee, in the heart of the capital, he approached the platform on which stood the wooden statue of Hindenburg, now completely abandoned.

It had long been my wish to have a closer view of this figure, not for the purpose of adding a nail or two to it but, if possible, of extracting some. Here and now, I thought, was my opportunity, while everybody was looking the other way. I approached the platform on which the colossal figure stood. For once it was completely deserted. I hastily mounted the stairs that led to it and found that the giant's knees were still several feet above my head. That meant that all the silver and golden (or gilded) nails covering the choicer parts of the figure, like the face, hands and sword, were well out of my reach; and the ladders leading to them had been removed. But there were still heaps of the commoner steel-headed kind to have a go at. So edging round to the side of a leg where I was most likely to escape observation, I started digging at the nails with my walking-stick. There were no loose ones; they were all well hammered in and not easy to get out. But in a minute or two I had got half-a-dozen or more of them safely in my pocket.

I was trying to get more when suddenly there was a tremendous burst of heavy firing. It must have been from artillery by the 'Reichstag' just across the Platz. Instantly there was a wild commotion as the crowd began to scatter and run, mostly in my direction, men shouting and women screaming and some of them, as I noticed, leaving their hats behind them in the scramble to get away. I managed to slip down the stairs and join the scurrying fugitives without being challenged, and hurried home, delighted with my trophy.

Having reached Berlin, Brigadier General Rees was uncertain as to what to do next. 'It did not appear to be an easy thing to find anyone who could put us in touch with the authorities. I interviewed Mr Mayne of the Red Cross and Sir Edward Ewart who had just arrived but they were unable to give me much information.'

Eventually Rees was pointed in the direction of the Netherlands ambassador who told him he was arranging on behalf of the British government for the safe passage of British prisoners and that he would try to repatriate the officers at Bad Coburg within ten days. In the meantime, he would send food. Rees saw no point in returning to the camp and decided instead to walk around Berlin as a 'free agent' with another officer named Campbell. What he saw as he walked down the Unter den Linden was in stark contrast to the scene which the Reverend Henry Williams had witnessed four years before. Then, the Kaiser had driven through the excited civilian throng, and young men had walked arm in arm singing the national anthem.

We turned into the Unter den Linden where we found ourselves faced with a line of revolutionary troops armed with rifles who were clearing everyone off the street. Campbell, rather boldly, made his way through the crowd and told the commander that a British General wished to go to the Adlon Hotel. The commander after inspecting us waved us through his line and we set off up the empty street. We called in at the Adlon and then finding ourselves again in the Unter den Linden facing the Brandenburg Gate we marched straight ahead through the centre archway, which, prior to the revolution, had been reserved exclusively for the use of the Kaiser.

[Later that day] We found that crowds were beginning to line the streets and that the Prussian Guards were about to make their celebrated entry into Berlin. Having a vantage point where our uniforms would not be too conspicuous we watched the march. Much was subsequently written about their 'victorious' entry but the right word seemed to me to be pathetic. It was merely a home coming. Companies much under strength and composed of boys and men over age. Officers without swords, who were turned out into the street as soon as they reached their barracks. Weapons rusty and equipment stained. Machine gun limbers drawn by a motley collection of broken down horses. As a military spectacle it was lamentable.

That evening we went to see a ballet on skates which had in it a skit on the Hohenzollern family, which passed without comment from the audience. After the theatre we visited a bar in the building to get a drink. It was a long narrow room with the bar counter at one end and a solitary fiddler at the other. Between the counter and the fiddler were a number of chairs fairly well occupied, a large group of German officers being prominent. We got our drinks and found seats, but we had not been there long when something made me turn to look at the fiddler and found that he was facing me and playing 'It's a long way to Tipperary'. Not only that but after a few moments half the people in the bar joined in. The officers did not stand and as we had no wish to be mixed up in any demonstration we left.

The next day Rees was given his papers to leave Germany. They were signed by the new War Minister whose previous job, Rees was amused to hear (erroneously, as it appears) had been that of a bartender in New York.

It would be many months before German prisoners would begin their journey home. Until a peace treaty was signed and the war officially over, the Allies were not about to deliver hundreds of thousands of combat-hardened soldiers to the enemy. Those Germans taken prisoner in the last spasms of fighting in October and November, and who were still in France and Belgium, would be used as orderlies in hospitals or as labour out on the battlefields clearing up the mess that they had helped create.

At the end of November 1918 John and Eliza Brewster received a letter from Sergeant Egbert Wagner. In May 1915, Wagner had saved the life of their son, Lieutenant James Brewster, after heavy fighting at Ypres, and through correspondence a friendship was established. The Brewsters had fervently hoped that Sergeant Wagner would survive the war 'to do other good work' and that hope had been realised: Egbert had been transferred to the Russian Front and taken prisoner but was released after Russia sued for peace.

Sergeant Wagner, through his Danish intermediary, contacted the Brewsters once more. His brother, Lieutenant Theobald Wagner, serving with the 16th Infantry Regiment, 12th Company, had been badly wounded in the chest and captured at the end of August 1918. At the end of the war, Theobald Wagner, having been shipped to England, was still in a military hospital in Sutton Veny, in Wiltshire, but was soon to be removed to an officers' camp.

Egbert Wagner wrote,

> My request is as follows: would it be in any way possible for you to adopt my brother on your estate in any capacity as 'worker', in order that under more favourable conditions he might have the opportunity to get his lung trouble mended?
>
> The assistance I was able to render your son claims no recompense, but our hearts would be rejoiced by any possibility of the return of a like kindness.

Lieutenant James Brewster had been exchanged as unfit for active service, although by the Armistice he had recovered sufficiently to take up duty with a home squadron of the RAF in Norfolk. On receiving a letter from his father, he travelled to Taunton to the officers' POW camp where Theobald Wagner had been taken, and although he was unable to see Lieutenant Wagner personally he managed to get a message through and with it an offer of help. It appears that the Brewster family could not employ Lieutenant Wagner after all, but they lent him some money and managed to get hold of a considerable number of clothes for him; with winter closing in, he had nothing to wear other than the hospital uniform he stood up in.

Germany and Britain remained technically at war, but the Wagners and the Brewsters had long since been at peace.

I I

An Expedient Divorce

After leaving Berlin, Brigadier General Rees proceeded to The Hague where he reported to the British Embassy the following day. He fully expected to find the staff 'thoroughly cheerful with the successful conclusion to the war' but instead he arrived in an atmosphere of anxiety and rumour. Everyone was convinced that Field Marshal Hindenburg was creating a new army outside Hanover with which to renew the fight. It took Rees the best part of two hours to convince the ambassador that no such army existed. This achieved, Rees was packed off to the War Office in London to see and reassure the Foreign Secretary, Arthur Balfour, that 'We really had won the war and [that] the Germans knew it'. Rees remained perplexed by the paranoia.

> My only explanation of what seems a curious phenomenon is that, the armies having lost contact with each other, the Allies were solely dependent on the reports of secret agents. The agents who knew perfectly well that the war was over saw no object in making further reports. The result was a state of intense anxiety amongst responsible people who, faced with a complete absence of any real news, were half inclined to give credence to the wildest rumours.

For two days after the ceasefire there was no communication between the Allies and the Germans. The latter were clear about what the terms of the Armistice obliged them to do. The Allies would hold their line while the German army began its march home, abandoning vast quantities of weaponry as they went. The Germans' head start was in order to avoid any possible clashes between opposing armies but, as Rees pointed out, this created uncertainty and the ridiculous conjecture that the Germans might opt to fight on.

The British Army's senior command had far more pressing problems to deal with than to take notice of idle fears. Before the ceasefire, the Germans had laid booby-traps in towns and villages through which Allied troops would pass. They also planted explosives to blow up important road junctions and these would have to be dealt with by engineers and, where necessary, roads rebuilt. River crossings had been destroyed and pontoons were needed; smashed railway signalling and switching equipment required immediate repair. The first wireless traffic post-11 November was in response to the Allies' urgent need to know where German delayed-action mines were hidden and which roads were currently impassable or badly damaged.

On the ground, the Allied infantry remained on the defensive and instructions were issued forbidding fraternisation; spare time would be used by the men to clean up. In what became known as the 'pomp and polish order', all arms were to achieve a level of smartness that brought home to the enemy the reality of its defeat and, correspondingly, the high morale and battle-readiness of the Allies.

Although the 'talk' had been of waging war to Berlin's gates, there was no appetite to cross the greater part of Germany to reach the enemy's capital, despite the symbolism attached to entering the city. Instead, the Allies would march on the Rhineland but no further: of the British Expeditionary Force's five armies, only the Second Army was given the privilege of crossing the border.

The Allied occupation and control of the industrial and commercial jewel of Germany would undoubtedly focus the attention of Germany's politicians on a lasting peace settlement. The

Germans knew that the Armistice was simply a cessation of hostilities, the Allies reserving the right to reignite the campaign should the Germans become non-compliant.

On 1 December 1918, the first Allied troops crossed into Germany. Stephen Graham, a Scots Guards private, was one of the first over the border.

> We were thoroughly proud of ourselves, as if we ourselves had won the war, and we entered each German village with the air of conscious pride and with that *élan* which might well characterise the first British troops to enter. We believed always that we dazzled the Germans, and that they were rubbing their eyes and asking in surprise, 'Are these the English whom we once despised?'

The Rhineland was partitioned: the Belgians took Düsseldorf to the north of Cologne, the French the region of the Eiffel, including Koblenz to the south, and the Americans occupied Wiesbaden, sixty miles south-east of Koblenz. Haig, in a masterstroke of negotiation, took control of the Rhineland's most important commercial hub, Cologne. He allowed the French, still boiling at the destruction of northern France, to forgo judgement and seize by far the biggest chunk of the Rhineland, including swathes of unimportant farmland and forests: the French had landmass but at the cost of influence. By contrast, the British held a relatively small portion of ground that included a city that was the industrial, financial and transport centre of the region.

At the beginning of December, the citizens of Cologne welcomed home German troops as heroes. Rhenish flags were raised and bunting and banners draped across city streets, reassuring truculent soldiers that civilians honoured their sacrifice. Those flags came down as the final soldiers crossed the Rhine, and the city prepared for British troops.

During the hiatus, trouble broke out as gangs of radicalised former soldiers roamed the streets. City security was threatened and the mayor, Konrad Adenauer, politely asked the British to hurry up in order to restore calm. The 4th (Royal Irish) Dragoon Guards, the regiment that had taken part in the first action four years before, rode into Cologne on 6 December with one squadron forming up outside the cathedral under the gaze of curious civilians. By the terms of the ceasefire, all serving German soldiers were marched east of the Rhine, leaving the city open. To ensure this had happened, two troops under Second Lieutenant Kenneth Stanley rode over the giant river-spanning Hohenzollern Bridge.

After posting sentries at the bridge's western end, Stanley crossed to find a ten-man German guard on the far side where, using a mixture of hand signals and pidgin French, he conveyed his belief that the Germans should not be there. Some minutes later a staff car drew up and out stepped a much-decorated German general who assured Stanley that the British were not meant to cross the river until 12 December. A compromise was reached with the Germans ceding two-thirds of the bridge to enable the British to keep observation. A chalk line was drawn to signify the divide, while a German officer was ordered to report each sunrise to the British until he and his men were withdrawn.

The Second Army fanned out through Cologne and into neighbouring towns such as Bonn. The men took up residence in abandoned barracks, freezing halls, theatres and schoolrooms: eighty-eight schools were requisitioned for troops. Officers were sent to live in private homes, and the population of Cologne grew by a quarter. Where necessary, NCOs and even privates were ordered to sleep under the same roof as German families, some of whom still expected their own soldier sons home at any time.

Living cheek by jowl with British soldiers was not the great hardship it first appeared to be, for hungry families quickly discovered their 'guests' brought with them much-needed food and toiletries purchased from the army's well-stocked canteens.

Military law was introduced, with a 6 p.m. to 9 a.m. curfew. Identity cards were compulsory and freedom of movement restricted. Letters were subject to censorship and telephone calls forbidden. No newspapers or leaflets could be printed without express military permission. The rule of non-fraternisation continued and British soldiers were expected to walk about in twos or more and bearing side arms. No disrespect, intended or otherwise, would be tolerated. As a result, civilians who failed to remove their hats in the presence of British officers had them firmly clipped from their heads; a truculent policeman who attempted to cross the road between companies of a marching battalion was left lying in the gutter. As one journalist wrote, 'British rule settles on a district as softly as snow, but freezes as hard as ice.'

Britain's military leaders and politicians worried unnecessarily about the Bolshevik contagion in Germany spreading among British ranks. To stifle its influence, the British steadfastly refused to work with anyone except existing, properly constituted civil authorities. They declined to recognise any revolutionary governments such as those that briefly existed in Bavaria or Mainz, while within the British Bridgehead, Rhenish separatists and communist Sparticists were watched and, if necessary, expelled. To remain broadly dispassionate, the British were equally firm with right-wing units of the German Freikorps and determinedly refused to sanction the chasing of suspected left-wing 'felons' who escaped into the safety of the British zone.

'The people welcomed us as rescuers from anarchy,' wrote Guardsman Norman Cliff. When he came across a gang terrorising a shopkeeper, he and fellow Guardsmen 'weighed in' until the thugs dispersed. 'The gratitude of the weeping family was overwhelming, and nothing would satisfy them until the father fetched the Iron Cross he had won and handed it to me, emphatically rejecting my appeals to take it back.'

As with most soldiers, the primary concern was for their own welfare and a chance to enjoy the trappings of a beautiful, largely untouched city. The ban on fraternisation was subverted as soldiers mixed with civilians, especially those fortunate enough to be in private billets, although, as Private Stephen Graham saw, the losses of war touched many families.

When we entered into the German houses we saw on many walls and shelves the photographs of soldiers, and as we asked of each we learned the melancholy story – wounded, dead, dead, wounded. Death had paused at every German home. The women brought out their family albums and showed us portraits of themselves as they were before the war, and asked us to compare that with what they looked like now.

In bars and cafés, British soldiers met former German service-men, many of whom wore their greatcoats. Initial frostiness thawed as all understood that while they had been enemies on the battlefields they were, and remained, comrades in arms. It was only weeks since they had been at each other's throats in France and Belgium but German and British soldiers soon shared tables and talked, using, as Graham recalled, the international language of hand gestures and schoolboy French.

We were all agog to find out where Fritz had fought against us, where we had faced one another.
'You at Ypres.'
'Moi aussi at Ypres.'
'Compris Bourlon Wood? Moi at Bourlon Wood.'
'Bapaume? Yes I know that fine, M'sewer. He's been at Bapaume. Wounded, M'sewer? Twice? Moi three times.'
Our fellows would unloose their tunics and show the scars on their bodies. The German boys would do the same. Then, being unable to express themselves, both would grin in a sort of

mutual satisfaction . . . We met a young man who had actually been opposed to our very unit in the Cambrai fighting of a year before.

Racial affinity certainly greatly contributed to bring about this reconciliation between the rank and file and the German people they met. The cleanliness of German towns and villages and of the people, the fair complexions of the women, the first-class state of German civilisation from an artisan's point of view . . . 'Well, Stephen,' said a dour Scottish corporal to me at Zulpich, 'I have been four and a half years out here, and have lived in France and in Belgium and now in Germany, and I can tell you the people I feel nearest to me are these. They are honester and cleaner, and somehow I feel I understand them better.'

He was ordinarily a very reserved fellow, but I know he had hated the Germans.

One man with reason to hate the Germans was Private Ginger Byrne. It was nearly two and a half years since he had seen the slaughter on the first day of the Battle of the Somme. That day he had been pinned down in no-man's-land by a German machine-gunner who made it his personal aspiration to kill the young British private, but Byrne was not one to hold grudges.

I had been given a two-ounce packet of tobacco with a gold label on the front. You could chew it if you wanted. But I smoked fags and I'd had this packet in my pocket for six months. So I thought I'll give old Jerry a present. Well, it was Christmas Eve and we'd been heaving quite different sorts of presents at each other for the previous four Christmases, hadn't we?

So off I trudged through the snow. I went by myself, because if it turned out to be a little old lady by herself she might've been frightened if there'd been more than one soldier. I opened the gate and walked down the footpath and knocked on the door. An old German with one of those big pipes opened the

door and he just looked at me. I didn't know any German except
'Gut morgen' so I said that. Then I took this packet of baccy out
of my pocket and offered it to him, and I held out my hand. So
we shook hands. Then he stood back and motioned me to go
inside.

His wife was there and his two sons. They all welcomed me and
we all shook hands. They didn't have much food, but they had a
good fire and we all sat round the fire. The language barrier was
terrible, but we tried speaking to each other in what bit of French
we had. The old lady obviously couldn't understand anything.
The two sons gave me to understand they'd been machine-gunners
in the German army. I said I'd been a machine-gunner too and we
all nodded our heads. It was a pity I'd no German; we could have
had a nice professional chat. I wondered afterwards if either of
them could have been that gunner on the Somme in 1916. I'd
willingly have shaken him by the hand; he knew his job all
right . . .

I'd spotted a little accordion on one of the kitchen shelves. So I
pointed to it and the old farmer got it down and gave it to me. I
played 'Silent Night' and they sang it in German and I sang it in
English. They really loved that. We enjoyed it so much we sang it
twice. Their national anthem is one of our hymn tunes, you know.
I learned all the words of the German national anthem when I was
in school – in English, of course. In those days they were sort of
relations of ours; still are . . . Funny really.

As barracks were occupied by men of the cavalry and infantry,
so numerous aerodromes on the outskirts of Cologne were taken
over by squadrons of the recently renamed Royal Air Force. The
respect which opposing pilots accorded one another in combat
was uninterrupted during the Occupation. Ernst Udet, the
German ace whose sixty-two victories placed him second only to
the great Baron von Richthofen, was a welcome visitor to RAF
messes. At Bickendorf in early 1919, Udet spoke at length to

British pilots including Captain Edward Crundall, recipient of the Distinguished Flying Cross and with seven victories to his name. Crundall recalled how Udet was 'treated to drinks and talked about the war days when he was stationed at Douai and flying Albatross Scouts'.

Not everyone shared such tolerant views. There was low-level and persistent trouble in the city's back streets, shops and bars, and brawls were common. There was petty and vindictive damage, too. One unidentified private whose portrait was taken by a German photographer wrote on the reverse. 'This [picture] cost me two marks and it cost the man that took it 300 marks for a new camera.' There was theft, soldiers helping themselves to cigarettes in shops with the self-serving excuse that, just as Germans had stripped Belgium bare, so British soldiers were entitled to dish out reciprocal medicine. Complaints poured into the civilian-run Occupation Office about the thoughtlessness of soldiers taking shortcuts across private gardens, trampling on plants. In private billets, homeowners submitted innumerable claims for broken china, damaged furniture, carpets ruined by spurs and cigarette burns. Low-level antagonism was to be expected. What surprised everybody was how well, in general, Britain's Tommies rubbed along with the Germans.

Within months of the Versailles Peace Treaty being signed in June 1919, the number of British troops in Germany shrank to fewer than 10,000. The occupation gradually became another peacetime posting, albeit an attractive one as British soldiers saw their buying power rise concomitant to the declining value of the German currency, which faltered, then freefell. Families were allowed to join the occupying forces and a new source of friction developed between army wives and proud German *Hausfrauen*.

In the end, around 700 soldiers married German girls, and life-long friendships were forged between soldiers and the families with whom they came into contact. Alfred Henn, a driver in the artillery, struck up a friendship with a German soldier that continued until the late 1990s. The pragmatic people of Cologne appreciated the security the British brought, not just for resisting interference from the political extremes tearing the rest of Germany apart, but from the French, whose bitterness at the damage wrought in northern France and the profligate loss of life poisoned post-war contact.

Violet Markham, who visited the Cologne Bridgehead in late 1919, was astonished at the calmness and relative tranquillity on the city's bustling streets.

> The outstanding fact in the occupied territory, and one which fills an English visitor with ever-growing amazement, is the complete acquiescence of the Germans in the situation. Life is astonishingly normal. These amazing people, outwardly at least, do not appear to mind that their country is occupied by hostile armies . . . A picture rose before my eyes of an English station occupied by German troops: would equal apathy and indifference have been shown under such conditions? In this as in many other aspects the German psychology is a riddle to which no answer seems forthcoming, and it is a riddle the perplexity of which will be found to deepen with every hour spent in the occupied territory.

Of course these were not 'Germans' inasmuch as they were not Bavarians, Hannoverians or Schwaben. These civilians were Rhinelanders, and Rhinelanders prided themselves on an easy nature and gentle pragmatism. Security and relative stability brought by the British after such a devastating war was worth more at that moment than unfettered freedom and probable chaos. No population enjoys being occupied but the Germans had come to call the British-controlled Cologne Bridgehead 'the Island of the Blessed', and for good reason.

*   *   *

The wartime blockade on Germany remained in force while the victorious nations met at Versailles to wrangle over a treaty to be presented to the German nation as a fait accompli. Meanwhile, the acute food shortages in Germany continued and in January 1919 the British government acted to alleviate the suffering. In the Rhineland, the average daily civilian intake had shrunk to barely 1,000 calories per person. Orders were given that surplus stores, including 12,000 tons of meat and 100,000 tons of potatoes, were to be shipped from Rotterdam and Antwerp to the west bank of the Rhine. The situation was just as dire in Berlin where there remained a small British contingent, including Princess Evelyn Blücher and the Reverend Henry Williams. In response, the British government authorised surplus Red Cross supplies to be distributed among British residents in the capital, but included an important rider: 'Beneficiaries must be genuine British subjects and not include British born wives whose husbands are of enemy nationality.' It meant that naturalised British subjects of German birth living in Germany had a greater right to these parcels than women born in Britain and married to Germans, as long as they could prove 'a satisfactory connection with the British Empire during residence in Germany', whatever that was supposed to mean.

Ada Crosley was desperately worried about her daughter, Lillian Stephan, and her young grandson. Lillian married a German in 1910 and had, prior to the war, moved to Arnstadt where she remained. Although she was considered German by British authorities, her mother insisted her daughter had never been naturalised and neither had her grandson. By January 1919 mother and daughter were practically starving. In a letter to the Red Cross Society, Ada pleaded for help.

I had a letter today from her begging very hard for food for herself and child whose health is a great anxiety for her for want of food and milk. She has tried to get home to England for the sake of the child's life. We have no wish nor has she for her husband, only herself and child. Can she soon come home to be fed before it's too late or can I send her food for the child, please, please can you help in some way to do something . . . she has no German sympathies, but is a thorough true Englishwoman. I have had three sons at the war all wounded severely, one a prisoner, but my daughter's plight is my greatest trial.

A reply came shortly afterwards: 'The Minister of Blockade has been consulted regarding this matter, and has decided that food should only be supplied, for the present, to genuine British subjects. Accordingly assistance should not be given to Mrs Stephan.'

British-born women who had married for love effectively remained outcasts. By contrast, a German-born woman, Malvina Mendelssohn, received aid once the authorities had checked that her German husband was naturalised British in the 1870s. He had died in the 1890s and his wife moved to Wiesbaden. On the outbreak of war, and owing to her British nationality, she was forced to leave Wiesbaden, spending the rest of the war in Frankfurt. Old and in ill health, she was in a desperate plight but food parcels would be on their way to her. 'Inform the CPWC [Central Prisoners of War Committee] that Mrs Mendelssohn is a British subject and that there is no objection to their supplying her with food from Berlin.'

Government policy angered some senior British officers working in Berlin. One, Major General Sir Richard Ewart, complained about the extreme unfairness involved in the 'hard and fast rule' that penalised these British-born women. 'The result was to exclude a considerable number of very deserving cases and to include many which were clearly not so deserving.' Despite his protestations, Sir Richard was given his instructions: there was to be no change, although he was at least given the courtesy of a three-point explanation.

1. If once we begin to allow food to go freely to wives of Germans, there will be an end to the blockade.

2. To relieve the wife is to relieve the husband and I think the principle is unsound, especially as we hear from the Netherlands Minister in Berlin of the number of British subjects there who are in need of relief.

3. The British-born wife of a German is no longer a British subject ... German subjects should be helped by their own Government out of the supplies allowed under the terms of the armistice and any such future supplies – not by the British Red Cross.

If these British-born women were going to be fed, they would have to return to Britain. In March 1919, in a Foreign Office file, an official set out the prevailing view. 'It's a Home Office matter, but their attitude we know is that British born <u>widows</u> of Boches may be permitted to come to this country provided that they undertake to apply for naturalisation as soon as possible after arrival. I do not think any children who were German nationals would be admitted.' It was a stance that would not alter until peace was signed; until then, it was unlikely that any British-born 'German' mother was about to leave her children behind.

In Berlin, Princess Blücher addressed the plight of such women in her journal, asking why it was that British and American wives were being made to suffer through no fault of their own. Her journal was coming to a close after four and a half years of jotting down disasters great and small, for 'there was hardly ever a ray of light to vary the long gloomy chapter of history', she believed.

We English or Americans who happen to have alien husbands are subject to mistrust and suspicion everywhere. Instead of our position being alleviated by the end of actual hostilities, we shall be treated as pariahs and outsiders in every country.

From the very outbreak of the war our position was difficult, and the more conscientiously we tried to act up to our feeling of duty to both countries, the more keenly did we feel the slights and insults we often had to bear. Destiny devolved upon us the task of trying to be impartial (as far as this was possible) to both countries, and of endeavoring to keep up some shred of courteous feeling between them.

It was not an easy moment for many of us, when, loving our country and our families with every fibre of our being, we followed our husbands abroad into their own land, urged by loyalty to them to try and be just in our opinions, at a moment when our relatives were falling at their hands, and all the evil spirits of hatred and resentment were let loose on the world.

True, our relations in England and America remained faithful, but very often their partisanship for us made them liable to petty persecutions themselves. Here, where we were subject to suspicion and mistrust at every step, and our simplest sayings were wilfully misconstrued, our husbands fought our battles loyally, and although they were patriotic in the best sense of the word, were regarded with doubt in both countries. Now, at this time of spurious peace, we are worse off than ever. We may not return to the home of our youth, even for the most fleeting visit to our parents who are dying to see us, because our husbands, no matter what their way of thinking may be, happen to be aliens; for the same reason our money and belongings are kept back from us. In Germany again we are looked upon doubtfully because our sympathies may be too international; in neutral countries we may not visit or associate with society for fear of compromising our friends; whilst in order not to compromise our husbands we may not be seen talking to English or American friends or relatives anywhere in public. Thus, everywhere we feel banished and in exile, and long for a time when a more charitable feeling shall prevail in the world. These complaints are of course not to be limited to the English wives of Germans, but may be applied to all women married to aliens. There is indeed no place under the sun for us, and absolutely no laws to protect us . . .

Feelings of alienation and displacement held another group in its thrall, although in many people's eyes this group had done nothing other than bring trouble down on its own collective head. The Reverend Henry Williams knew about them, the 'renegades', he called them, the men of the Irish Brigade as they knew themselves – the four dozen or so who signed up under Sir Roger Casement's encouragement to fight for Ireland. These men had ended up abandoned and segregated from all other prisoners, sitting out the war in military barracks at Zossen, spending time in pubs, as Williams was led to believe.

The last I heard of these Irishmen was that they were still in Germany for some time after the end of the war because they daren't go home for fear of being shot. One of them, a big fat fellow, made himself conspicuous when the Revolution broke out by finding his way with a Machine Gun on to the top of the Brandenburg Tor in Berlin and remaining perched up here for two or three days. For the sake of that machine gun it is to be hoped he kept fairly sober.

Whether Williams actually saw the Irishman or not is unclear. If it was second-hand information, it certainly appears reliable and may have come from Major General Sir Richard Ewart, with whom Williams was well acquainted. Through Sir Richard, a more detailed story of Casement and his ill-fated Brigade emerged. In early February 1919, Sir Richard met Princess Evelyn Blücher and her husband at the Continental Hotel in Berlin. Over dinner a number of topics were discussed: Princess Blücher spoke first of the military campaign in Africa where her brother-in-law, Admiral Sir Edward Charlton, had been serving alongside Sir Richard

during operations. And then the talk turned to Casement, as Sir
Richard recorded.

> She mentioned that they [the Prince and Princess] had seen a
> good deal of Casement. They looked at him as a most misguided
> man, and practically off his head . . . Before Casement left for
> the final trip [to Ireland], he gave Prince Blücher some hand-
> written papers . . . Princess Blücher asked me to read the
> papers . . . They are interesting as showing that Casement was
> averse to any attempted uprising in Ireland unless supported
> by organized foreign assistance in the shape of men, arms,
> supplies etc. The Irish Revolutionaries on the other hand asked
> Germany to send arms alone. Casement thought this a mad
> scheme, and refused to endanger the men of his 'Brigade' by
> sending them on the venture. The German Government then
> rounded on him, and threatened to throw the whole blame on
> him by reporting him to the Irish Revolutionaries . . . it was
> interesting to see that Ireland was in constant communication
> with Germany.

Three days after this convivial dinner, Sir Richard came across
five Irish Brigade volunteers; by this time the hand-made green
uniforms were gone. Now they were 'a rough looking lot in civilian clothes', and included one of the original ringleaders, Henry
Burke.

> Our discovery of Burke was interesting. During the fighting in
> Berlin, the Government troops picketed the Brandenburg Gate at
> the end of the Unter den Linden and all motors were stopped.
> Lieutenant Breen went through in a car and to his astonishment
> the NCO of the picket challenged in a broad Irish brogue!
> This was Private Burke of the Connaught Rangers [he was
> actually of the Royal Dublin Fusiliers]. In the evening he came
> round to the Embassy and told his story. It appeared that when the

Revolution took place and the German guards were slack, many prisoners got out of their camps and Burke, knowing he was a marked man as belonging to the Casement 'Brigade', disappeared with the others. He hung about in Berlin thereafter till one day he saw, during the fighting, a Government soldier throw down his rifle and join the [communist-inspired] Sparticists and he said it was more than he could stand to remain idle when a fight was on so he joined up with the Government troops and fought with them!

The men had little to do, nowhere to go and in the end they became compliant. Whether they were cajoled or threatened, the five left Berlin and headed for Cologne to report to Second Army Headquarters for repatriation. More men of the Irish Brigade followed and within weeks most of the men who had enlisted into the Irish Brigade were back in Britain. Four never returned. One died of natural causes in 1916; one committed suicide; one more died in a fight with another Irish Brigade recruit, and the last was shot dead during the continued unrest in Germany in February 1919.

The survivors had every reason to feel nervous returning to Britain after the punishment handed out to the Irish rebels of Easter 1916. In fact they need not have worried. The majority of those who had joined the Brigade had, by providence, achieved absolutely nothing and that in a sense was their saving grace.

In February 1919, the government considered the fate of Casement's Brigade. There was little inclination to pursue the men for treason or desertion. The recent amnesty and release of Irish rebels from prison weakened the case for a prosecution, and a trial would, it was acknowledged, only inflame feelings once again in Ireland. Lawyers working for the Crown believed that any trial would have to be pursued through the civil courts and not by court martial, as many of the cases would be disbarred owing to the lapse of time. Section 161 of the Army Act, lawyers advised, stipulated that a court martial had to take place within three years of an offence.

> We are of the opinion that it is highly improbable that a jury would convict anybody of this offence against whom it could only be said that he had joined the Irish Brigade. It would be open to any such a person to say, and to say without the possibility of contradiction, that his reason for joining was not disloyalty to the Crown, but a desire to get a favourable opportunity for escape, or more lenient treatment from the Germans.

On the same day as the Law Officers' report, Winston Churchill stood up in the House of Commons and told MPs that as far as the government was aware, thirty-three of the Brigade were now back in Britain and, while their whereabouts were known, none was in custody. A month later at least six of the Brigade had returned to Ireland and the decision was quickly taken not to proceed against any of them for 'technical reasons'. In reality the best prosecution evidence would either have had to come from members of the Brigade who chose to turn on their comrades, which was unlikely, or from the Germans themselves, and that was out of the question. The Allies' expressed determination was to prosecute Germans for war crimes, not to call them as witnesses in a trial of British citizens.

The Versailles Peace Treaty included specific clauses to deal with the thorny issue of war criminals and their prosecution. By signing the Treaty, the Germans committed themselves to Articles 228, 229 and 230 which required them to hand over alleged criminals for trial in Allied courts. Yet, despite Germany receiving a combined Allied list of 854 names, including German war heroes such as Hindenburg and Ludendorff, not one senior ranking politician or soldier was ever prosecuted.

Fleet Street fury over enemy atrocities led the public to believe that British politicians would lead the way in demanding the handover of war criminals; there had certainly been enough vitriolic political speeches made after the ceasefire to gave that impression. Britain would take the lead but, ironically, not in prosecutions. Among the Allies, Britain backed out of putting anyone on trial who had or still held any significant political or military standing in Germany.

By contrast to France or Belgium, Britain was effectively untouched by the destruction of property. Significantly, Britain's war aims were broadly satisfied by the end of June 1919. Germany's High Seas fleet, interned at the Royal Naval base in Scapa Flow, had been scuttled by the ships' skeleton crews. Without a navy and shorn by the Treaty of all colonial possessions, Germany would never again threaten the Empire, or so it was thought. The political imperative to hunt down German war criminals faded with declining public pressure at home and the general desire to move on and address domestic economic and social problems. When the Dutch refused to hand over Kaiser Wilhelm, the British huffed and puffed but ultimately accepted the decision. Indeed, in time the British strove to ameliorate the far more aggressive stance of French and Belgian politicians towards the realisation of war crimes trials, fearing that prosecution of senior German officers would cause a right-wing backlash and further destabilise the country. The truth was that the British fear of Bolshevik ideology spreading from the east, rather than the issue of war criminals, held the attention of politicians. In a note found amongst Foreign Office papers and dated March 1920, Winston Churchill made clear where his sympathies lay.

In my view the objective which we should pursue at the present time is the building up of a strong but peaceful Germany who will not attack our French allies, but will at the same time act

as a moral bulwark against the Bolshevism of Russia . . . The
advice of the War Office throughout the last fifteen months has
consistently [con]tended that recovery, stability and [the] tran-
quilization of Europe, will enable Britain to enjoy the fruits of
victory . . .

It was a pragmatic statement. Even so, after all the politicians'
promises, some attempt to prosecute would have to be made, and
each nation drew up its list of targets, starting from the top.

British military intelligence officer Stewart Roddie was a man
acutely aware of Germany's precarious political position. In early
1920, six months after Versailles, he attended a supper at the
home of a prominent businessman who acted as host to the country's political elite. The President and Prime Minister of Germany
were to be there, as was the country's Defence Minister, Gustav
Noske. According to Roddie, using this private house allowed
people to speak frankly and openly.

As Roddie was about leave his hotel that evening, his batman
handed him his coat. In the pocket, he had placed a loaded service
revolver and half a dozen rounds of spare ammunition. Roddie
was surprised, seeing no reason for such extravagant precautions.
'Much to his [the batman's] disgust I refused to be armed to the
teeth, but when I reached the rendezvous and found the house
surrounded by detectives who certainly were, I wondered if I had
not been unduly rash.'

At dinner, Roddie spoke at length to the Defence Minister.
Noske impressed upon Roddie that his government had struggled
for a year to build even the semblance of stability and now the
Allies demanded the one thing that would make the German
people fulminate.

'You want us to arrest the Kaiser, the Crown Prince, Hindenburg,
Ludendorff, hundreds of officers, high and low, and deliver them
over to you to be tried for crimes against you. Since when has it

been the custom for the accuser to be the judge? What would our people think of those who made such a foul demand of them, and what would the world think of the people who complied? . . . I can easily afford to risk my life; I have little to live for. My only son you shot to pieces . . . Oh, he's not dead. He's only in a madhouse. That is the end of my family.'

His face grew hard and his voice metallic, and he brought out those last words as if he were biting grit. And something cold shivered down my spine as I felt what this being of seemingly steel and iron was enduring.

'Get your country to see that they ask an impossibility; they will if things are explained.'

Noske was a member of the Social Democratic Party and was seen as a moderate figure. Yet, in Germany's turmoil, he had used his hidden inner steel to ruthlessly crush a myriad communist uprisings in 1919 while working as closely as he dare with the army's traditional right-wing officer class.

After dinner, Noske offered to give Roddie a lift back to the Adlon Hotel and Roddie told the Defence Minister about the precautions his batman had taken. '"Well," Noske said, putting his hand in his coat pocket and producing a deadly looking automatic, "you are not as careful as I am. Not that this would save me, but I should like the satisfaction of having a shot at whoever got me."' The necessity of carrying a gun, and the seriousness of Noske's words, were not lost on Roddie who reported back what he had seen and heard. He was immediately ordered to England to meet senior military officers, including Field Marshal Henry Wilson, and politicians of the stature of Winston Churchill and Sir Arthur Balfour. 'Mr Churchill appeared to me to be the most alive to the seriousness of the internal conditions in Germany,' Roddie wrote in his memoirs, adding that he believed his evidence was circulated within the Cabinet.

Roddie could not know whether his evidence was key to modifying British policy on the prosecution of war criminals, but it seems likely that it had some unquantifiable effect. Less than four weeks later, in March 1920, Roddie had a two-hour private meeting with Ludendorff in Berlin. Roddie became convinced that the ageing Field Marshal was as fearful of, and as trenchant against, the baleful influences of Bolshevism as any British politician. Incredibly, Ludendorff even suggested to Roddie the merit of a joint Allied/German army under the command of Field Marshal Haig that could march on Moscow.

Despite Gustav Noske's fear, Ludendorff was not a man that the British were about to arrest and bring to trial. Continued German protests encouraged the Allies to shorten their lists, with the Germans paying especial attention to cajoling the British, who were rightfully seen as diffident prosecutors, and the country seen as amenable to rational argument.

When the Allies demanded the surrender of Germans for trial, the British fought to persuade the French and Belgians simultaneously to hand over the right to try the accused to the Germans. 'It was,' wrote an observer, 'simply a case of Germans being tried in Germany by a German court for offences against German law.' When these rights were reluctantly granted, the Germans, not surprisingly, chose to try defendants in the Supreme Court in the Saxon town of Leipzig, a city about as far away from Allied influence as it was possible to get.

In March 1919 the Commanding Officer of the 3rd Infantry Labour Company bade farewell to his men. It was two years since Major William Renwick had been ordered to take command of a unit made distinctive by its composition primarily of men with German surnames. Although Renwick may once have seen this appointment as a dubious honour, in the intervening time he grew both to respect and rely on the men under his command.

It was time to leave, and Major Renwick wrote a letter to be posted on the barracks notice board. Renwick was returning to civilian life. He had been in the army since 1914 and had served three years in France away from his wife, children and business, but in saying goodbye to his men, he made clear his feelings.

I feel regret that I sever my connection with such a splendid Company, which I had the pleasure and honour to command from its formation. During the whole time I was C.O. I was most loyally supported by all ranks, and few men had an easier task. That the company had a good name for discipline, work, appearance and efficiency was in no manner due to me, but the credit lies with my platoon commanders, senior NCOs, and men who combined so well to make the Company a name.

We had to fight down a prejudice and I think I can truthfully say we did so . . . to the end of my time I will look back with pleasure to the days which brought me into close association with so many good fellows, and no words I can express here will convey the thanks I should wish to tender to you all for the support I always looked for and never failed to receive.

Renwick was genuinely proud. In September 1917 he had been recommended for the Military Cross while three others, Company Sergeant Major Wiehl, Company Quarter Master Sergeant Korhaus and Corporal King were put up for the Meritorious Service Medal. Renwick received his MC but of the others only King received any recognition, being Mentioned in Dispatches. A case of the prejudice he had fought hard against? Maybe. But the next year, in May 1918, Meritorious Service Medals were awarded to Privates Malzer and Kriehn of 1st ILC.

Major Renwick might be going home but the men under his command were remaining in uniform, at least for the time being. In mid-January 1919, a confidential memo was received from the Adjutant General that personnel from these companies were 'on no account to be demobilized' until further instruction. No reason is given for the order but the general dissatisfaction among the British Army's rank and file at the slow pace of demobilisation had to be addressed and the ILCs were unlikely to receive preferential consideration. In the febrile anti-German atmosphere apparent in early 1919, no one could be sure what the future held for these men. It was better, perhaps, that they stayed together rather than return to Britain to disperse to all corners of the country. Many of these men, including the 1st, 2nd and 4th ILCs, remained in and around the Ypres Salient and near Courtrai until November, when commanding officers received orders that no more leave was to be allotted as instructions were anticipated ordering the companies back to Britain.

Only in mid-December did the men of the 3rd Infantry Labour Company receive permission to disband and a final message of farewell was read out to the men.

> Now that the time has come for you to leave the army and go back to civilian life, I wish, both personally and officially, to thank you for the service which you have given.
>
> You take away with you the priceless knowledge that you have played a man's part in this Great War for freedom and fair play. You take away with you also your remembrance of your comrades, your pride in your Company, and your love for your Country.
>
> You have played the game: go on playing it and all will be well with the great Empire which you have helped to save.
>
> I wish you every prosperity and happiness.
>
> F.O. Clarke for O.C. 80th Labour Group

Unlike Renwick's heartfelt message, this 'farewell' must have sounded perfunctory. It could have been written for any disbanding company, and probably was. Not that these men would have cared; they were going home but it was over a year since the Armistice and six months since the Versailles Peace Treaty and the question must have been on the lips of many: what were they going home to? Would attitudes to Germans have changed, would there be work for these men? The omens were not good.

Although life had to move on, public bitterness against Germans bubbled below the surface, and, as politicians tend to do, they fell into line with public sentiment. One manifestation of this attitude was a deliberate policy of obstruction, hindering the return of naturalised British nationals of German birth, and there was no better example of this than the ongoing saga of Carl Fuchs, world-renowned cellist and friend of Sir Edward Elgar.

Carl Fuchs had been detained in Germany since the outbreak of war and his British wife had made a determined effort to have her husband exchanged, but to no avail. On his release from open detention, Nellie Fuchs applied for a British passport for her husband. However, the British government, aware that returning citizens would have to pass through neutral Holland, advised the Dutch government to withhold facilities from such people as the British government deemed them only 'technically British subjects'.

There was a pervasive belief in the Home Office that such individuals wished purely to escape the dire economic situation in Germany and would become a burden on the British taxpayer. It was important to ensure that anyone who returned was considered a 'suitable person to receive a British passport and the protection therein', a useful delaying tool if required. By February 1919, Nellie Fuchs was exasperated.

'Sir,' she wrote to the Home Office, 'May I remind you that I am still without a reply to my letter of January 10th, the receipt of which you acknowledged on January 11th. I urgently asked for a passport for my husband, Professor Carl Fuchs, to enable him to return to England and support his family . . . A request for a passport was sent on December 10th . . .' Only in March was permission grudgingly given and authorisation passed to the Dutch Legation in Berlin to issue a passport to Fuchs. Later that month he returned to Britain, almost five years after he had left to visit his sick mother.

Politicians were almost as one in their desire to see all such enemy aliens sent home and government policy was to repatriate Germans. In December 1918, just days before the General Election, Andrew Bonar Law, the Coalition's Chancellor of the Exchequer, made a speech promising action over the subject of repatriation. 'I do not believe that people who have had to be locked up in our time of deadly peril are good citizens and if this Government is returned to power at the conclusion of peace, we shall send them back to their own country . . .'

The government was returned to power and repatriation carried out as quickly as shipping facilities permitted. Bonar Law had good reason to want Germans repatriated: he lost his two eldest sons in the fighting. And while all MPs were mindful of the electorate, many others had lost sons, too, including the new Home Secretary, Liberal MP Sir Edward Shortt, whose only son, Lieutenant William Shortt of the Scots Guards, had been killed in October 1917. As Home Secretary, Sir Edward regularly updated an interested House on the repatriation of enemy aliens, and the figures were startling.

By February 1919, the number of internees had fallen from around 24,250 to 19,800. By March, Shortt told the Commons that just six internment camps remained operational, holding 12,500 internees, of whom 10,500 were German. By October 1919, 84 per cent of all enemy alien internees had been sent back to Germany and Austria.

In a Statement made by Shortt in April 1919, he told the House that only forty-one internees had been released from detention and granted leave to remain in Britain on the recommendation of an Advisory Committee set up to look at all cases. This left around 5,000 Germans who were unwilling to leave Britain. Of these nearly 3,900 were granted permission to remain, usually on grounds such as family ties or long residence. Of course, many thousands more uninterned Germans stayed, too. In July, Shortt, in response to MPs' questions, revealed that, of those, 5,785 males and 5,965 females were exempted from repatriation on advice since 1915. The net result of government policy cut the German population in Britain from 57,500 in 1914 to 22,250 by the end of the decade.

The strategy of repatriation did not extend to providing passage for German British-born wives and children to leave alongside their husbands. These wives followed or in some cases preceded their husbands, although no British-born wives were sent away against their will.

The offices of the Friends Emergency Committee had remained busy throughout the war, helping families of enemy aliens as they struggled to survive in Britain or, often reluctantly, left British shores to return to Germany. In October 1919, the FEC issued its seventh and final Report, revisiting its work in the previous year including the plight of women whose husbands had been interned. The Report's author referred to the Armistice and the hope, expressed through a flood of letters written to the FEC by these women, that normal life would be restored: a hope misplaced.

Peace had come at last, their husbands would be set free then and there and they would see the end of all their anxieties and trials! But husbands were not released as they expected, and suspense weighed down the women more than all that they had endured in the past had done. Later, as the repatriation of interned men was accelerated, many more of our acquaintances had to face a dreadful dilemma – should they join their husbands in lands where food was terribly scarce, where, even if the man had work and was earning well, household effects were unobtainable, or only to be bought at prohibitive cost? Or, if they delayed the family reunion and remained in Britain, what would they live on when the special grants ceased? Must they become paupers? Would delay possibly lead to permanent separation? It speaks volumes for the courage and devotion of these women that numbers of them never hesitated, but were only too anxious to start off at once for a strange country so that they might be with their husbands at the earliest moment possible. Those who find it most difficult to come to a decision are English-born wives with older children settled in employment here, or with sons serving in the British Army. They have to face the fact that, if they join their husbands abroad, these children are left behind them; so, naturally, they are strongly drawn both ways at once.

Such terrible problems as these are often put before the visitors who have become very valued friends to many desolate women. Indeed our visitors form a most important personal link between committees and their cases in all manner of vicissitudes, and a wonderful work has been done by them in ministering to moral and spiritual needs, in addition to physical wants. When, in consequence of talks with some of the mothers who were going to rejoin their husbands, it was realised how greatly they dreaded the plunge into the unknown which they were yet determined to make, a series of teas, with talks from helpers who knew Germany, were arranged in the office. At these, Mrs Schmidt, shall we say, a native of East London, gleaned some details of such mythical places as Hanover or Berlin, and of everyday life there. Classes for simple conversational German were also arranged, so that the women should be able, on arrival in their new homes, at least to ask for the necessaries of life. Expressions of gratitude from the women we have helped grow more frequent, as they realise what benefits they receive from 'St. Stephen's' friends.

Ethel Druhm and her eight-year-old daughter Elfreda were resigned to leaving London for a new life in Germany. Since their hairdressing shop had been smashed by a baying mob in autumn 1914, the family had lived with chronic hardship. Richard Druhm was interned and his wife and child largely abandoned by the rest of her English family, a family that had always disapproved of Ethel's pre-war marriage. By reverting to her maiden name of Norris, Ethel found work in London but while she was willing, temporarily, to give up her married title, she was not about to give up her husband, as Elfreda recalled.

When the war was over, my father was sent back to Germany, directly. Now the wives could easily have divorced their husbands and stayed in England. Some did and some didn't. My mother wouldn't, so she left for Germany, and of course I went with her. I was very close to my mother, and very trusting, and what she did was right.

It was February, and it was really cold, making it a terrible journey. Miss Elsie Hope, my mother's one dear friend, came and saw us off from the station. She loved me as if I was her daughter and she brought me an eiderdown, a coat and a pair of boots because she knew it would be cold. But my grandmother and my mother's sisters didn't come to the station to wave goodbye. There was bad feeling about that for many years; they knew we were being sent to Germany.

When we were in Germany in 1919 we kept contact with some of the families Father had met in the internment camp. Stalenbrusher was one family we met up with, another family was the Stemlers. They used to live nearby and they had a daughter whom I used to meet. But she went back to England. Germany was terrible in those days with the riots and skirmishes and the food situation being so awful, that Frau Stemler left her husband and went back home taking their daughter with her. She couldn't stand it any longer.

I do not recall the crossing but the trains we went in on the other side were war-damaged, with their windows all broken and no heating; it was pretty bleak and freezing. We went through Holland and each evening we got out of the train where the

Quakers or Dutch Red Cross helped us until we got into Germany. It took nearly a week to get there, waiting in Germany for trains to take us on towards Berlin and the little town of Lugenwaldt, about 50 kilometres south of the city.

We went to the place where my father's parents were, and they welcomed me. My grandfather sat me on his lap and tried to teach me a few words of German. They said the best way for me to learn the language was to go to school, so the week after, they took me to school. The first lesson we had was French, imagine, out of German into French, and I only knew English. Yet the children were so nice they rivalled each other to take me around, there was no anti-English feeling whatsoever. They really couldn't do enough for us.

It was nearly a year since Richard Noschke had chosen to be repatriated. He missed his wife and five children and was unsure when he would see them again even though there was peace. In his memoirs, written after returning to Germany, he had had time to think.

Now that I am here safe, away from all the horrors of this terrible war I have time for reflection. I often wonder how was it possible that the English people, after being resident in that country for 25 years with an English wife, a grown up family, the best of character, 20 years in one situation, could be so bitter, but the answer I have never found. I have made many friends, as I had spent the best part of my life over there, but I am sorry to say, that nearly all, with very few exceptions have turned against me . . .

I am now over three years torn away from my family, and no sign that I shall ever see them again. By these few lines I give my children a clear impression of what I have gone through, how many sleepless nights I have had, and hoped against hope.   •

Noschke's memoirs were written for his children, including his eldest son, William, conscripted to serve in one of the Infantry

Labour Companies, in his case the 6th ILC. Interestingly, although written in Germany the diary is in English, not presumably because Noschke was so anglicised that English came more naturally, but probably because his children could not read German particularly well and perhaps not at all.

Richard Noschke did return to England and a home in East Ham, London, although precisely when this was permitted is not known. He was still living there when the Second World War broke out.

Too many British MPs were rabidly keen to purge Britain of almost anything German or German-tainted. The British Nationality and Status of Aliens Act of August 1918 had contained many anti-German provisions including the right to revoke a certificate of naturalisation, and cases of revocation, as already noted, were pursued before the Armistice.

It is not known how many civilians lost their British citizenship, although if the cases reported in *The Times* were *all* those on which the Home Secretary revoked certificates, then it would appear that fewer than a hundred men were affected, excluding wives and children. The majority lost their certificates in the two years following the war, although there were cases as late as October 1923.

If the law as exercised against German-born Britons appeared harsh and even vindictive, it was benign in comparison to the way it made victims of those women whose only crime was to marry enemy aliens. Back in 1870, the debate in the House of Commons about women's nationality was considered largely a matter of sentiment.

During the war, the likely humiliation and punitive restrictions placed on these women became abundantly clear: they lost their rights as British citizens, and to diplomatic protection when travelling overseas. An Act passed in 1918 forbade the employment of these women in the Civil Service. And when the franchise was extended these women were ineligible to vote even if they fulfilled other criteria. It was hardly surprising that pressure grew to change the law so as to revert to the status quo pre-1870, in other words that status in respect of nationality was unaffected by marriage. By 1923 the House of Commons appointed a Joint Select Committee to look into the issue, but it failed to agree on the best path to take. Six years later, the Nationality of Married Women Bill was put before the House but, despite cross-bench support from 222 MPs, it fell by the wayside. Only in 1946, after twenty-five years of agitation, did the government finally agree that women should keep their own nationality on marriage, and all the protections that naturally accrued with citizenship.

In May 1920, a final list of alleged German war criminals was sent to Berlin but owing to legal technicalities – and German foot-dragging – the cases were not brought to court for another year. In the end, the British authorities put forward seven cases, a ludicrously small number reduced to four owing to an inability to locate three of the accused. Those due for trial were low-ranking officers and men who were directly implicated in acts of criminality, the cases being taken forward owing to the strength of the evidence. Of the four cases, three were for the mistreatment of prisoners of war: Sergeant Karl Heinen, Private Robert Neumann, and finally Captain Emil Müller, whose brutality at Flavy-le-Martel POW camp was witnessed by many men, including former Private Nathan Sacof, captured in March 1918 and interpreter for Müller.

Most of the British witnesses taken to Germany had resumed civilian lives and wished to forget about the war. Former Private Arthur Hoyland was to give evidence against Robert Neumann, but Hoyland ignored the notice requiring him to go to Leipzig until two Scotland Yard police officers were sent to collect him. As a prisoner, Hoyland had been hung by his thumbs and whipped with wire after trying to escape. He had also been put through a mock execution and starved.

Several government representatives including the Solicitor General, Sir Ernest Pollock, joined the witnesses on their journey to Leipzig. Two police sergeants under the command of an Inspector A. C. Collins gave added security, Collins speaking to the witnesses before they left. 'They were addressed by me regarding the importance and serious nature of their mission to Germany, and the necessity of conducting themselves in a proper manner whilst on the journey and during their stay at Leipzig in order to prevent any hostility, and not to provoke any ill-feeling on the part of the Germans.' Collins's words were eminently sensible but if anything was indicative of the government's melting attitude to the Germans, then the last sentence was abysmally illustrative and may well have caused bitter reflection among the party.

Those giving testimony would be in Leipzig only a matter of days. In the meantime, 'in order not to attract the attention of the populace it was considered desirable', wrote Inspector Collins, 'that the witnesses should walk the street in small numbers with observation of their movements being kept by [both British] and German police officers.'

The Supreme Court consisted of a long assembly room adorned with giant imperial paintings of Frederick the Great and Kaiser Wilhelm I. There were seven judges and two prosecutors, all dressed in full regalia. The court was packed with journalists from eighty newspapers from across the globe and the judges sat at a horseshoe-shaped table within which space witnesses stood to give testimony.

The first witnesses attended court on 23 May. The case concerned Sergeant Karl Heinen who ran the Frederick-der-Grosse coal mine. He was charged with cruelly and inhumanely treating prisoners of war under his charge. Witnesses gave their evidence and then the defence rose to argue that the POWs were refractory in refusing to work and that no more violence was used than absolutely necessary. The German Attorney General said the case was proven and asked for a sentence of two years. The President in giving judgement praised the manner in which the men gave their evidence and proceeded to sentence Heinen to just ten months in prison. The German court had treated each assault as individual infringements of the law and, as one observer noted, 'sentence merely represented the aggregate punishment for a series of assaults, and gave no consideration to the long course of brutal conduct involved'.

As the case was concluded, witnesses were permitted to leave Leipzig for London. On their arrival, the second batch of witnesses was sent out for the trial of Captain Emil Müller. Deaths at Flavy-le-Martel camp had been frequent, averaging six men each day, the court was told. The deaths were directly or indirectly attributable to the camp's appalling conditions, caused by a lack of food and water, dire sanitation, excessive work and brutal treatment.

Several German sentries under Müller gave evidence for the prosecution, including one who directly contradicted Müller's testimony. In his defence, the former commandant claimed he had no control over conditions (rather embarrassingly it was revealed that the camp was British-built and had been overrun by the Germans) and that chaos reigned owing to the number of prisoners. He claimed to have reported conditions to his superiors but that nothing was done. Müller was found not responsible for conditions but guilty of cruelty. The Attorney General called for fifteen months in prison; the President awarded six months for crimes that, British observers noted, were substantially the same as those committed by Sergeant Heinen.

Of the other British cases, Private Robert Neumann was found guilty of beating British prisoners and received six months in prison, while the last case, that of U-boat commander Lieutenant Karl Neumann, descended into farce when the whole case was dealt with in two hours. Neumann was accused of sinking a hospital ship. He claimed that he was acting on orders, a lawful defence the court accepted. No witnesses were called and Neumann was released. The British cases were done and dusted in a week.

Despite the unsatisfactory outcome of the Karl Neumann trial, the British cases were expedited without rancour, unlike those of the Belgians and French that descended into courtroom mayhem, such was the depth of mutual hatred and recrimination. Outside, crowds spat at and taunted members of the French and Belgian missions, and trials were abandoned.

The Germans understood that their own best interests were served by treating Britain's handful of cases with respect: witnesses and observers were not jostled outside court. It was relatively easy to sentence two other ranks to short periods in prison, and the one officer convicted of crimes had had his professional character protected during the President's summary.

As the British mission was about to leave Leipzig, the Germans, in an attempt to 'make up' for the decision to free Karl Neumann, informed the British that they would be pursuing another criminal case against two U-boat officers. These men had been party to an indisputably criminal attack against another hospital ship, the Llandovery Castle, in which survivors, including nurses, had been attacked while sitting in lifeboats. Both officers were found guilty and sentenced to four years in prison. With the ending of this case, the British drew a line under the whole issue of war crimes trials and normalised relations with Germany. Well-documented crimes, such as those against the prisoners sent to the Russian Front in February 1917, were allowed to pass into oblivion.

The British press reported the proceedings and labelled them farcical, The Times calling them a 'scandalous failure of justice'. In the Commons, the government was asked about the light sentences and whether anything was going to be done about the failure of justice.

Sir Ernest Pollock, the Attorney General, who had attended the trials, answered on behalf of the Prime Minister and, while he felt it improper to make a statement when the French and Belgian cases were still in court, he nevertheless added:

> Perhaps the Hon. Members may care to know that the sentence which was delivered in my presence excited great dejection amongst the military party of Germany, and the officers there certainly did not think it was a small sentence to have one of their number sent to an ordinary prison to carry out the sentence of 10 months among thieves and other felons.

Listening MPs may have struggled to see why German thoughts and feelings were of any relevance. Surely it was right to presume that sentencing had everything to do with the crimes for which conviction was secured and nothing whatsoever to do with the conditions under which that sentence might be served? It did not really matter. MPs blew off some steam, but there was no appetite to pursue the matter further. Politicians lost interest in the subject of war crimes because the British public lost interest. The war was over.

So did Britain acquire the 'fruits of victory' as anticipated by Winston Churchill? If she did, then most Britons did not share in any obvious harvest. Broken families would have to find ways to re-adjust to living with people who had often become strangers especially to their children. It was a re-adjustment made all the harder by the post-war era of austerity. Years of extraordinary financial outlay resulted in the need for fiscal restraint. Unemployment, poverty and depression resulted; returning soldiers' claims to pensions and support were ungratefully received and frugally rewarded. Historians have debated and will continue to debate the gross and net price of the conflict between Britain and Germany. Both nations were physically and emotionally drained, though Germany had come off much the worse. In 1917 and 1918 it is estimated that Germany lost as many civilians through the effects of hunger and associated illness as Britain lost in battle. What happened to both nations politically and strategically has been well documented. Less well recorded are the myriad stories of lives fractured by continuing physical and mental scars including those caused by enforced separation and isolation: the human face of the Great War.

Acknowledgements

I would like to thank the enthusiastic and supportive staff at Bloomsbury, particularly Bill Swainson, the senior commissioning editor, for their encouragement and continued belief in my books. I am also very grateful to Liz Woabank for her keen interest and kind assistance, Oliver Holden-Rea, Tess Viljoen, Maria Hammershoy, Holly Macdonald, Paul Nash and Anya Rosenberg for their collective skill in helping to bring *Meeting the Enemy* to publication. I would also like to express my gratitude to Richard Collins for his careful and insightful editorial comments on this, the fifth of my books he has edited.

Especial mention should be made of my excellent agent, Jane Turnbull, whose astute thoughts and insights have been of invaluable help this year; I greatly value her friendship. Once again, I am very grateful to my great friend Taff Gillingham for his technical reading of the text and the discovery, as always, of small but important errors on my part; his kindness is much appreciated. My appreciation also goes to Peter Johnston for excellent additional research work.

My warmest thanks must go to my family: to my mother, Joan van Emden, whose support is unquantifiable and whose deft literary comments are, once again, of immeasurable help. Thank you, Mum. I am indebted also to my wife, Anna, who is a tower of support and who never makes adverse comments other than that I should try to tidy my study now and again – will do!

I would like to thank the following people for permission to reproduce photographs, extracts from diaries, letters or memoirs:

Calista Lucy at Dulwich College for background information on Wilford Wells; fellow author Jack Sheldon whose expert knowledge of the German language and German military units helped decipher Wilford Wells's military records; Christine Leighton, College Archivist at Cheltenham College for her generous permission to reproduce the image of Henry Hadley. I would also like to thank Margaret Tyler and Kevin C. Dowson for permission to reproduce the picture of Major Renwick and fellow officers of the 3rd Infantry Labour Company; Liz Howell for the image of men of the 30th Middlesex Regiment and Private Charles Kuhr, taken at Reading in 1917; Kevin Northover for his picture of fraternisation at Beaumont Hamel and Kevin Varty for the image of Captain Richard Hawkins. Thanks also to Fergus Johnston and Ellen Campbell, both distant relatives of Henry Hadley, and Christopher Jage-Bowler, priest at St George's Church, Berlin. My gratitude for help and advice goes to my good friends Mary Freeman, Jeremy and Mark Banning for their thoughts and useful tip-offs! Thanks, too, to Dave Empson, William Spencer, Stephen Chambers, Duncan Mirylees and Gaby Chaudry.

As always, I am very grateful to the families of those I have interviewed who have also been most kind in forwarding precious family photographs and documents.

Sources

Published Memoirs

Andrews, Albert, *Orders are Orders: A Manchester Pal on the Somme*, ed. Sue Richardson, privately published, 1987

Barnett, Denis Oliver, *In Happy Memory*, privately published, 1915

Binding, Rudolph, *A Fatalist at War*, George Allen & Unwin, 1929

Bloem, Walter, *The Advance from Mons*, Peter Davies, 1930

Blücher, Princess Evelyn, *An English Wife in Berlin*, Constable, 1921

Buckler, Julius, *Malaula! The Battle Cry of Jasta 17*, Grub Street, 2007

Buxton, Andrew, *The Rifle Brigade, A Memoir*, Robert Scott, 1918

Byrne, Ginger, *I Survived Didn't I?*, ed. Joy Cave, Leo Cooper, 1993

Chapman, Guy, *A Passionate Prodigality*, Buchan & Enright, 1985

Clark, Andrew, Revd, *Echoes of the Great War*, Oxford University Press, 1985

Cliff, Norman, *To Hell and Back with the Guards*, Merlin Books, 1988

Collins, Norman, *Last Man Standing*, Pen & Sword, 2002

Courtney, Lady, *War Diary*, privately published, 1927

Crundell, Edward, *Fighter Pilot on the Western Front*, William Kimber, 1975

Dundas, Henry, *Scots Guards, A Memoir*, Blackwood, 1921

Evans, Alfred, *The Escaping Club*, John Lane, 1941

Ewart, Wilfrid, *Scots Guard*, Strong Oak Press, 2001

Fielding, Rowland, *War Letters to a Wife*, Spellmount Classics, 2001

Foley, G. A., *On Active Service*, privately published, Bridgewater, 1920

Gerard, James W., *My Four Years in Germany*, Hodder & Stoughton, 1917

Gillespie, Alexander, *Letters from Flanders*, Smith, Elder & Co, 1916

Graham, Stephen, *A Private in the Guards*, William Heinemann, 1928

Grinnell-Milne, Duncan, *An Escaper's Log*, John Lane, 1926

Hitchcock, Frank, *'Stand To' A Diary of the Trenches*, Hurst & Blackett, 1937

Hodges, Frederick James, *Men of 18 in 1918*, Arthur H. Stockwell Ltd, 1988

Hutchison, Graham Seton, *Footslogger*, Hutchinson & Co., 1933

Jünger, Ernst, *Storm of Steel*, Allen Lane, 2003

Lucy, John, *There's a Devil in the Drum*, The Naval and Military Press, 1993

Markham, Violet, *A Woman's Watch on the Rhine*, Hodder & Stoughton, 1921

Martin, Jack, *The Secret War Diary of Jack Martin*, Bloomsbury, 2009

McCudden, James, *Flying Fury: Five Years in the Royal Flying Corps*, The Aeroplane Publishing 1918

Muddock, J. E. Preston, *All Clear, A Brief Record of the London Special Constabulary 1914–19*, Everett & Co., 1920

Osburn, Arthur, *Unwilling Passenger*, Faber & Faber, 1926

Peel, Mrs C., *How We Lived Then*, The Bodley Head, 1929

Pickard-Cambridge, Hilda, *An Englishwoman's Experiences in Germany, August 1914*, privately published, 1931

Richard, Frank, *Old Soldiers Never Die*, Faber & Faber, 1942

Roddie, Stewart, *Peace Patrol*, Christophers, 1932

Siepmann, Harry, *Echo of the Guns*, Robert Hale, 1987

Stoffa, Pal, *Round the World to Freedom*, John Lane, 1933

Troyte-Bullock, C. J., in *History of the Somerset Light Infantry 1914-1919*, Everard Wyrall, Methuen & Co, 1927

Vischer, A. L., *Barbed Wire Disease*, John Bale & Co., 1919

Vivian, A. P. G., *The Phantom Brigade*, Ernest Benn, 1930

Walkinton, M. L., *Twice in a Lifetime*, Samson Books, 1980

Unpublished Memoirs

Cole, Vic, Lance Corporal, 7th Royal West Kent Regiment, *An Englishman's Life*

Parke, C. G. A., 2nd Gordon Highlanders, *Memories of an Old Contemptible*

Smith, Francis Nimmo, 1st Scots Guards, *Diary*

Newspapers

Bournemouth Guardian 11 January 1916: reported court appearance of Julia Jacobitz

East London Observer 8 August 1914: editorial on East London Germans

Manchester Guardian 10 August 1914: Aliens' Restriction Act; 26 September
 1914: letter from Charles Eshborn

The Times online 27 June 1904: King George's visit to Kiel; 6 August 1914:
 Florence Phillips; 8 August 1914: Bampfylde Fuller; 26 December 1914:
 Hensley Henson; 26 December 1914: Reverend Henry Woods; 12 May
 1915: Sir Felix Semon, Sir Carl Meyer and Leopold Hirsch; 7 July 1916:
 Jellicoe's Despatch; 8 March 1918: Lord Newton's speech to the House of
 Lords; 12 July 1918: Sir George Cave and Brigadier Page Croft; 2 November
 1918: Udo Willmore-Wittner

Magazines

Account of Private Robert Nisbet, published in *The New Chequers*, magazine of
 the Friends of Lochnagar

Memoirs of Corporal Walter Crookes, 1st Cheshire Regiment, published in
 the Regimental magazine *The Oak Leaf*, date unknown

Memories of Lieutenant Alexander Gallaher and Private Alfred Tilney,
 published in the Regimental Magazine of the 4/7th Royal Irish Dragoon
 Guards

Memories of Private William Gordon, published in *The Beam*, December 1969

Other Reading

Brown, Malcolm & Seaton, Shirley, *Christmas Truce*, Papermac, 1994

Holmes, Richard, *Tommy: The British Soldier on the Western Front 1914 – 1918*,
 Harper Collins, 2004

Housman, Laurence, *War Letters of Fallen Englishmen*, Victor Gollancz, 1930
 (incl. letters of Captain Edward Hulse and Lt Colonel John Hawksley)

Marlow, Joyce, *Women and the Great War*, Virago, 1998

Panayi, Panikos, *The Enemy in our Midst*, Berg, 1991

van Emden, Richard, *All Quiet on the Home Front*, Headline, 2003

van Emden, Richard, *The Soldier's War*, Bloomsbury, 2008

W. A. S. and J. D. N., eds, *Wycliffe and the War 1914–1918*, including letters
 of Melville Hastings, privately printed, 1923

Willis, James F., *Prologue to Nuremberg*, Greenwood Press, 1982

Winter, John, *Death's Men*, Allen Lane, 1978

Archives

Author's private collection: Letters of Rifleman Ernest Blake; photocopied diary of Private Tom Tolson, 8th King's Own Yorkshire Light Infantry

Hansard: Reginald McKenna and Joseph King (HC Debate 5/8/1914 vol. 65 c1987-90); Winston Churchill (HC Debate 15/4/1919 vol. 114 cc2713-4); Edward Shortt (18/2/1919 vol. 112 cc741-3 and HC Debate 13/3/1919 vol. 112 cc260 and 01/04/1919 vol. 114 cc1054-5 and HC Debate 15/7/1919 vol. 118 cc210-11); Caroline Hanemann (HC Debate 7/8/1919 vol. 119 cc527-8)

Imperial War Museum: By kind permission of the Department of Documents, with grateful thanks to Tony Richards: private papers of Captain Charles Carrington – Documents 20614; private papers of Major General Sir Richard Ewart – Documents 683; account by an English Woman (Miss Waring) of the Outbreak of War in Germany, August 1914 – Documents 12426; private papers of EV Stibbe – Documents 11786; private papers of Lieutenant Thomas Hughes – Documents 12244; private papers of Richard Noschke – Documents 11229; jingoistic letter from Lotte to Dorothy September 1914 – Documents 1962; private papers of Lieutenant Colonel Sir Iain Colquhoun – Documents 6373; private papers of Brigadier General H. C. Hubert Rees – Documents 7166; Royal Dragoons Letter Book, 1914 – Documents 12546; private papers of Miss W. L. B. Tower incl. reference to 3rd Marquess of Ormonde – Documents 6322; private papers of Private Martyn Evans – Documents 9766; letter from a German soldier (Wiengartner) to the family of a wounded British soldier (Mole), March 1916 – Documents 12451; private papers of Private Samuel Fielding – Documents 12810; private papers of Major General Sir John Laurie – Documents 1713; private papers of Reverend Montague Bere – Documents 12105; private papers of Brigadier T. I. Dun – Documents 12179; private papers of Private Frank Harris – Documents 14979; private papers of Brigadier Philip Mortimer – Documents 12327; private papers of Private Percy Clare – Documents 15030; private papers of Private Arthur Wrench – Documents 3834; private papers of Captain Arthur Pick – Documents 4672; private papers of H. G. R. Williams – Documents 11514

By kind permission of the Department of Sound, Imperial War Museum, and with thanks to Peter Hart: Lance Corporal Harry Hopthrow – Catalogue Number 11581. Every effort has been made to trace copyright holders and the author and the Imperial War Museum would be grateful for any information which might help to trace those whose identities or addresses are not currently known.

The Liddle Archive: By kind permission of the Liddle Collection, Leeds University Library, www.leeds.ac.uk., with thanks to Richard Davies: Private Charles Eshborn GS 0526; Reverend Henry Williams GE 37; C. A. M. Dunlop GS 0480; Lieutenant J. A. Brewster GS0196; Private Percy Ogley GS1200

The National Archives: Kew, www.nationalarchives.gov.uk. In the 1920s the following officers corresponded with the Great War's official historian, Brigadier General Sir James E. Edmonds (Cab45), and extracts from their letters have been used in the book.

Cab45 (Cabinet Papers): unknown officer quoting Lieutenant George Edwards 1/6th Seaforth Highlanders; Lieutenant Bradford Gordon 9th Kings Own Yorkshire Light Infantry; Lieutenant Colonel John Hall, 16th Middlesex Regiment; Lieutenant Aubrey Herbert, 1st Irish Guards; Captain William Carden-Roe, 1st Royal Irish Fusiliers; Captain J. G. Smyth-Osbourne, 1st Royal Welsh Fusiliers; Colonel Roger Tempest, 2nd Scots Guards

FO (Foreign Office files): FO383/17 Annie Reiser; FO383 23/81/169/207/315/521 Carl Fuchs; FO383/48/182/294 Henry Hadley; FO383/53 Hermann Waetjen; FO383/55 C. F. Just; FO383/60 Albert Cresswell/Edgar Gillon/ David Russell; FO383/80 Mrs W. D. Burnyeat; FO383/80 Wilford Wells; FO383/80/151 Julia Jacobitz; FO383/80/149 Corporal Alfred Felton; FO383/81 Julius Ring, /197 William Kunz, /197 Wilhelm Roderwald, /194 Bartholomus Eid, /192 Carl Martini, /193 Henry Steinke, /442 Hubert Biskeborn; FO383/180 Lt Col. Godfrey Goodman, Captains Hans Roser/ Reinhardt/Maffett; FO383/202 Mary Harthaus; FO383/203 Captain Robert Campbell; FO383/289 Captain Bushby Erskine; FO383/203/289 Peter Gastreich; FO383/292 Adam Ultsch; FO383/522 Lilian Stephan; FO383/522 Malvina Mendelssohn

MEPO (Metropolitan Police Office): MEPO 2/10662: attempts by Casement to form an Irish Brigade; MEPO 3/1166 German War Criminals: police enquiries and action on behalf of H. M. Procurator General for Leipzig Trials

WO (War Office files): WO32/5783: interviews with Field Marshal von Ludendorff and General Hoffman by Lieut. Col. W. Stewart Roddie on Bolshevik menace; WO95 (War Diaries): WO95/2215/1 – 9th East Surrey Regiment; WO95/2695/1 – 1/5th Sherwood Foresters; WO95/1971/2 – 8th Royal Munster Fusiliers; WO95/1371/1 – 1st Royal Berkshire Regiment; WO95/1972/2 – 8th Royal Dublin Fusiliers; WO95/1972/2 – 7th Royal Irish Rifles; WO95/1972 – 48 Brigade; WO95/1975/5 – 9th Royal Munster Fusiliers; WO95/1535/2 – Diary of Lieutenant James Pennycuik, held within war diary of 59th Field Company Royal Engineers; WO141/9: Formation of the Irish Brigade; WO141/36: Trial of members of German Irish Brigade; WO141/67: German Irish Brigade; WO161 Prisoner of War Interview Reports 1914–1918, interviews with the following POWs: Private John Harrison, 1st Cheshire Regiment; Private John Cooper, 1st Coldstream Guards; Captain Thomas Sotherton-Estcourt; Captain R. F. Peskett, 2nd Dragoon Guards, Lincolnshire Regiment; Private George Winkworth, Rifle Brigade; Private Charles Duder, 4th Royal Fusiliers; Captain Arthur Hargreaves, 1st Somerset Light Infantry; Private James Harrold, 2nd East Kent Regiment; Lance Corporal Herbert Lewin, 1st Royal Berkshire Regiment; Private James McDaid, 1/10th Argyle and Sutherland Highlanders; Private Thomas Dickinson, 8th Durham Light Infantry; Private George Kitson, 12th Royal Scots Fusiliers; Private Patrick Leavy, 14th Highland Light Infantry; Private Alfred Hoare, 1st Hampshire Regiment; Private James Harlock, 17th Royal Fusiliers; Private Ernest Barton, 2nd Manchester Regiment; Crewman Alfred Amey, HMS *Nomad*; Private Ernest Brown, 20th Machine Gun Corps; Private Andrew Duffy, RAMC; Private Tim Macarthy, RAMC; Private Daniel Merry, 7th Battalion Canadian Infantry; Private Patrick Cullen, 2nd Royal Munster Fusiliers; Sergeant James Morrison, Royal Marine Light Infantry; CSM Alexander Gibb, 2nd Argyle and Sutherland Highlanders; Corporal Robert Steele, 5th Signal Troop Royal Engineers; Private Arthur Soder, 1st Dorset Regiment; Lance Corporal Harold Sugden, Army Service Corps attd 6th Field Ambulance; Corporal Charles Wright, 5th Lancers; Private Charles Brown, 1st West Yorks; Private Frank Barlow, 1st West Yorks; Lieutenant Patrick

(Pat) O'Brien, Royal Flying Corps; Lieutenant John Howey, Royal Flying Corps; Captain Francis Don, Royal Flying Corps; Private George Wash, 8th Durham Light Infantry; Private Henry Webb, RAMC; Private James Whiteside, 36th Machine Gun Corps; Private Ernest Hart, 2nd East Kent Regiment; Captain Harold Rushworth, Royal Flying Corps; Lieutenant Harvey Frost, Royal Flying Corps; Lieutenant Geoffrey Parker, Royal Flying Corps; Private George Allen, 1st Rifle Brigade; WO339 & WO374 Officers' Files concerning: WO339/16499 – Captain William Renwick; WO339/60685 – 2nd Lt Frederick Ruscoe; WO339/26578 – Captain David Burles; WO339/17037 – 2nd Lt John Brewster; WO374/77437 – Major Charles Yate

The National Army Museum: NAM 1999-11-216-1 – War Diary, 1 Infantry Labour Company, Middlesex Regiment, 5 March 1917–30 January 1918; NAM 1999-11-216-2 – War Diary, 2 Infantry Labour Company, Middlesex Regiment, 2 April 1917–30 November 1917

Regimental Museum of the Royal Welsh: Private Charles Heare, 1/2nd Monmouthshire Regiment

Society of Friends: Annual reports of the Friends Emergency Committee

Surrey History Centre: By kind permission of Surrey History Centre: Captain Wilfred Birt – ESR/25/Birt/4; Captain William Morritt, 1st East Surrey Regiment – ESR/25/Morrwg

The Tank Museum, Bovington: Driver Ernest Reader – WW1/Readerer

Trustees of the Army Medical Services Museum: Diary of Capt. Henry Wynyard Kaye, MD, RAMC – RAMC/739

Interviews conducted by the author

Soldiers and Seamen: Able Seaman Alfred Bastin, Royal Naval Division; Lance Corporal Andrew Bowie, 1st Cameron Highlanders; Lance Corporal Vic Cole, 7th Royal West Kent Regiment; Private Bill Easton, 77th Field Ambulance RAMC; Private George Gadsby, 1/18th London Regiment; Lieutenant Richard Hawkins, 11th Royal Fusiliers; Private Walter Humphreys, 1/15th London Regiment; Private Jack Rogers, 1/7th Sherwood Foresters; Private Ernest Stevens, 20th Middlesex Regiment; Private Frank Sumpter, 1st Rifle Brigade

Civilians: Percy Johnson; Elfreda Druhm

Index

A NOTE ON THE TYPE

Linotype Garamond Three – based on seventeenth-century copies of Claude Garamond's types, cut by Jean Jannon. This version was designed for American Type Founders in 1917, by Morris Fuller Benton and Thomas Maitland Cleland and adapted for mechanical composition by Linotype in 1936.